# With Friends Like These

This book is dedicated to the memory of Phil Sheldon,
who died tragically young in 2005, and whose photographs
here are only a tiny part of the reason he is so greatly
missed by so many people.

# With Friends Like These

*A Selective History of the Ryder Cup*

## MARTIN VOUSDEN

TIME WARNER
BOOKS

First published in Great Britain in 2006 by Time Warner Books

Copyright © 2006 Martin Vousden
Foreword copyright © 2006 Sam Torrance

A CIP catalogue record for this book
is available from the British Library.

ISBN 0-316-73096-3

Typeset in Minion by M Rules
Printed and bound in Great Britain by The Bath Press, Bath

Time Warner Books
An imprint of
Little, Brown Book Group
Brettenham House
Lancaster Place
London WC2E 7EN

A member of the Hachette Livre Group of Companies

www.littlebrown.co.uk

Time Warner Books is a trademark of Time Warner Inc. or an affiliated
company. Used under licence by Little, Brown Book Group, which is not
affiliated with Time Warner Inc.

All photographs are courtesy of the Phil Sheldon Golf Picture
Library, with the exception of: p. x, p. 206 Corbis; p. 26
Popperfoto; p. 63, p. 135, p. 142, p. 165, p. 185 Empics; p. 104,
p. 126 Getty Images; p. 37, p. 43, p. 202 Action Images. The
publisher would like to take this opportunity to thank Gill
Sheldon for her time and much appreciated help.

# Contents

# Acknowledgements

My thanks go in particular to the golfers from both sides of the Atlantic who so willingly gave their time to speak about their Ryder Cup experiences – Peter Baker, Seve Ballesteros, Brian Barnes, Paul Broadhurst, Billy Casper, Luke Donald, Bernard Gallacher, David Gilford, Peter Jacobsen, Sandy Lyle, Corey Pavin, Ian Poulter, Dave Thomas, Sam Torrance, Tom Watson, Paul Way, Lee Westwood. My thanks also to everyone who has represented their country or continent in the Ryder Cup and, in the process, brought some of the most exciting, vibrant and vivid memories into my otherwise dull life.

Stephen Guise at Time Warner Books not only commissioned me to write this but also had the skill, patience and tact to guide me through.

A debt of gratitude is owed to Iestyn George and all at *Golf Punk*, especially editor Tim Southwell, for commissioning me to write the booklet that gave birth to the idea of this book, and for allowing me to use some of the material from that booklet here. My enduring thanks also go to Bill Robertson at *Golf Links* for always having more advice, ideas and enthusiasm than anyone I know but who nonetheless allows me to get the occasional word in.

My big-bottomed friend should be thanked for her non-stop support, wrapped in a cocoon of abuse and psychological trauma – you know who you are.

A mention also to Andrew Griffin, who had no part in this book whatsoever but always wanted an acknowledgement in one. This, Andy, is yours.

Finally, a special thank you to two special players. Sam Torrance has almost made the Ryder Cup his own property and his involvement as both player and captain has done nothing but add even more lustre to an already gleaming trophy. But particular mention should go to Seve Ballesteros, who for so long was the inspiration for European Ryder Cup teams and who convinced us all that this moribund contest could become competitive. Tony Jacklin's was the calculating mind that demanded equality and convinced his players they could achieve or better it. but Seve's was the beating heart of the wondrous revival that has seen the Ryder Cup become the most dramatic and exciting event in sport.

# Foreword by Sam Torrance OBE

I have always loved the Ryder Cup. Throughout my career, from the day I became a professional golfer at the age of seventeen, one of my overriding ambitions was to play in the competition that I regard as the greatest team event in sport. I like people, enjoy company and love the banter and camaraderie that can be found in clubhouses and bars throughout the world – what the Irish like to call 'the craic'. So to play alongside and against some of the finest people I have met, representing our country or continent, was always going to have a particular appeal.

A golf course can be a lonely place. With only a caddy at your side you take on the rest of the field with whatever talent you may have. Play well and you might make the halfway cut, which at least means you will be paid that week. Play very well and you might get into the top 10, and have a good payday. Play to your potential and you could win, and for any professional sportsperson there is no better feeling than winning. If you're lucky, a few people outside your immediate friends and family, who for whatever reason support you, share in the success.

And then comes the Ryder Cup, and for one week every two years you are not competing for yourself but alongside eleven others, always conscious that outside that select group comes the captain, officials and helpers, the people who usually support you, and then millions of others, for whom the competition is much, much more than another golf event. As a player you can feel the weight of expectation and hope they invest in you. It flows from the grandstands, is reported in every newspaper and dominates the television coverage the competition generates.

And then there are the golfers. Over the years both teams have fielded some of the most talented people ever to play the game, and I've been lucky enough to tee it up alongside and opposite them. People like Peter Oosterhuis, Nick Faldo, Sandy Lyle, Howard Clark, Ian Woosnam, Seve Ballesteros, José Maria Olazábal, Mark James, Bernhard Langer, Colin Montgomerie and many, many others, with whom, for three days, you are joined in order to play for something much bigger and more important than personal glory. For 103 weeks you line up against them, with the intention of beating their brains out, and then find yourself on a podium, wearing the same uniform, being introduced to the crowd as a team, and your heart swells with pride at being included among their number.

And you look across at the other team, which may contain people like Freddy Couples or Curtis Strange or Lee Trevino – to name but three who have become dear friends – and you can't wait to take them on because they are among the finest people and best golfers the world has produced, and who doesn't want to measure themselves against the best?

I have won twenty-one events on the European Tour and thankfully have continued to win now that I have joined the ranks of the Seniors, but none of those victories can equal the joy I have felt in the Ryder Cup. When I holed the winning putt on the Belfry's eighteenth green in 1985 to end twenty-eight years of American domination, I thought, simply, that a golfer's life doesn't get much better than this. Because we had gone so close two years before at PGA National in Florida, and because we had such a great crop of talented players, there was a real feeling of optimism and the air crackled with the expectation that we might actually win this thing. But to be the man who delivered the *coup de grace* exceeded even my hopes and I remember thinking that this was, by a margin, the best moment of my career.

The idea that it could be surpassed – as it was seventeen years later, when I captained the team – was too preposterous to contemplate. And yet on that same green, Paul McGinley added another chapter to the remarkable story of Irish contributions to Samuel Ryder's competition, and I felt a sense of pride, achievement and pure happiness that was clearly shared by golfers all over Europe. I still get asked about it now and will never tire of remembering those

magical few September days in 2002.

It has not been all happy memories – my own personal low point coming in 1993 when I had to withdraw with an injured toe – and there have been times when the passion of competition has boiled over, which has caused some people to question whether the spirit of the Ryder Cup is in danger of being forgotten. Let me reassure them, that is never going to happen. When you have a competition as partisan and intense as this one, it is bound to boil over on occasion. This is not to condone bad behaviour, and we all know where and when it has happened, but golf remains a sport of honour and integrity, played by gentlemen, so on those few occasions when things get out of hand we all know how important it is to get them back under control, and we do.

But thankfully, for every bad memory there are ten good ones. When I was asked to name the best Ryder Cup I ever played in I had no hesitation in saying, 'Muirfield Village, 1987'. Nick Faldo and Woosie forged an almost unbeatable partnership, we saw Seve and Ollie together for the first time, in what would become the greatest Ryder

Cup pairing in history, and Eamonn Darcy grabbed that vital point in the singles against Ben Crenshaw. Not only that, but we won in America for the first time ever, on a tough course that the Americans play every year on their Tour, against a good team, captained by the finest golfer there has ever been, Jack Nicklaus. We were, quite simply, magnificent that week.

We all have our favourite Ryder Cup memories because the event is littered with special moments, and I have been fortunate enough to have my two greatest moments in golf in the Ryder Cup. In this book Martin Vousden has gathered more than sixty other such moments. From the captaincy of Walter Hagen at the very beginning of the competition, to the unexpected and dramatic GB&I win at Lindrick in 1957, to Craig Stadler's missed putt at the Belfry in 1985 and beyond, he has collected the most dramatic, remarkable and, in some cases, almost forgotten moments of a competition that has had more than its fair share.

I hope you enjoy reading about them as much as I have enjoyed being a small part of that history.

# Introduction

Golf has the reputation of being a gentle game. It prides itself on its etiquette, manners and good sportsmanship and, with the exception of snooker, is probably the last big-money sport in which contestants are not only prepared to call a penalty on themselves, but would be vilified if they did not. It is a game in which players will offer advice and help on the practice ground, applaud good shots on the course and genuinely wish each other well.

And then there's matchplay.

Matchplay golf is red of tooth and sharp of claw, a man-on-man, knock-'em-down-and-keep-them-there duel in which no quarter is asked or given. Seve Ballesteros, one of the greatest exponents of matchplay golf, once said of it: 'If you ever feel sorry for somebody on a golf course, you better go home. If you don't kill them, they'll kill you.' In the 1991 Ryder Cup, Raymond Floyd, another great match player, admonished his partner, Fred Couples, who had complimented their opponents on a good shot. 'You can

be friendly with them another time,' Floyd said, 'but this week we're trying to beat these guys.' Actually, Ray and Fred were trying to beat them (or someone like them) every working week of their lives, so what he really meant to say was: 'This week is matchplay, and the Ryder Cup.'

But it's not all hatred and enmity, or it wasn't supposed to be. When a British seed merchant from the Midlands of Britain decided in the early 1920s to put up a prize for an international golf competition between America and Great Britain & Ireland, it was to foster a spirit of goodwill and sporting endeavour. But nobody, least of all Samuel Ryder himself, could have possibly imagined what he was starting, not that the competition has always been as vitally important as it seems today. As recently as the 1970s the event was threatened by extinction because it had become such a one-sided affair. America won with such monotonous regularity and ease that some of its best players couldn't even be bothered to take part.

That changed in 1979 when the Great Britain & Ireland team became Europe, the continent produced a crop of players – Nick Faldo, Seve Ballesteros, Sandy Lyle, Bernhard Langer, Ian Woosnam and José Maria Olazábal among them – capable of taking on the world. Since then the Ryder Cup has become arguably the most intense, competitive and compelling sporting contest anywhere in the world. It is watched by over a billion people around the globe and has become the third biggest sporting occasion in the calendar, bested only by the Olympic Games and football's World Cup.

That, in itself, would be a phenomenon but the Ryder Cup doesn't end there. It creates heroes out of men who would struggle to be recognised in their own homes, who if not competing would otherwise be attending meetings of Undistinguished Anonymous. It sees superstars humbled, underdogs triumph and above all, offers the world a three-day fiesta of astonishing, unbelievable golf of a standard seen in no other event. Somehow the act of representing one's country or continent, and, in this most singular game, of playing with and for eleven team-mates, allows some of the best golfers in the world to consistently demonstrate the superb play of which they are capable.

Their life is built around 72-hole stroke play events, in which the man who makes fewest mistakes is likely to win, especially in the four premier events of the year, the Majors. The watchword of the professional golfer is 'patience', which means don't attack the flagstick, lay up from the tee, avoid hazards, play the percentages and let the other guys make mistakes. But in the Ryder Cup all that changes.

Each contest is staged over the sprint distance of eighteen holes, and involves the man-on-man duel of matchplay – in which two combatants look each other in the eye and play only each other. In stroke play they compete against 155 others, and it's only at the end of the day or week that they see how well they have done in comparison to the field. In matchplay you know instantly if you go a hole ahead, or fall behind, and how many holes remain in order for you to maintain or increase the advantage, or

overcome the deficit. As a consequence matchplay golfers know that in a competition lasting five hours rather than four days, it is essential to get off to a fast start and be aggressive from the outset. If it works, and an early lead is established, the opponent(s) know they must quickly counter with their own attacking play, and so it goes on, with punch and counter-punch until only one man or team is left standing. For many golfers the idea of carrying other players' expectations, as well as their own, can become either a burden or give them a new sense of belief.

Golf, despite its camaraderie, is a selfish, lonely, intensely private affair in which it is you against the world. It is not (although it has been and may be again) an Olympic sport in which you march behind your national flag and represent a nation. You live and die, prosper or perish by your own efforts. It is a nomadic, egocentric world lived in hotel rooms and on practice grounds all around the world, where each week involves a ruthless analysis of exactly how well you are playing. Fall below the most exacting standards imaginable for even one hole and you could miss the cut that week, which means no payday and an early flight home. You are up

against the best in the world at what they do and must consistently be as good, if not better, in order to earn a living. It is a singular game for singular, driven obsessives who often sacrifice family and normality in the quest to prove just how good they are.

And then comes the Ryder Cup, in which the team is everything, ego is left at the door and when suddenly, instead of your own devoted fans, you are playing for country, continent and national pride. Some of the greatest players the world has ever seen find it difficult to adapt (hi Tiger) and their Ryder Cup record becomes a pale shadow of their individual achievements. Others find a sense of belonging, companionship and brotherhood that lifts their performance above anything even they believed possible (Phillip Price, we salute you).

Because of this, the Ryder Cup has had more drama, more heartache, more excitement, more tears, more animosity, more sportsmanship, more unexpected heroes and humbled superstars than any other sporting competition. It has produced more memorable moments than just about any other sporting event, in much less time. This is their (selective) history.

# 1926 An idea is born, and from tiny acorns . . .

Samuel Ryder did not create the event that has borne his name for almost eighty years but he will be forever remembered for providing the trophy and helping, in 1927, to formalise a competition that was happening already. By the time the Ryder Cup officially started, it had already been held twice without ceremony. The idea itself was the brainchild of James Harnett, a circulation representative with *Golf Illustrated* magazine. He had been unsuccessful in raising money to underwrite a competition between the leading men golfers of Britain and America, so took his idea to the United States Professional Golfers' Association (US PGA), and in December 1920 it put up enough money to pay for the expenses of its players. An unofficial match took place in 1921 at Gleneagles, Scotland, and James Harnett selected the American team (probably with the help of team captain, Walter Hagen), so

it is he that we have to thank for the subsequent thirty-five matches that were created to foster a spirit of good-will, but which often set the two continents at each other's throats in the sporting equivalent of war.

Great Britain and Ireland (GB&I) won that first, informal contest 9–3 without apparently breaking sweat, and while this may seem remarkable now because we have become so used to the idea of American dominance in golf, in 1920 things were a little different. Despite what the Dutch may say, the game was invented in Scotland, and the earliest professionals and club makers in America were from places like Carnoustie and St Andrews. The roll call of winners inscribed on the US Open trophy, a championship founded in 1894, was dominated by names like Willie Anderson and Laurie Auchterlonie. The seismic event that changed everything was the 1913 US

Open, in which an unknown amateur from Brookline, Massachusetts called Francis Ouimet took on two of the greatest players ever – Englishmen Harry Vardon and Ted Ray – and not only matched them over 72 holes but thoroughly trounced them in an eighteen-hole play off. As well as being one of the most magnificent performances by an underdog in sporting history, it served to ignite in American hearts and minds a belief that they could take on the best and beat them – something they have been doing ever since. But seven years after Ouimet's victory, and to a large extent inspired by it, American talent was flowering but not yet in full bloom, and so they succumbed to Britain at Gleneagles. And to complete that coincidental circle by which sport so often seems to thrive, the first GB&I captain was the same Ted Ray that Ouimet had defeated in that 1913 US Open.

One thing is clear though: the first unofficial match between the nations failed to generate a great deal of interest, or financial backing, and there would be a five-year gap between Gleneagles and the second unofficial encounter, which came about more through luck than judgement. The governing body of the Open Championship, the Royal & Ancient Golf Club of St Andrews (R&A) decided, for the first time, to stage regional qualifying rounds before the Open. This meant that players from overseas – which in those days usually meant America – had to travel to Europe one week early. Samuel Ryder attended the Open qualifying as a spectator and afterwards was apparently dismayed to see American and home players standing apart from each other. Because they had extra time on their hands, Ryder suggested they form teams for an unofficial match. He put up a prize fund of £5 for each member of the winning team and provided a chicken sandwich and champagne buffet afterwards.

The match was clearly enjoyed by the participants because later that same evening in a pub, George Duncan, a member of the British team, suggested that it become a regular, formal competition, saying to Ryder: 'This is wonderful. It's too bad we don't have a match like this which is official.'

An so one of the greatest sporting events in the world was born because an enthusiastic Scotsman had a few too many drams in a pub and, in the manner of inebriated men before and since, decided that the fellows he was with were the damned finest in the world, and wouldn't it be great if they could all meet up more often? Ryder replied: 'Why not?' and agreed to donate a £250 solid gold cup.

If the Gleneagles contest had been a little one-sided, Wentworth in 1926 was even worse, with GB&I again being the home side and winning by 13½–1½. Looking back on that second encounter, it is remarkable to think that Walter Hagen, one of the greatest match players golf has even seen, was beaten 6&5 in the singles (by our friend the tipsy George Duncan) and 9&8 in the foursomes where, partnered by Jim Barnes, he was thrashed again by Duncan, who was partnered by Abe Mitchell. It was even worse for the USA's Fred McLeod, who went down 10&9 to Arthur Havers, but luckily for McLeod his humiliation does not appear in the official record books because of the unofficial nature of the match – sorry to bring it up here, Fred. Equally lucky for American pride was the fact that neither McLeod nor his team-mates Tommy Armour and Jim Barnes had been born in the US; the first two were expatriate Scots while Barnes was a Cornishman by birth. When the two team captains and Ryder met to discuss the practicalities of a regular encounter, it was agreed that players had to be born in (later amended to 'a citizen of') the country they were representing. It was further agreed that the contest would be held in alternate years beginning in 1927, and that Samuel Ryder would commission a trophy for which they would play.

The first official Ryder Cup matches were arranged for 3–4 June 1927, at the Worcester Country Club, Massachusetts, USA.

Samuel Ryder has said that, had Abe Mitchell died from the appendicitis he contracted on the eve of the first official match, the trophy would have been named in his honour and two teams would now be battling it out in alternate years for the Mitchell Cup. Just doesn't sound right, does it?

*The tipsy Scotsman who may be responsible for the whole thing, George Duncan*

# 1927  Now we can start getting excited

In contrast to the ballyhoo that surrounds today's contests, the GB&I team send-off from Southampton docks for the first-ever Ryder Cup was modest and one that, frankly, met with apathy, even from golfers. In order to finance the trip *Golf Illustrated* launched an appeal to raise £3,000 to pay the British team's expenses, but it fell £500 short and Samuel Ryder had to fork out the balance. After this, the biggest single contribution came from the Stock Exchange Golf Society for the sum of £210. There was also the difficulty of team selection. With no such criteria as an Order of Merit or official earnings to be taken into consideration, the great triumvirate of Harry Vardon, James Braid and James Taylor were pressed into action as selectors.

A historical aside: on that summer's day, as the British team boarded the liner *Aquitania* for the six-day Atlantic crossing, the Ryder Cup itself made its first public appearance. It bore the figure of a golfer on the lid, a man called Abe Mitchell who was honoured at the insistence of Samuel Ryder, who paid Abe £1,000 a year to be his personal golf tutor. Ryder was a late convert to golf, but like many who discover the game after their fiftieth birthday, became one of its most zealous advocates.

Born in 1858, he was the son of a Manchester corn merchant, but when he moved into the family business he found that his father was scornful of his newfangled ways. In particular, young Samuel wanted to sell penny seed packets by mail order so, in the face of his father's resistance, went into business for himself, moving south to St Albans in Hertfordshire (which he chose for its central location and three railway stations) to establish the Heath and Heather Seed Company. He was a workaholic, even if the word hadn't been coined then, and in 1906 was elected mayor of his adopted town. But his long working hours took their toll and when he fell ill, fresh air and light exercise were part of the prescription for recovery: it was suggested that he take up golf. A cricket lover, he initially scorned the idea but in only a short while he was so hooked that he would practise six days a week in all weather (but never on a Sunday). After a year at his local municipal course he joined Verulam Golf Club in 1910 and he clearly had something that either attracted or intimidated his fellow men because within twelve months he had reduced his handicap to six and been elected captain of the club, an honour he was also given in 1926 and 1927. His company sponsored the Heath and Heather Tournament in 1923, and among the field of professionals was Abe Mitchell, regarded as one of the best players who hadn't won an Open Championship.

Ryder befriended the golfer and four years after their first meeting, the GB&I side gathered at Southampton docks for

*The man on top of the cup, Abe Mitchell*

the journey to Worcester, Massachusetts. Unfortunately, Abe Mitchell was not among their number. He had been appointed GB&I captain but a bout of appendicitis that proved nearly fatal put paid to any possibility of travel, so Ted Ray, one of the three-man selection committee, was drafted in as a replacement. His opposite number was Walter Hagen, who would go on to become the longest-serving US captain ever, eventually taking charge of six US teams and remaining involved up to and including the 1937 contest, which was the only one in which he didn't play. Only American-born players were supposedly allowed to represent US but somehow Johnny Golden, an immigrant from Eastern Europe, slipped through the vetting process. Joining him and Hagen were Leo Diegel, Johnny Farrell, Bill Mehlhorn, Gene Sarazen, Al Espinosa, Joe Turnesa and Al Watrous. They were opposed by Ted Ray, Aubrey Boomer, Archie Compston, George Duncan, Arthur Havers, George Gadd, Fred Robson, Herbert Jolly and Charles Whitcombe, but this opposition was pretty weak and found it difficult to adapt to American conditions, and US won 9½–2½. A member of each respective team – Al Espinosa for America and George Gadd of GB&I – did not play at all, and two years later Walter Hagen instituted the American policy, which has remained in place ever since, that all team members would play at least once.

In foursomes play only Boomer and Whitcombe for GB&I managed a win (over Diegel and Mehlhorn), while their team's solitary singles point came from George Duncan, who beat Joe Turnesa by one hole (Whitcombe managed a half with Sarazen). The visitors were as thoroughly outclassed as the Americans had been in the previous year's unofficial match at Wentworth. Some felt that home advantage was a big factor, while others believed that a stormy six-day Atlantic crossing was not the best preparation for such a contest. A more prosaic truth, however, probably rests in the words of GB&I captain Ted Ray, who said: 'One of the chief reasons for our failure was the superior putting of the American team. They holed out much better than we did.' It was to become a familiar litany.

Samuel Ryder was not at that inaugural contest but lived to see two Ryder Cups – those of 1929 and 1933 – on home soil. On 2 January 1936, three years after that second match, he died at the age of seventy-seven from a massive haemorrhage. It happened while he was on holiday with his family in London and his eldest daughter, Marjorie Claisen, arranged for him to be buried with his beloved mashie (5-iron). His youngest daughter, Joan, travelled with her father to all the golf events he attended. She not only continued to attend all the Ryder Cup matches held in Britain but was also in America in 1983 when the US barely beat Europe at PGA National Golf Club in Palm Beach Gardens, Florida. That contest represented the beginning of the end of American dominance and, while the first Ryder Cup in 1927 couldn't match it for competitiveness or drama, Samuel Ryder had sown a seed from which great things would grow.

# 1929  A contest is born – GB&I can play this game too, you know

The first ever match was won by the Americans at a stroll but the return encounter in 1929 at Moortown, Leeds, proved that GB&I could compete too. In the singles, relatively modest home players like Charlie Whitcombe, George Duncan and Archie Compston beat vaunted opponents Johnny Farrell, Walter Hagen and Gene Sarazen respectively. And then the youngest member of the side, Henry Cotton, wrapped it up against Al Watrous, coming from behind to set the seal on a 7–5 win.

American captain Walter Hagen's approach – 'Don't hurry, don't worry. And be sure to smell the flowers along the way' – was so laidback he made Ernie Els look like the Road Runner but it was, like so much of his behaviour, an act. He later revealed that from the moment he woke up on an important day of competition he forced himself to do everything – wash, shave, dress, eat breakfast – with deliberate calm and as slowly as possible, so that by the time he reached the first tee he was as unruffled as a duck paddling quietly across a pond. He was also a master of gamesmanship and at his imperious best in the one-to-one combat of matchplay, which is why he won the US PGA Championship, five times between 1921 and 1927 in the days when it was the only matchplay event to be accorded Major status. During that sequence he won four in a row, becoming the only twentieth-century golfer to achieve this feat in any Major. Hagen famously said he didn't want to be a millionaire, simply to live like one, and he railed against the snobbery of the day, which saw golf professionals as artisans who were not to be allowed into the clubhouse with the lady and gentlemen members. He refused to enter the clubhouse at Royal Troon in 1923 when he won the Open Championship because he, and all the other competing pros, had been barred from it all week. Three years earlier at Deal he hired a Rolls Royce, parked it outside the clubhouse door and ostentatiously changed his shoes in it because he was not allowed access to the locker room. Later, he arranged to eat a sumptuous meal, complete with silver cutlery, in full view of the members' dining room, where he was also unwelcome.

His gamesmanship on the course never amounted to cheating but was borne of supreme confidence in his own ability – he was not above playing to the galleries, who loved his showmanship. On one occasion he faced a shot that was well within his compass – over a tree to a green – but he made a great fuss about changing his club selection, shaking his head and pacing anxiously, as if caught in a great dilemma as to whether or not he should take the shot on. When he eventually put the ball onto the green the crowd cheered him to

the rafters and his opponent no doubt allowed himself a rueful shake of the head.

Hagen would have been a genius of marketing or advertising because he recognised that appearance creates an attitude, and that there is no such thing as objective truth – if people believe it to be so, then it is. So your opponent is much more likely to be defeated if he thinks you are the best player in the world. In all likelihood, whenever Hagen walked (slowly) onto the first tee for a matchplay contest, he would look his opponent in the eye and think the 1920s equivalent of: 'You're mine and you should call me Daddy.' While his foe was probably thinking: 'You're absolutely right Pater.' In 1927, at the first official Ryder Cup, Hagen had paid out of his own pocket for his entire team to be fitted with blazers and trousers from a New York tailor, with the words 'Ryder Cup team' stitched on the jacket breast pocket. Their GB&I counterparts looked shabby in comparison and behaved throughout like the underdogs they were, even to the point of letting themselves be thrashed like miscreant public school boys 9½–2½.

In the face of such a one-sided humiliation, the Europeans, with Britain to the fore, usually respond with niggling, whining complaints and in this 1929 contest, the British PGA refused to allow the visiting Americans to use their newfangled steel-shafted clubs. Hagen's arrogance did nothing to alleviate the British sense of injustice, which can often be sparked for the most trivial of reasons, but this time the braggard's own words came back to haunt him. When he heard he was playing GB&I captain George Duncan in the singles, he said to his players: 'There's a point for our team right there.' It was a remarkable show of arrogance considering that three years earlier, in the unofficial Wentworth match, he had lost heavily to Duncan 6&5 in the singles and previously in foursomes. Not only that, but his cocksure remark was overheard by Duncan and fired him up to the point where he walloped Hagen 10&8 over thirty-six holes. Similar success came to Charles Whitcombe (8&6 over Johnny Farrell), Archie Compston (6&4 over Gene Sarazen), and Henry Cotton (4&3 over Al Watrous). In what was subsequently proven to be an extremely uncharacteristic move, GB&I dominated the singles, overturning a first day deficit to set up overall victory. It was one Ryder Cup apiece and already this infant competition was shaping up to produce a rivalry to match anything in sport.

This Moortown Ryder Cup is probably the first time that the spectators became so involved, and partisan, that their behaviour could affect the result. The 10,000 people who turned out to watch were enthusiastic and vociferous in supporting the home team but, to the disgust and disapproval of many, also cheered the bad shots of the Americans. Europeans like to claim the moral high ground when it comes to crowd behaviour, and especially in Britain there is a myth that 'our' fans are the most knowledgeable and respectful in golf, but this is certainly not always the case and here were the early signs of what was to follow – although no one could begin to guess quite how carried away we would all become.

# 1931 Shooting ourselves in the foot, it's what we're good at

After the first two matches had been shared, hopes were high for a real contest at Scioto, Ohio, in 1931, but GB&I imploded before ever getting on the boat. An original clause of the competition rules said that team members had not only to have been born in Britain or Ireland to represent their country but also had to live there – so two of our strongest players, Percy Alliss and Aubrey Boomer, were omitted because they were attached to clubs in Germany and France. The idea was to reward players who worked in Britain, but, as in later years when full-time membership of the European Tour was seen as a prerequisite for selection, it simply excluded potential match-winners and gave the Americans an enormous advantage they didn't need. It was becoming clear that the USA was now the dominant force in world golf, and the chasm that had opened up between American and British pros was wide and broadening with each passing year. In

America, led by flamboyant crowd pleasers like Walter Hagen, the first player to make $1 million from the game, they 'competed' in lucrative exhibition matches and earned significant income from manufacturers, who wanted the burgeoning stars to play and endorse their products. As a result they were full-time touring pros facing stiff competition week in and out. In contrast, pro golfers in Britain were attached to golf clubs and their main source of income came from club members, to whom they gave lessons, and sold and repaired golf equipment. Their social status was somewhere between that of scullery maid and butler and in most instances they weren't allowed into the clubhouse unless as the guest of a member.

And then just to make sure that whatever slim chance of victory GB&I might have had was quickly removed, the British PGA then insisted all our players had to travel together and

return home immediately after the match. Not only that, but any money they might make in America was to be shared equally among them all. Henry Cotton, who was a conceited and supercilious character at the best of times, took umbrage at being told what to do and refused to agree, so three of the strongest players from Britain were either excluded or withdrew. Cotton had made his own travel arrangements because he wanted to arrive in America early, get used to the conditions and grab a piece of the pie available from big-money exhibition matches. The PGA belatedly realised that his absence would be a major blow to the team and tried to broker a compromise but offered too little, too late and the ever-haughty Cotton went instead as a reporter, and persuaded Percy Alliss to do the same.

If this catalogue of self-inflicted disaster wasn't bad enough, nature

*George Duncan putts in the sweltering heat of mid-summer Ohio*

decided to get in on the act and arranged a heat wave, with temperatures up to 100°F that disconcerted the visitors far more than it did the hosts. Bernard Darwin wrote that 'heat is our worst enemy' and the GB&I team was so badly affected that the British PGA raised a protest and it was agreed that the competition would never again be staged in America in midsummer. Of the matches themselves, they were notable for the fact that America not only won at a canter, taking the overall contest by 9–3, but in many of the matches the margin of victory was insultingly easy. Two of the Americans' foursomes victories were by 10&9 and 8&7, and in the singles there were two 7&6 victories, and one by 8&6.

American captain Hagen didn't have too much time for his opposite number, Charles Whitcombe, regarding him as stuck-up and snobbish. As they stood on the first tee waiting to start their singles match, a waiter bearing a small tray and a cocktail delivered the drink to Hagen, who promptly necked it before hitting his drive down the middle. Whether he pulled the stunt to unsettle a disliked opponent or make a point about his perceived arrogance is not clear, but Hagen won 3&2. It has been suggested that the glass contained nothing more than coloured water, but whatever the motive it served to underline The Hague's reputation as a man who lived fast and would likely die young.

On that sorry second day, GB&I won only two of eight singles matches – William Davies had the better of Johnny Farrell and Arthur Havers beat Craig Wood, both by 4&3 margins. In the previous day's foursomes, only Fred Robson and Abe Mitchell had managed to secure a point. If GB&I had fielded its strongest team the chances are they would have been beaten, but petty, internecine bickering pretty much guaranteed a loss. What next, making the players wear manacles and leg-irons?

Gene Sarazen was on the American team and is best known for his exploit four years later in hitting the 'shot that echoed around the world' in the second ever staging of The Masters, in 1935. On the par-5 fifteenth he hit a 4-wood 220 yards over water, and holed it for an albatross two (which the Americans insist on calling a 'double eagle', but surely that would be four-under par for a hole?). It led him to victory and established The Masters. And yet the man himself says it was not the best shot he ever hit – that accolade falls to a stroke he played in this 1931 Ryder Cup. It came in his singles match against Fred Robson and Sarazen recalled: 'On this short hole, I hooked my tee shot over the green into a refreshment stand. I found my ball in the middle of the stand in a crevice in the concrete. No free drops back then, but a window toward the green was open. I played the ball through the window and onto the green about eight feet from the hole.'

Robson's state of mind can only be guessed at and he three-putted to lose the hole with a bogey and Sarazen, not surprisingly, won the match 7&6.

# 1933 A close encounter, with no hint of what was to come

The uneasy relationship between the two teams was embodied in the 1930s by the battle between J. H. Taylor and his opposite number Walter Hagen (who seemed to make a habit of disliking GB&I captains). Taylor, a Devonian of humble origins, took life deadly seriously and probably looked on frivolity as a hanging offence. In a move not wholeheartedly endorsed by his team – actually, they hated it and were livid with their skipper as a result – he hired a physical-fitness specialist and had them up at 6 a.m. doing cross-country runs. Hagen's chief exercise came from being measured for suits. In all probability the animosity between the two stemmed from several years earlier when Hagen became the first truly independent professional golfer, as opposed to golf club professional. He neither liked nor was prepared to tolerate being treated as the second-class citizen, which was the lot of golf club pros, so he struck out on his own and became the first ever 'unattached' touring pro, confident that he could make a living from tournament winnings, exhibition matches and endorsement deals alone. The move, made with Hagen's inevitable brash cocksureness, was not entirely welcomed, especially by some of the more snotty clubs, which felt that 'their' professional should choose to remain tied to the club and be grateful for the honour that such an attachment bestowed on his (probably undeserving) head. There was also a feeling that this noble sport of gentlemen would become tainted by base motives such as increased commercialisation and the desire to make a living from it. As ever, Hagen didn't give a flying fig what they thought.

Into this debate stepped J. H. Taylor who rebuked Hagen for his unattached status, suggesting that people like himself (that is, those who knew their place) were happy to work for the dignity and status that was theirs by association with a famous club. Unlike his predecessors as captain, however, Taylor would not compete as a player, a move that would be quickly copied by the Americans. In this case it was a pragmatic decision because not only had GB&I been beaten like an old carpet two years before but, with the exception of his resounding loss to George Duncan in 1929, Hagen consistently got the better of his opposite number, and in most cases whoever else they lined up against him as well. In addition, Taylor was sixty-two years-of-age, twenty-two years older than Hagen, so playing was never an option and the age difference probably served to exacerbate whatever disparity of attitude the two men had. This emerged most strikingly before the matches even began, when Hagen failed to turn up at the agreed time and place to exchange the order of play. A second meeting was hastily arranged and again

the American captain failed to show, causing an almost apoplectic Taylor to threaten to withdraw his team and cancel the event. Hagen, who was almost certainly engaging in his usual games-manship and trying to slip a burr under Taylor's saddle, had a good idea how to get his man riled.

It worked too, because Taylor was a stiff, formal character who thrived on adversity and seemed at his happiest when he was miserable. Bernard Darwin wrote of him: 'I do not believe that anyone, not even the great Bobby [Jones] himself, suffered more over champi-onships than he did.' This inner fire made him his own harshest critic but it could be a close-run thing – it is not likely to endear you to successful oppo-nents if you say of them afterwards, with a shake of the head: 'He did not beat me, Sir, I beat myself.'

And so, no doubt with sulphur from Taylor's nostrils still hanging in the air, the matches started and to no one's surprise the first day ended with a 2½ to 1½ lead – but, to the consternation of some, the advantage favoured GB&I. As has so often been the case, the US team of Billy Burke, Leo Diegel, Ed Dudley, Olin Doutra, Hagen, Paul Runyan, Gene Sarazen, Densmore

Shute, Horton Smith and Craig Wood looked much more powerful on paper than the home contingent of Allan Dailey, William Davies, Syd Easterbrook, Arthur Havers, Arthur Lacey, Abe Mitchell, Alf Padgham, Alf Perry and Charles Whitcombe. They were, bolstered though, by the return of Percy Alliss who was back in the UK from his continental sojourn and made himself again eligible for selection. Most tellingly on that first day, the 'dream team' duo of Hagen and Sarazen could scrape only a most unlikely half against Alliss and Whitcombe, having recovered from an almost unimaginable position of four down with only nine left to play.

On day two the people of Lancashire came out in droves – estimates as to their numbers vary but it was at least fifteen thousand and possibly as many as twenty-five thousand. However, a good percentage of them were as much there to see Edward, Prince of Wales, who had agreed to present the trophy, as they were for the golf. Unfortunately, for his Prince-ness he attracted such a large and noisy crowd of his own that he felt it unfair to inflict them on a match and was obliged to beat a (presumably stately) retreat to the clubhouse. Having

lost their point of focus, the spectators started wandering where they pleased, often disrupting matches in the process because there hadn't previously been a need for gallery ropes. Such was the chaos that on the sixth hole Arthur Lacey's tee shot was found by a spectator who put it in his pocket and strolled away, presumably whistling a merry tune, although in fairness the drive was reportedly so bloody awful that no one could have reasonably expected it to finish where it did. To try to cope, stew-ards were equipped with long wooden staffs that had red and white flags attached. They were immediately dubbed the 'Lancashire Lancers' and otherwise largely ignored by a gallery that increased the British reputation for being rather too enthusiastic in support of its team – or, more accurately, not

Walter Hagen wanted to advise Shute on his final green putt because, having seen several matches through the eighteenth, he knew it was quicker than it looked. But the Prince of Wales was talking with the US captain, who thought it would be ill mannered to excuse himself to speak with his player. Shute charged the putt 7 feet past and missed the one coming back.

*Captains Hagen (left) and Taylor in a show of camaraderie for the benefit of Samuel Ryder*

averse to cheering their opponents' mistakes.

Despite or because of this chaos, the singles ended in a nail-biting tie at four each, and the day was decided when Syd Easterbrook holed a tricky 4-footer to beat Densmore Shute one-up, so that the overall score was 6½–5½ in Britain's favour. The Ryder Cup had now been played four times and won twice by each side. This was the closest contest yet and no one could have predicted that the trophy would not make its way to Europe again for just about a quarter of a century.

# 1947    An American to the rescue

The 1935 and 1937 matches had both been won comfortably by the Americans – the second being the first ever 'away' victory by either team – and after a ten-year hiatus forced upon us by the Second World War, the golfing contest resumed at Portland, Oregon. But in 1947, two years after the end of the war, Britain and British golf was almost destitute. The PGA couldn't afford to send a team to the US, and knew it couldn't launch a public appeal with so many of the population living on or below the poverty line. After a few years of American domination and the interregnum forced by the war, it looked as if the cup was slipping into oblivion. And then up stepped Robert Hudson, an American fruit grower who sponsored the Portland Beach Open and was a great supporter of the biennial contest. He underwrote all the costs of the GB&I team, and it has been suggested, with considerable justification, that while Samuel Ryder created the official competition, Robert Hudson saved it from oblivion. He not only paid for the GB&I team (and officials) to board the *Queen Mary* (the ship that is, not the monarch) but also met them when they docked at New York, threw a welcome party at the Waldorf Astoria Hotel and accompanied them on the four-day cross-country train trip to Oregon, in which rich food and good spirits – in both senses of the term – figured prominently (and for which, of course, he also paid). In addition, he provided all their travel and out-of-pocket expenses and picked up the tab for their caddies. It was and remains a remarkable act of generosity from a man who did it all simply because he loved golf in general and the Ryder Cup in particular, and wanted to see the contest staged at his home course. Less well known is that for several years afterwards each member of the GB&I team received a Christmas

*The GB&I team at the pre-match banquet largely provided by Robert Hudson*

hamper of fruit from the man who is the almost anonymous hero of Ryder Cup history.

Unfortunately, Hudson's generosity was not reciprocated on the course, where GB&I were humiliated 11–1. It is not difficult to see why because so many things conspired against them. First, after a long lay-off in which most of the team had rarely seen a golf course and many had been actively engaged in military service, their game was not quite as sharp as it could be. No, let us correct that. In terms of international competition, they couldn't hit a cow's backside with a banjo. In contrast, the Americans had retained their competitive edge throughout the war years and had even continued to select 'Ryder Cup' teams, which then took on other American pros as challengers, with the proceeds raised by ticket receipts going to the American Red Cross. In addition, while the Open Championship in Britain was not played between 1940 and 1945, the US Open continued in 1940 and 1941, the Masters was also held in 1943, and the US PGA Championship was cancelled only once during the war years. The result was that the Americans continued to face top-notch competition from each other while in Britain, as

Max Faulkner said, with rather fetching understatement: 'There was too much else going on and we were rather distracted. The survival of the Ryder Cup was not a priority.'

And then there was the American team, which turned out to be one of the strongest ever fielded. Ben Hogan, Sam Snead, Byron Nelson, Jimmy Demaret, Lloyd Mangrum, Ed Oliver, Lew Worsham Herman Kaiser, Herman Barron and Dutch Harrison were formidable, to say the least, with five of them Major winners to one on the GB&I team (Max Faulkner would not win his Open Championship for another four years). And although GB&I could boast Henry Cotton, who had already won the Open, Fred Daly, Dai Rees, Arthur Lees and Max Faulkner, the other five members – Jimmy Adams, Eric Green, Reg Horne, Sam King and Charles Ward would struggle to be recognised at their own golf clubs. So uncertain was their ability that the team captain, Cotton, didn't play Green and Horne at all, so they had a three-week round trip in order to be privileged spectators. You may be seeing a pattern emerge here and the tapestry it weaves spells out the legend 'Never give a sucker an even break.'

Into this combination of ill fortune

stepped the bumptious Henry Cotton, who demanded that Ben Hogan's clubs be inspected to see if the grooves on his irons were legal. They were, and the rest of the American team's clubs were also offered for inspection, so Cotton examined their golf balls too – it would appear that he simply couldn't believe that the ball-striking of his opponents was so much superior to that of his own side.

When the golfing gods decide that it is not to be your day they can be utterly without mercy, and the 1947 Ryder Cup demonstrated this to perfection – over

In a strange reversal of the norm, Britain in the summer of 1947 faced one of its greatest heat waves of the twentieth century, so that the little golf the GB&I team had been able to play was over hard, dry, fast-running courses. In the days before fairway and even green irrigation systems were commonplace, it would have been like trying to play golf on an airport runway. In absolute contrast, Portland had experienced the sort of late-summer weather that caused Noah to go looking for two of every animal known to man, and the golf course was soaked, soft and sodden. Even Mother Nature, it seemed, was a supporter of the Americans.

two days of foursomes and singles competition, Sam King was the only GB&I player to record a point, which came in the penultimate singles, when he beat Herman Kaiser 4&3. Perhaps he took umbrage at his opponent's name.

Or perhaps it was simply that Kaiser was bored by the absolute ease with which he and his team-mates despatched the challenge. Had he been a bit more motivated he could have been part of the only clean sweep in the history of the competition.

In every other regard the Americans were sharper, better and more focussed. It would be nice to report that this pattern would not continue. But we can't always have what we would like.

# 1949  Are you looking at me?

Animosity and antagonism between Ryder Cup teams (and flowing from the galleries) is not, as we have seen, a recent phenomenon. In 1949, Ben Hogan, who was again the American captain, rightly questioned the legality of the GB&I players' clubs, on which the clubface grooves were too deep, and as a consequence they had to be filed down overnight by Jock Ballantine, the resident pro of the host club, Ganton. It was seen by many to be a retaliatory gesture from Hogan because of the event in 1947. Bear in mind also that the match two years before, in which USA had been totally

dominant, had been made possible only by the generosity of an American benefactor – and no one enjoys being the recipient of charity – and we had a rich stew of resentment starting to simmer.

Four years after the end of the war there was still food rationing in Britain, so the Americans had brought most of their own grub, including six hundred steaks, twelve racks of ribs, twelve hams and twelve boxes of bacon. This generosity was once again provided by Mr Hudson on the assumption that if the British couldn't afford to feed themselves it was asking a great deal to expect

them to play host to a bunch of over-fed, (presumably) over-sexed and over-there Americans. This feast was so exotic that it was at first impounded at Liverpool Docks by Customs officials, who probably hadn't seen such delights for so long that they didn't recognise the shipment for what it was.

When the food was eventually released after a bit of high-level intervention that probably averted a major international incident, instead of tucking in and saying to the home team, 'Look and weep, guys,' the Americans did something even more outrageous: they followed the wishes of

the donor, Robert Hudson, and shared it with their opponents at the pre-tournament dinner. But if they expected the stiff upper (and now well-fed) lips of the British to be grateful they were in for a big disappointment. The mood was summed up by one GB&I team member, Max Faulkner, who said: 'It made us feel rather sick,' but what no doubt really sickened him was the idea of being patronised by the upstarts from across the water – we taught 'em everything they know, you know. It's a great shame because the visitors were making a sincere gesture, but pride is the father of many sins and their actions only served, if you will pardon the culinary connection, to rub salt into the GB&I wound of inferiority. What was almost certainly at the heart of the matter was the perception that plucky Britain had stood single-handed against Nazi Germany for three years, before the American cavalry deigned to ride to victory.

The Americans were captained by Ben Hogan, who only seven months before had the car accident that almost killed him when he flung himself across his wife, Valerie, to save her as their car met a Greyhound bus head-on in fog. He was still on crutches and moving with great pain, but his bloody-minded desire to win

was undiminished and he insisted that his team rise at dawn and practise hard for as long as there was light. But it didn't do them much good because, no doubt stoked by the fires of self-righteous indignation, GB&I hit the ground running and took the first-day foursomes 3–1. It was quite an achievement as the US was by now, without doubt, the pre-eminent golfing nation. It had the climate for year-round play, a huge population, an explosion of course building and popular interest in the game, a college education system that valued and rewarded competitive sport and a full-time professional Tour. Britain had some nice courses.

Actually, it also had some pretty useful golfers but after their first day heroics they were slaughtered in the singles – largely through the inspired play of their opponents rather than any lassitude of their own. For example, Fred Daly shot a superb 66 over the morning eighteen holes against his singles opponent Lloyd Mangrum. Sadly for Fred, Mangrum shot 65 and lunched one-up. The pair then continued to match each other throughout the afternoon eighteen but Mangrum put in a burst of 3, 3, 2, 4, 3 to break Daly's heart and take the match 4&3. Almost equally good play was seen all over the course, but despite diminutive

Welshman Dai Rees also shooting 65 in the morning and eventually beating Bob Hamilton 6&4, while Jimmy Adams saw off Johnny Palmer 2&1, they were the sole home successes of the second day, and the Americans took the singles 6–2 for an overall winning margin of 7–5.

It can be reasonably surmised that Ben Hogan, who was probably the most uncompromising and flinty man ever to pull on a pair of golf shoes, gave his team such a blistering after the first day that they were more intimidated by him than they could ever be by their opponents. Two things became clear on this glorious, sunny day. First, no matter how well GB&I played – and in some instances they played exceptionally – the Americans seemed always to have an answer. Second, the upstarts from across the pond were at their absolute peerless best in singles competition, where they seemed to relish regarding an opponent on the first tee with the thought that they were better golfers, before going out to prove it.

To establish whether the British players' clubs were legal or not, the chairman of the R&A Rules committee was summoned from his Scarborough hotel bath to give a ruling.

*Max Faulkner in typically flamboyant mood at a dinner during the 1949 contest*

# 1957 Oh Lord, a win at last

In 1957 America had ten times the population of Great Britain and Ireland, ten times the number of golfers and courses and nearly ten times the number of Tour events and prize money. Our professional events had to finish on a Friday so that the pros could hurry back to their home clubs in time to sell Colonel Farquharson a few tees and re-grip Mrs McGonagle's putter. A few cock-eyed optimists had seen, in the 1953 and 1955 encounters, evidence that the huge gulf was narrowing – but you had to be mildly myopic or extremely xenophobic to convince yourself, as a Brit, that we really stood much of a chance. For example, in 1955 GB&I recorded four points, their highest ever total on American soil. Sadly, it was only half the Americans' score so they still lost convincingly. There were, it seemed, three types of golf supporter on this side of the Atlantic – optimists, wildly psychotic hopefuls, and those who thought we could win the Ryder Cup.

After the first day, the US inevitably strode into a 3–1 lead and all that remained was the second-day singles and, as every golfer knows, the Americans always win the singles. There are the Rules of Golf, by which we are all obliged to play, and then there are the Laws of Golf, from which we are all meant to suffer. For example it is a Rule of Golf that you may repair a pitchmark on the green but not a spike mark (don't ask – if they made sense, the Royal & Ancient and United States Golf Association would be out of business). But it is a Law of Golf that you never hit a good shot when you are called through; that your best ever round is always followed by a disastrous one; and that the Americans perpetually win the Ryder Cup singles.

Except on this day, when pictures were in black and white and before Doris Day became a virgin, we trounced 'em. After the foursomes GB&I captain Dai Rees called for a team meeting to discuss what to do next. As only eight of the ten-man team could compete in the singles, Max Faulkner asked to be benched because he was, by his own admission, playing 'rubbish'; Harry Weetman also apparently suggested that he should sit out the second day. Rees drew up his order of play but shortly afterwards was astounded to learn that Harry Weetman had told journalists that he would never again serve in a team under the captaincy of Rees. It created a hell of a stink and Weetman was eventually suspended from all official events for a year, later reduced to a few months. What lay behind Weetman's outburst remains in some doubt but reports at the time suggest he was simply aggrieved at being omitted – although he did later apologise.

*Max Faulkner and Harry Bradshaw have an 'informal' discussion for the camera*

Perhaps the furore, in which the players almost universally backed their popular and respected captain, fired up the home team but whatever the cause, they played like men possessed – albeit against a team that some suggested was one of the weakest ever fielded by the US. Eric Brown, a feisty Scotsman who detested the 'Yanks', started things off by dusting Tommy Bolt 4&3, and the rout had begun. Peter Alliss was the only home player not to win and only one match was halved.

Tommy Bolt was incensed by what he regarded as the partisan behaviour of the Lindrick crowds and famously said to Eric Brown after their match: 'I guess you won but I did not enjoy it one bit.' Brown replied: 'And nor would I after the licking I have just given you.' Everyone knew that this match had the potential to be one of the most tempestuous encounters ever – before it started, former Ryder Cup player Jimmy Demaret, who was working as a TV commentator, said the protagonists had last been seen standing fifty paces apart throwing clubs at each other.

Brown would feature in more Ryder Cups but had first come to prominence in 1953 at Wentworth when he beat Lloyd Mangrum in the singles. His captain, Henry Cotton, had said: 'All I want from you is a point,' and Brown, in typically pugnacious style, replied: 'And you are bloody going to get it.'

Two years later in the first-day foursomes he partnered Syd Scott, whose straight, reliable play was a perfect counterfoil to Brown's more aggressive but potentially more wayward style. In that same contest Brown beat Jerry Barber and now, in his third Ryder Cup appearance, his singles record was played three, won three, a tradition he would continue, because in four appearances as a player he never lost in one-on-one combat against another man, but equally never tasted success when in tandem with another player.

His opponent on this day, the famously mercurial Tommy ('Thunder') Bolt, whose superb play was often overshadowed by his tendency to throw clubs in disgust or break them over his knee when he failed to hit the shot of which he knew he was capable. Bolt was once playing in a tournament in America and was about 130 yards from the green on the last hole. He asked his caddy what club he thought was needed and was told: 'A wedge or 3-iron,' to which Bolt responded with a string of epithets, demanding to know why he was being given such a ludicrous choice. The caddy timorously replied: 'Because they're the only ones left.'

On this day Bolt was equally livid and continued to rage against the behaviour of the Lindrick fans. 'They roared when their guys won,' he said, 'cheered when I missed a putt and sat on their hands if I played a good shot.' At one point in the match he missed the green with an approach shot and, in typical style, flung the offending club up the fairway. His opponent, Brown, then put his ball onto the green quite close and, to the delight of the gallery, hurled his own club towards the hole.

Five other Americans were beaten, with one win and a half, with the result that the day's net result was 1½ to 6½. Actually, that wasn't a beating, it was one-sided, non-stop flagellation, and they didn't even have to pay £200 to someone called Miss Whiplash for the

In the first day foursomes Syd Scott faced a long putt on the first green but laid it stone dead – in the middle of the cup, but a few inches short. His partner, Eric Brown, spat at him, through clenched teeth: 'It'll never go in the fucking hole if you don't fucking hit it.'

privilege. Almost a quarter of a century had passed since GB&I had taken the Ryder Cup and it was beginning to look as if they might never hold it again, except in a few ceremonial photographs before the contest began. But now, spurred on by a partisan, rollicking, belligerent crowd at one of Britain's best courses, they had confounded their critics and caused one of the biggest upsets since Cleopatra demonstrated that women can enjoy sex, too. Allegedly. Credit should also go to Max Faulkner, the man who asked not be picked in the singles because of his poor play on day one. In contrast to the aggrieved Weetman, who ran to the press, Faulkner was all over the golf course on that day, like a hyped-up cheerleader, encouraging and cajoling his team-mates and, in the days before on-course scoreboards, relaying details of every other match. He was the unsung hero of that wonderful performance and later, not surprisingly, described it as the highlight of his Ryder Cup career.

After twenty-four long years we had the cup back. Surely it was now, once again, game on.

# 1959    Never mind the cup, we're lucky to be alive

The 1959 match is now best remembered for an episode that happened before the Ryder Cup got under way, before the GB&I team had even reached the venue, and it remains one of the incidents of the competition's folklore that is recalled most vividly – especially by those most directly involved. Talk to any of them and they recount a terrifying story that even today causes an involuntary shudder of horror because, although none of them died, almost all thought they were about to meet their maker. In cold, prosaic terms, the aeroplane in which they were travelling plunged 4000 feet – virtually the height of Britain's largest mountain, Ben Nevis – in a matter of seconds (although Dave Thomas says to this day it was 6000). But that description can hardly begin to tell of the terror on board.

The team had already endured a five-day Atlantic crossing by ship, of which stormy weather had been the most notable feature, and anyone who has been the victim of sea-sickness will testify how debilitating it can be, often causing the sufferer to wish for a quick death rather than a continuation of the agony. Next these bedraggled, weary and nauseous travellers went to Augusta for some exhibition matches with the great Bob Jones, from where they moved on to

Los Angeles and boarded the fateful plane for the routine 150-mile flight to Palm Springs. Unfortunately, they met a hurricane as they crossed the San Jacinto Mountains. Bear in mind also that the Munich air disaster, in which twenty-three of forty-five passengers had died, ripping the heart out of the Manchester United football team known as the Busby Babes, had happened only the year before, and it is easy to appreciate the fear of the Ryder Cup team.

When the first intimations of severe turbulence were felt, Bernard Hunt gave his seat to a flight attendant. He was rewarded for this act of selflessness by being suddenly catapulted upward – or rather, the aeroplane plummeted downward with such speed that he was flattened against the ceiling. Peter Mills, a team-mate, managed to grab hold of another flight attendant to prevent her joining Hunt, as anything loose in the cabin – including luggage from overhead lockers – was thrown around like orange juice in a blender. A vice-president of the PGA, Lou Freedman, was quoted as shouting: 'Let it crash, I can't stand this any longer,' while all around him passengers in various states of panic or resignation either screamed in fear, spoke a few prayers, or muttered

some private last words to their loved ones.

Peter Alliss later said: 'To say it was rough on that plane would be an understatement. It was awful. I remember looking at the roof and seeing all the coats and bags up there – that was the time when you had open racks, and they all just flew up there. The pilot had cut his head. A stewardess had broken her leg or hip. It was total bloody chaos.'

And then, after a great deal of struggle and the passage of several minutes that must have felt like many lifetimes, the pilot managed to regain control of his aircraft and a semblance of order was restored. He guided the plane to Palm Springs but in the course of his final approach was told by air-traffic control that the airport was closed due to the tornado with which he had just gone ten rounds and that he would have to return to Los Angeles. When the plane eventually touched down, without further incident, several of its passengers rushed down the gangway and kissed the ground in gratitude. The GB&I team was told that an alternative flight was being arranged for later in the day, but team captain Dai Rees, no doubt to the unending gratitude of his fellow passengers,

declined the offer and chartered a Greyhound bus for the remainder of their journey. But at least the people who shared this horrific experience could later laugh about it: they subsequently formed the Long Drop Club, complete with club tie, and would meet for dinner whenever they could. History does not record if they threw food at each other or the ceiling in order to reconstruct that memorable journey.

Dave Thomas was on that flight and told me: 'Everything went straight up to the ceiling but you didn't really have time to be scared; it was afterwards that you were really worried. It was John Letters [a club manufacturer] who formed the Long Drop Club. We all became members and Doug Ford (the only American on the flight) was the only American eligible to join.'

When the bedraggled GB&I team got off the aeroplane in which they had thought they would die, a journalist approached the same Lou Freedman who had been praying for early death and said that he had almost wet himself. Lou replied: 'I did,' and ran off to find a safe haven and, presumably, a clean pair of trousers.

*The Long Drop Club, formed in 1959*

With that episode behind them it will come as little surprise to learn that once the team reached the golf course it was only to receive the regulation humbling, this time by a margin of 8½-3½. Frankly, there is not much of interest to recall from the golf except for one aberration by Harry Weetman, who had served his PGA-imposed suspension and who now seemed happy to play once more under captain Dai Rees. If a happy relationship between the two was now restored, its limits must have been tested by Weetman's attitude in the foursomes. Playing alongside Dave Thomas, and against Sam Snead and Cary Middlecoff, the GB&I pair were 2 up with two to play in the only match on the first day that showed any fluctuating fortunes, with a classic nip-and-tuck contest in which both sides gained and then relinquished a lead. Thomas could have sealed the win on the seventeenth green but missed a 5-foot putt. Despite this he drove well up the last, while Middlecoff pulled his tee shot into the rough. Being one-down on the last hole Snead had little choice but to try to reach the green in two, but was asking too much of even his magnificent stroke-making and dumped his ball into the water guarding the putting surface. The best his team could now realistically hope for was to take a penalty drop, play onto the green and hole the putt for a bogey five. Weetman, therefore, could afford to lay up with his approach, leaving a simple pitch over the water and a one-putt par or two-putt bogey, to either win or halve the hole, and therefore win the match. He went for the green.

You could probably write the rest yourself but, for the record, Weetman's ball also found the bottom of the lake, the US made their unlikely five, Weetman and Thomas took six, lost the hole and halved the match. Ordinarily this would constitute a Ryder Cup disaster, but after the flight he had endured only a few days earlier, Weetman probably whistled a happy tune as he strolled nonchalantly from the green.

# 1967 Hogan's swansong

Without putting too fine a point on it, the 1961, 1963 and 1965 matches were one-sided processions in which the US dominated with such nonchalant ease that the competition was again in serious danger of fizzling out. Because the one thing it didn't offer was competition. A number of changes to format had been introduced to try to give GB&I a fighting chance – such as reducing matches to eighteen rather than thirty-six holes (the theory being that there was more chance of an upset over the shorter, sprint distance), increasing the number of points available from twelve to twenty-four, and then to thirty-six, and adding two series of fourball matches. The changes did make a difference – they served to emphasise quite how large the gulf between the sides had become and gave US even bigger winning margins (14½–9½; 23–9; and 19½–12½ respectively). And then, as if to seriously underline a point that didn't need to be made, Ben Hogan was appointed captain.

Hogan is, without question, one of the finest players ever to have swung a club, and in the opinion of many he is the absolute best. Words like 'focused', 'flinty' and 'uncompromising' might have been minted for him, and he was all of these things and more. He seemed genuinely not to care what others thought of him and marched resolutely to his own tune, doing things his way and to hell with the consequences or anyone who thought differently. Not only had he won nine Majors, but he was the first person to take three in a calendar year (only Tiger Woods has matched the feat) and in 1953 was only prevented from chasing the elusive Grand Slam of golf (all four in a season) by a clash of dates between The Open and US PGA Championships. He had recovered from an horrific car accident, after which it was feared he would never walk again, to take six further Majors, and he became only the second player, behind Gene Sarazen, to win all four during his career (they have subsequently been joined by Gary Player, Jack Nicklaus and Tiger Woods). He never played in the US PGA after his accident because the gruelling 36 holes-a-day format was too much for his injured legs, but if he had there is every chance that he would have improved his position as joint fourth in the list of all-time Major winners, behind Tiger Woods, (ten), Walter Hagen (eleven) and Jack Nicklaus (eighteen). And there was the matter of his Ryder Cup record, which was faultless. He had played three times, twice as captain, and in three matches had won all three contests in which he was involved. So when the Ryder Cup was brought to Hogan's home state of Texas, to be played at Champions GC, Houston, it seemed only right to ask the great man to be non-playing captain.

Johnny Pott was in the American side and later recalled his captain's team meeting with the words: 'He said, "Boys, there's nothing to being the captain of the Ryder Cup. You guys are all great players. Pairing is real easy. I'm going to pair together you boys who drive crooked. I'm going to pair together you boys who drive straight. And the first ball's going to be hit by Julius Boros because he don't give a shit about anything. So y'all just go play your game.

"You got these uniforms here. If you don't like the way they fit or whatnot, don't wear them. I never could play in somebody else's clothes. [Doug] Sanders, if you want to come out here and dress like a peacock, that's fine. Whatever you want. But let me tell you boys one thing – I don't want my name on that trophy as a losing captain."'

But he delivered the *coup de grace* for his side at the opening gala dinner. As visiting captain, Dai Rees got to speak first and introduced his team members one by one, extolling their abilities and listing virtually every event they had won, or in which they had done well. It was a long-winded peroration that must have smacked a little of desperation, as he bravely struggled to paint his side as world-beaters, using a comparatively meagre palette. When he eventually sat down Hogan took to the microphone and gestured, as if by pre-arranged signal, for his team to stand – Julius Boros, Gay Brewer, Billy Casper, Gardner Dickinson, Al Geiberger, Gene Littler, Bobby Nichols, Arnold Palmer, Johnny Pott and Doug Sanders all got to their feet. Hogan then simply said: 'Ladies and gentlemen, the United States Ryder Cup team – the finest golfers in the world.'

Peter Alliss, a member of the GB&I side, summed up the effect with the words: 'The British were 2-down before a ball had been hit'. The fifteen-point margin of victory (23½–8½) remains the biggest ever seen. It was an appropriate farewell from the Ryder Cup to Ben Hogan, one of the greatest golfers to compete in the event. And he ensured his team won before they finished their prawn cocktails at the pre-tournament dinner.

Doug Sanders, who was famous for the flamboyance of his clothes, later confessed that Hogan said to him before his singles matches: 'Doug, you will win today, won't you?' Sanders replied that he would and later added: 'One thing you did not want to tell Ben Hogan was "I lost."' Sadly, he did lose – beaten twice on the same day, by the same margin, to the same opponent – 2&1 to Neil Coles at a time when there were two series of singles matches on the final day.

# 1969 (1)   Still a pain

Ken Still of America thankfully played in only one Ryder Cup – at Royal Birkdale, Lancashire, in 1969 – if he'd been in any more it could have resulted in a blood-bath. Over the years many players from both teams have had a particular ability to get under the skin of their opponents, but Still had a talent to antagonise that surpassed even his capacity to hit a golf ball, which was considerable, especially around the greens. This tied encounter is best remembered for Jack Nicklaus' act of sportsmanship on the final hole when he conceded Tony Jacklin's putt; but the overall competition was in stark contrast to that gentlemanly concession. In fact, until the Kiawah Island street fight twenty-two years later, it remained the most antagonistic Ryder Cup ever seen. And a lot of that discord was down to Ken Still. On the first-day foursomes, he was partnered with Lee Trevino against Maurice Bembridge and Bernard Gallacher, and on the thirteenth tee

Bembridge asked Still to move a little as he was standing in his eyeline. Play was stopped for several minutes while Still ostentatiously moved other players, offi-cials and caddies as far away as possible, rather than simply step back the couple of paces that were required. A few minutes later, having been put in a bunker by Trevino, Still attempted a recovery shot that bounced back from the lip and appeared to hit him on the shoulder. When Trevino asked if he had been struck by the ball, Still refused to answer, so Trevino, to his great credit, told him to pick it up and conceded the hole. The Americans lost the match 2&1.

To put the incident in context, though, we need to remind ourselves that Still wasn't the only source of aggra-vation. GB&I were captained by Scotsman Eric Brown, who admitted that for 103 weeks every two years he liked Americans, but when it came to the

Ryder Cup he wanted to tan their arses in the worst possible way. So he began the week with the shameful instruction to his team not to help the Americans look for their golf balls if they should find the rough. He subsequently tried to suggest that it was tiring to be wandering all over the course looking for balls and he did not want his team members to accrue a penalty if they should acciden-tally step on one. But this was a load of hogwash. There is no penalty in such a circumstance, as the GB&I team would surely have known (if you step on your own or a team-mate's ball during a search it's an infringement, but not if you step on that of an opponent).

This instruction quickly leaked to the Press, who were more than happy to fan a few flames of resentment, and then Ken Still proceeded to pour petrol all over them. If his early-morning antics weren't bad enough he then, along with Dave Hill, took part in what was

*Eric Brown determinedly displaying his tartan roots*

probably the most antagonistic, bad-tempered display the cup has ever seen later that afternoon in the foursomes. They were pitted against Bernard Gallacher, a twenty-year-old debutant who, possibly because of his Scots heritage, considered himself the equal of any man alive, and Brian Huggett, one of the long line of combative Welshmen who have graced the Ryder Cup and have never taken a backward step, either on the golf course or anywhere else. He later said: 'If there was going to be a scrap, it'd be with our four – none of us were keen to lose. In fact, the one thing we wanted to do was beat them buggers and there was trouble right from the start.'

More than thirty-five years later Bernard Gallacher had an almost photographic memory of the match and said: 'The acrimony started early in the week when Ken Still and I played and he was guilty of gamesmanship. It started when he and Lee Trevino partnered Maurice Bembridge and I in a foursomes match and I was driving along with him; we were driving at the same holes. And we had quite a long walk up to the eighth tee and he said things like: "You put a great swing on that one, a really good swing." And so there was a bit of needle before we even played the Saturday match.'

*That does not sound like gamesmanship?*

'It may not sound like it, but it was. He's really only interested in beating me and interested in his own game so he doesn't need to interfere with a twenty-year-old playing in his first Ryder Cup. Anyone who knows anything about the game knows that when you get a comment like that, you start to think about your swing and think things like: "Maybe I am swinging well, perhaps I'm swinging slowly, maybe I should swing even slower and be even better." So it's a form of gamesmanship. He's a very highly-strung person and Dave Hill was even more highly strung. So we got to the third hole in this particular match. As I was about to hit my putt from about 20 feet on the third, Ken Still shouted: "Get your own caddy to hold the flag."'

Gallacher explains:

'He definitely waited until I was about to hit it before he said anything. In those days the caddies weren't as they are now; he was using a caddy that was given to him by the PGA of Britain and in those days the caddy who held the flag was probably whichever one was closest to the flag, irrespective of who he caddied for – that's just the way it was. So that irked us. Then on the seventh hole Dave Hill putted out of turn. He hit a good putt up from long distance to about two feet and continued to putt even though I was away. Both Brian and I said: "Sorry, you can't do that." Ken Still just flipped; he said: "If that's the way you guys want to play, take the hole and take the cup." The referee didn't help because he couldn't find the rule. In those days it wasn't the professional referees you have today: they were club pros who were handed the rule book five minutes before they went on the tee; probably went over a few local rules and things like that, so it took him a long time to find out the rule about putting out of turn in a fourball match. Eventually, Eric Brown and Sam Snead their captain were asked to come out by Lord Derby to quieten the match down.'

Shortly after the Ryder Cup Brian Huggett was on the same plane as Ken Still flying to a tournament in the US when the American said to the Welshman: 'How about a practice round together?' As has so often been the case, Ryder Cup animosity is soon put aside when the event finishes.

Huggett recalled to the *Guardian* newspaper many years later: 'On the eighth Still was still arguing the toss and I wasn't about to back down. I suppose I'm quite a fiery bloke and Bernard was young then and a cocky little sod and didn't think anyone could beat him. There was definitely aggro on the eighth. We didn't quite come to blows but it was as near to it as you could get without doing it.'

Gallacher added: 'We weren't going to take that rubbish, we weren't going to be stood on. The Americans have a history of trying to intimidate, of trying to brush you aside. Well, it wasn't going to work.'

The temperature was cranked up a few more degrees on the green. Still had a short putt for par and his partner was on the same line, but further away, facing a birdie chance. Gallacher knew that Still wanted to take his putt to show his partner the line, so he picked up Still's ball and conceded the putt.

Again, Gallacher recalls: 'Ken Still flipped and went completely bananas because obviously he wanted to putt, he wanted to show Dave Hill the line and he didn't know the rule. I went across, flipped the ball across the green to him and said: "You can have that one." It wasn't a giveable putt. It was really one of those acrimonious matches that happened. I don't remember Eric ever telling us to calm down or that we were wrong.'

*He was no wallflower?*

'Oh, Eric was feisty and fiery. A lot of people would lie down and let the Americans stand all over them but Eric wasn't prepared to do that. The whole of that week was a case of stand up for yourself and show them that you're playing as well. We hadn't won the Ryder Cup since 1957; the Americans were dominating it and Eric was giving us strong pep talks every evening just to make sure we went out and played our game and didn't allow ourselves to be put off by these guys.'

The situation was almost out of control. The players were arguing and snapping at each other, the gallery had overheard many of the heated exchanges and were almost a baying mob, and the two team captains, Lord Derby, the president of the PGA, and a number of police were summoned to try and restore calm.

A semblance of order was established and the United States – largely due to the superb play of Dave Hill – took the honours 2&1. Hill went on to compete in two more Ryder Cups but, mercifully, his team-mate on that infamous day did not.

# 1969 (2)  What it should be like?

The Ryder Cup is warfare with different weapons, and while everyone gets injured on the course, the trick, as golf writer Peter Dobereiner pointed out, is not to bleed. But it wasn't always thus. There was a time when sportsmanship, grace under pressure and love of the game counted for more than mere victory – and if you believe that then come here, I've got a car I want to sell you. Golf is rightly proud of its ethics, morality, etiquette and values but that doesn't mean that golfers put style over substance. Yes, they want to win in the right manner, but the bottom line is: they want to win.

Without doubt one of the greatest sporting gestures of all time occurred in 1969 at Royal Birkdale when Jack Nicklaus conceded a very missable putt to Tony Jacklin with the words: 'I don't think you would have missed that, Tony, but I didn't want to give you the opportunity.' Ever since, Nicklaus has

been lauded and honoured for remembering the ethos of golf and reminding us all that the manner in which you play is at least as important as the result. Well . . .

The truth is that some of Big Jack's team-mates were furious with him, and his captain, Sam Snead, wouldn't talk to him for the rest of the day – which included the post-match celebratory dinner. Their attitude was that the Ryder Cup is a team event and it is not up to one man, especially a rookie, to take such a unilateral decision on behalf of his colleagues. Snead said: 'When it happened all the boys thought it was ridiculous to give him that putt. We went over there to win, not to be good ol' boys. I never would have given a putt like that – except maybe to my brother.'

Calm down boys, the gesture came on the final day of the final singles and resulted, as Nicklaus knew it would, in a tied match, at 16–16, so America kept

the cup as holders. It therefore wasn't half as significant a concession as it would have been if the contest was in doubt but, nevertheless, it should be celebrated.

Billy Casper, the greatest ever American points scorer in the competition, told me: 'I wouldn't have given that putt under the circumstances to anyone. We'd worked so hard to get to that position and to have him give that putt didn't go too good with us. Looking back on it now, it was one of the greatest things that ever happened to the Ryder Cup – I was so close I couldn't see it at the time.'

Nicklaus himself later said: 'I'm amazed at the attention that got because at the time I didn't think it was a big deal, I simply thought it was the right thing to do. It didn't make any difference to the result because we were going to retain the cup either way, so I didn't want to take the chance that he

might miss the putt and have his stature diminished. Tony was a hero, and, as the then Open champion, was so important to the game of golf in Britain.'

Brian Barnes, who was making the first of six Ryder Cup appearances that year, says of the incident: 'I couldn't believe my eyes when that happened, because to be in the situation where there was that much pressure on him, because the Americans had been hammering us left, right and centre, and yet it only needed Tony to win that final hole and we'd won the Ryder Cup for the first time since Lindrick. And he conceded this two-foot putt under the most extreme pressure – I don't think I know of anybody in the history of the game who could have been that calm in that situation to realise that if Tony had missed the putt after just winning the Open Championship, it would have done more harm to British and European golf than anything else. And I know full well that that was what Jack was thinking about.'

What has often been overlooked in the aftermath of that most sporting of gestures is that the Nicklaus–Jacklin match, and the contest itself, was one of the most exciting for many years and the GB&I team was able to rouse itself to produce a performance that left the outcome in doubt until the very last match of the last day. There were a number of reasons for their resurgence. First, they were playing at home over a classic links at Royal Birkdale. Second, Tony Jacklin had lifted the Open championship claret jug just two months earlier and his victory had boosted the morale and expectations of both the home fans and players. Third, the larger, American ball, which was easier to manoeuvre, was compulsory for the first time, after a period of several years in which both had been permissible, British players were now well accustomed to using it. Fourth, there was a lingering resentment over Ben Hogan's accurate but hurtful introduction of his players two years earlier as the best golfers in the world, and a more powerful desire than usual to stick it up 'em (and they don't like it up 'em, you know). If you want to see the British at their best, give them a grudge and a sense of injustice, light the blue touch paper and retire to a safe distance. Fired up with a sense of missionary zeal they shot out of the blocks on the first morning like cheetahs on amphetamines and took three-and-a-half points of the four available in the foursomes. The Americans came back 3–1 in the afternoon series but at the end of the day the home side still held a half-point advantage. The next day's morning fourballs also went to GB&I, this time 2½–1½ and again the visitors fought back in the afternoon, taking two matches and halving the other two. This left the match poised at 8–8 going into the singles. But of course, the Americans always win the singles.

Except that in the first round of eight singles matches played on the final morning – they didn't. Lee Trevino beat Peter Alliss, Dave Hill knocked off Peter Townsend and Billy Casper beat Brian Barnes, and these three wins came from the first four

Just ahead of this game Brian Huggett was playing Billy Casper in a tense, tight match. They were all-square on the eighteenth green when a tremendous roar from the seventeenth indicated to Huggett that Jacklin had just won his match (in fact he'd holed an outrageous putt for eagle to draw all-square). So when Huggett stood over his four-and-a-half-foot putt for the half, he was convinced it was to win the Ryder Cup and when it went in, he broke down in tears.

matches on the course; but that was it for the Americans, who lost the other five games. Neil Coles, Christy O'Connor, Maurice Bembridge, Peter Butler and Tony Jacklin all won, and in the last match it was the mighty Jack Nicklaus who was despatched by the Open champion 4&3. With the inevitability of waves crashing on a seashore, the visitors came back at their hosts in the afternoon, but by heaven it was a close call, and it all came down to that pulsating final match. Neither player was on top form but when Nicklaus won the sixteenth to go one-up the omens were not good. Yet Jacklin is nothing if not a fighter and he immediately hit back with an eagle three at the par five seventeenth to pull them back to all square. After both had driven at the eighteenth Nicklaus asked his opponent: 'How do you feel?' and received the reply: 'Bloody awful.' Nicklaus responded with: 'I thought you might, and if it's any consolation, so do I.'

But perhaps the last word on that famous concession should go to the recipient, Jacklin, who said some time after the match: 'Jack saw that that putt on the last hole in 1969 meant a heck of a lot more to the Ryder Cup than who won or lost that particular match. It was a great moment.'

And in a fine gesture the Americans also allowed GB&I to keep the trophy for a year, rather than take it back to the States, which they were entitled to do.

# 1971 Awkward question

Ryder Cup encounters have turned on tiny incidents – someone standing in a player's eyeline, a missed putt here or bad bounce there; but one of the most absurd occurred in 1971 when Arnold Palmer and Gardner Dickinson were playing Bernard Gallacher (who does seem to feature regularly in these controversies, but, then again, he is a Scot) and Peter Oosterhuis. It was in the second-day fourballs at Old Warson Country Club, St Louis, and GB&I had enjoyed a fruitful first day, taking a one-point lead. Despite the fact they were playing away from home – where they had never won – there was a new confidence about the visitors. Tony Jacklin had proved that his 1969 Open Championship win had been no fluke by also taking the US Open in 1970, at a stroll. In addition, the team had plenty of fresh young talent, most notably the rookie Oosterhuis, who seemed to have all the game anyone needed to succeed

at the highest level. His inclusion meant that eight of the side were under thirty and following the historic tie two years before, British optimism seemed to be built on substantial foundations rather than the usual shifting sand.

But some things had not changed, and the British PGA's permanent state of near bankruptcy was one of them. As ever, money was tight and the players had to exist on a shoestring, so much so that the British team was obliged to use club members, who were so excited they nearly wet themselves, as caddies. Arnold Palmer and Gardner Dickinson had taken two points from the first day and so, not surprisingly, had been retained as a partnership for this second-day fourball match, where they faced Peter Oosterhuis and Bernard Gallacher. All went well until Palmer creamed a 5-iron to the green at the 208-yard seventh hole. Gallacher's caddy was so impressed that he said: 'Gee Mr Palmer, what did you hit there?' In doing so he unwittingly broke the rule that prohibits seeking advice and under the Rules of Golf, anything the caddy does is considered to be at the instigation or knowledge of the player, so if a rule is broken, the player is hit with a penalty.

Gallacher remembered the incident thus. 'Peter and I didn't hear him say anything. Whenever Palmer hit a shot in America someone would say "great shot" and this guy must have forgotten where he was because he said that and added: "What club did you hit?" It was a throwaway line that I didn't hear but what upset me – I don't know if it upset Oostie as much – was the fact that they didn't call the infringement on the tee.

'I don't think it was Arnold Palmer's fault either. When we got up on the green, Arnold was at the back of the green and I was lying 2–3 feet away; no one knew before we got there who's ball was closest – there had been a big cheer when both shots were played. It was Gardner Dickinson who brought the question to the attention of the referee who was compelled to ask the caddy and loss of hole was the result.'

What really irked Gallacher was his belief that it was only when the players reached the green, and could see that Gallacher's ball was within tap-in distance, while Palmer would have to hit a special shot to match an almost certain birdie, that Dickinson spoke out. The really puzzling aspect is that the players were allowed to complete the hole (in fact, both teams made par) before the referee announced that because of the rules infringement, GB&I had lost the hole. They went on to lose the match, too, by 5&4.

Gallacher said at the time that he lost all respect for Arnold Palmer but has subsequently decided, like most people in golf, that it is difficult to believe that Arnold Palmer could be guilty of games-manship.

Then again, Oosterhuis remembers that the following day he drew Arnold Palmer in the singles. The British player was having an excellent day and was two-up with four to play when a message was relayed to them out on the course that US had amassed enough points to retain the cup so theirs was, in effect, a dead rubber, which could no longer affect the outcome of the contest. Palmer said to Oosterhuis: 'Shall we walk in?'

In the afternoon singles Lee Trevino beat Brian Huggett 7&6. At one point Trevino's ball was up against a tree, and the only shot he could play was a left-hand reverse wedge shot. He hit it 120-yards onto the green, looked at his opponent and said: 'Don't look at me, I'm as surprised as you are.'

*Bernard Gallacher, who served as both player and captain*

and the young Englishman replied: 'Does that mean you are conceding the match?' If they had walked in without the concession, the match would have been halved and Palmer would have escaped jail – an attempted bit of kiddology on the part of a seasoned pro up against a young greenhorn?

Oosterhuis later said: 'He said "No" with a big grin on his face and I think he was just having fun with a twenty-three-year-old to see what reaction he would get.'

Oosterhuis won 3&2.

Oosty and his team-mates did well in the singles, taking 7½ points to the Americans' 8½ but because of a poor second day they lost the overall contest 18½–13½. To get thirteen-and-a-half points on US soil was an achievement but still nowhere near good enough. After the early parity, when the first four matches were shared two apiece, the US had now won thirteen contests to the lone GB&I success of Lindrick in 1957, and the 1969 tie at Royal Birkdale. In the process, the Americans had amassed a cumulative total in those matches of 187 points, to GB&I's 105.

This was getting serious.

# 1975   Barnesy does the double

Jack Nicklaus is the most successful golfer who ever lived. Brian Barnes is not. And yet on one glorious autumn day in 1975, the biggest underdog the world has seen since David picked up a stone and said to Goliath: 'Do you like hospital food?' faced the Golden Bear down and beat him. Twice. It has been said of golf's Major championships that good players can win them once – if they run into form at the right time and get the rub of the green, but only great players win more than one (a theory nevertheless disproved by Andy North and Lee Janzen, both of whom have won the US Open twice). The same can be said of matchplay. Over eighteen holes an underdog can get lucky or be inspired or meet a superior opponent having a poor round but over thirty-six holes, or two matches, it won't happen. Except it did. And it was not because Nicklaus had a bad day at the office or was having, by his standards, a poor season. He was at his absolute magnificent best that year, winning the Masters, the US PGA Championship (in the other two Majors he was tied third and tied seventh) and four other tournaments.

But while Nicklaus had already cemented his position as the most prolific player ever, using the only criteria that matters, Major

championships (he'd recently won his fifteenth as a pro), Barnes was a smiling bear of a man who too often let life get in the way of his golf. Legend has it that his caddies should have been on triple salary because in addition to carrying a full Tour bag with fourteen clubs, they often clinked their way around the course because of the booze they were obliged to pack just to keep their man going. In fact, his drinking didn't become a problem until 1989, when he was almost at the end of his playing career, but Barnes was a rebel who was frequently fined by his own Tour and we, of course, loved him for it; and we loved him even more because his greatest moments came in the Ryder Cup when we were perennial no-hopers. And his drinking was not just show-manship: 'I was completely rat-arsed, twenty-four hours every day,' he once said. Of the offences for which he was fined, one of the most colourful involved playing the second half of a hole one-handed, in a bet with his caddy. When he was fined he pointed out that pro golfers are in the entertain-ment business and the gallery had been mightily entertained, but this defence fell on deaf ears.

Perhaps his most celebrated incident came in 1981 at Dalmahoy during the Haig Whisky Tournament Players Championship, as recounted in the *Scotsman* newspaper some years later. The sponsors provided a six-pack of beer on the tenth tee. Barnes gratefully downed one and made eagle. So he then finished the beer while making birdies at 11, 13, 14 and 16, and yet another eagle on 17. He played the back nine in 28 en route to a course record 62. What else could a chap do but cele-brate with a few more pints in the clubhouse? Unfortunately for Barnes, after he had been in the bar for two hours, Brian Waites matched his score for the tournament and forced a play off. Barnes had, by most estimates, consumed enough beer to put most men, even John Daly, on their backs – so it was little surprise when he put his tee shot into water during the final play-off hole. Yet, after taking a penalty drop he pitched onto the green and holed out for the most unlikely par. In the face of such an outrageous performance it is little wonder that Waites eventually three-putted the fourth extra hole to hand Barnes the title.

A big man, 6 feet 2 inches and 17 stones in his prime, Barnes was a very pure ball-striker. Even so, when he strolled onto the tee on that September day in the Ryder Cup, wearing a pair of hideous check trousers and smoking a pipe (which he often kept clamped between his teeth while he played a shot), Nicklaus was probably not quaking in his spikes. He would soon have changed his attitude though because Barnes birdied the first two holes and never looked back, winning the match 4&2. Nicklaus was stung.

Barnes himself says: 'It wasn't until '95 or '96 that I heard about this, but Arnold [Palmer] had gone to Bernard Hunt [his opposing captain] the previous evening, the Saturday, and asked who he thought might give Jack a game on the Sunday, bearing in mind they only needed a couple of points or

Laurel Valley, the 1975 venue, did not allow women in its clubhouse – including players' wives. On the first evening at an American team meeting a furious Jack Nicklaus said to captain Palmer: 'Never mind the rules and all that crap, Arnold. If my wife is not sitting down to have lunch with me tomorrow, I'm going home.' The prohibition was relaxed for a week. Mighty big of them.

something to retain the cup. And Bernard thought the course is long and tight, Brian's a good driver of the golf ball, has played with Jack a few times in the Ryder Cup and maybe won't be quite as much in awe, so he's probably the guy, so they decided that Jack and I would be paired together. I beat him in the morning and we went in the Press tent after the game and Jack's asked a few questions and buggers off. I'm asked a few more questions and I couldn't believe the razzmatazz and what the American Press were making of this – it was only 18 holes matchplay, it would have been a far greater achievement in a 72-hole event.'

It is widely assumed that the Americans knew GB&I would put Barnes out as the last man in his team's singles line-up, so they did the same with Nicklaus to ensure a re-match. Jack himself said many years later: 'I'm sure they [the captains] just did it. I never even asked Arnold. I just assumed he went to the captain and said: "You know, Jack would really love to have Barnes again," and the captain said: "Barnesy would probably like another game with Jack."'

*And anyone can beat anyone over 18 holes – once.*

Barnes says: 'I'm more than capable of shooting two 67s. But I remember being asked how I'd like to take the Bear on again in the afternoon and remember saying that lightning doesn't strike in the same place twice. Unbeknown to me, Jack had gone to Arnold and said: "Look, the matches are over, there's only one match that the spectators want to see, and that's Barnesy against me again," so they changed the draw, which has never been done in the history of the Ryder Cup. So we went out to the first tee and of course Jack, with those ice-blue eyes, shook me by the hand and with a smile, in that slightly high-pitched voice, said: "Well done this morning Barnesy, but you ain't going to beat me this after-noon."'

He started birdie, birdie, just in case Brian thought he was kidding. But Barnes was like a terrier with a rat that day and would not let go. He kept pegging his illustrious rival back and then gained a narrow lead of his own with a birdie at the eleventh. The Blessed Brian hung on to his slim advantage and took the blond scalp for the second time, with a 2&1 victory. Yet, despite being, in Barnes' words, 'bloody mad', Nicklaus made a point of sincerely congratulating his opponent,

as he always did when he was beaten. But if the American was 'bloody mad' to be beaten twice he was even more annoyed later that evening. Early in the week his team-mate Bob Murphy had asked American captain Arnold Palmer if it would be acceptable for him to give a prize to the man who played the best for the GB&I side during the week. Palmer said it was okay but when the time came to make the presentation, Murphy gave it to Nicklaus.

Brian Barnes flirted twice with the idea of suicide and eventually won a long, tough battle against his alco-holism. He played for a while on the Seniors Tours on both sides of the Atlantic with much distinction but was forced to retire because of severe rheumatoid arthritis in his hands and feet. He hasn't hit a golf ball since 2000 and now commentates for Sky Television, but he will always be a hero to many because of those momentous two matches with Jack Nicklaus over thirty years ago.

It seemed appropriate to ask him if he thought that day overshadowed the many other achievements of his career and he said: 'I feel sorry for Jack in all honesty. When I was over there playing on the Champions Tour I would always be introduced as: "Brian Barnes, the guy who beat Jack Nicklaus twice in one day." And everywhere I went for the first couple of years it happened and I thought: "He must be really getting pissed off with this."'

*I wouldn't feel too much sympathy for Jack Nicklaus.*

'Exactly. But I did feel that everybody had gone a little overboard.'

Brian Barnes has always been modest about his achievement but for the rest of us it remains enduring proof of the attraction of sport, where just occasionally the form book, and expectations, are overturned in dramatic and memorable style.

# 1979 (1)    All together now

In order to understand the true significance of the 1979 match at The Greenbrier, West Virginia, we need to recall the previous encounter, when two important things happened at Royal Lytham & St Annes. First, in their increasingly desperate efforts to create some sort of drama, or competitiveness, the PGAs again tinkered with the format, making fewer matches (five foursomes, five fourballs and 10 singles). The idea was presumably to reduce the number of points, and therefore the margin of possible defeat that GB&I would inevitably suffer. As a creative solution it ranks right up there with the decision by the captain of the *Titanic* to turn sideways on when he spotted the iceberg, and it was equally unsuccessful. The contests had become a non-contest and, to stretch the *Titanic* analogy further than it probably deserves to go, altering the format was like rearranging the deckchairs of the doomed liner as it headed for the bottom. So bad had things become that Michael McDonnell, one of Britain's most respected and wisest golf commentators, wrote in the *Daily Mail* immediately after the 1975 contest: 'The Ryder Cup passed away yesterday. Not just for another two years, but almost certainly forever. There is no further point to this charade.'

He had a point. The first four Ryder Cups had been shared but in the following 18, America won 16, halved one and lost one. In 1975 the United States captain, Arnold Palmer, had been so bored by his side's routine march – or stroll – to victory that he attended an air show rather than watch the final afternoon's play. Britain had managed that shock win at Lindrick in 1957 and the famous tie in 1969, courtesy of the sportsmanship of Jack Nicklaus. But in

*The first ever European team, with Antonio Garrido (back row, second right) and Seve Ballesteros (front row, third right)*

close on half a century, that was all they could show for turning up every two years before being beaten like a furniture-chewing dog. The Ryder Cup was a complete non-event in America, where it wasn't even televised, and there had been mutterings of the need for change, but it fell to Jack Nicklaus, the dominant player in the game, to be the catalyst for that change. He recalled: 'We were playing in the 1977 event at [Royal] Lytham [& St Annes] and I sat down with Lord Derby, the head of the PGA in Britain, and I said: "John, you know that for everyone on the American team it's a great honour to play in these matches, but when the matches start there isn't much competition. We win every year [*sic*] and I don't think that's right. You've got a European Tour and if you included the European players we'd have some great matches that would really add to the Ryder Cup."'

Lord Derby said: 'Leave it with me,' and, good as his word, the necessary changes were not only made but completed in time for a pair of continental Europeans to be included at the next contest. Nicklaus said, many years after his invaluable intervention: 'There was a time when the American players would say it was a privilege to make the team but wouldn't think much of the matches themselves. Now we face a tough match every time.'

The second significant event of 1977 was the introduction of new, young players – notably Nick Faldo, Mark James and Ken Brown, who would form a strong nucleus for Europe over many years to come. Faldo, in particular, revelled in being the youngest player, at the age of twenty, to represent either side, and in partnership with Peter Oosterhuis he won his foursome and fourball matches (against Ray Floyd and Lou Graham, and Jack Nicklaus with Floyd again) before seeing off Tom Watson – then number one in the world – by one hole in the singles. It was an astonishing debut and one that foretold Faldo's future success, as he went on to become Europe's longest-serving and most successful player.

The match itself was the usual procession, with America winning 17–11 and never looking threatened. But it had enormous significance, not so much for itself but for what it foreshadowed, because this was the encounter in which GB&I ceased to exist and Europe came into being – at least as far as the Ryder Cup was concerned. The two continental trailblazers were Seve Ballesteros (naturally) and Antonio Garrido. Ballesteros was already the hottest prospect in golf but his teammate, Garrido was less awe-inspiring. He had won three times on the European Tour and was a steady, rather than spectacular player who has nevertheless enjoyed longevity, having played on the Senior Tour successfully since 1995. His eldest son, Ignacio, succeeded him as a Ryder Cup player in 1997. But when Antonio and Ballesteros made history for Europe there were few signs of what was to come because they lost two of the three matches they played in tandem, and both were beaten in the singles. But a sea change had occurred that would, before too long, alter the entire nature of the competition. It may also, perversely, have helped that Ballesteros got off to such a bad start, because the experience lit a fire of resentment against the Americans that was to smoulder, and often burst into flames, for twenty more years.

In order for Continental Europeans to be included, Samuel Ryder's daughter, Joan Ryder-Scarfe, had to agree, because it was she who needed to sign the legal agreement changing her father's original Deed of Trust.

One other small incident was to be the harbinger of things to come. The format changes meant that now there would be 12 singles matches, so every member of both sides would get at least one game. Because of this, a procedure had to be introduced should someone be unable to play because of illness or injury, and the infamous 'name in an envelope' formula was introduced. At the end of the second day each captain had to select a member of his team whose name would be placed in a sealed enve-lope. If a member of the opposing side became unable to play, the 'enveloped' player would also have to sit out the singles, and each side would get half a point. It therefore made absolute sense that the name that went in the envelope was the player considered by his captain to be the weakest. However, when European team-member Mark James failed to recover from a chest injury, and had to be withdrawn from the singles, it transpired that American captain Billy Casper had misunderstood the proce-dure and put the name of his strongest player (Lee Trevino) into the envelope, rather than his weakest (Gil Morgan, who was himself carrying a slight injury). To his great credit the European captain John Jacobs – admired every-where as much for his innate good manners as his abilities as a golfer – recognised that a genuine mistake had been made and did not insist that Trevino should sit out the final rubber. It was a decent gesture in a lost cause, but nevertheless something to be admired.

# 1979 (2)    Two little boys

America didn't usually need too much help in winning but at The Greenbrier in 1979 their assistance came from an unlikely source: two members of the European team, Ken Brown and Mark James. Neither was making his debut in the event, as both had been at Lytham two years before, but they appeared to have not the slightest interest in its history or traditions, the importance with which it was viewed by fans, partic-ularly in Europe, or the feelings of their team-mates. It began at the airport before they even left their home country, when Mark James arrived, in the words of captain John Jacobs, 'looking terrible'. This isn't difficult for James, who has worn a droopy moustache for most of his career, along with the facial expres-sion of a bloodhound that has stumbled onto a tin of dog food but forgotten his tin-opener. He and Brown were firm friends, room-mates and soul-mates, and James admits in his book *Into the*

*Bear Pit*: 'It did not bother us if people took a dislike to us because we had a don't-give-a-damn attitude which was fairly evident in some of our behaviour.'

He goes on to discuss several fines he incurred on the European Tour (few of which were his fault, he suggests), and adds that, by the time the Ryder Cup came around, officials had him and Brown singled out for special treatment. 'There was a tangible feeling that they were determined to keep an eye on us,' he writes. 'And didn't they just.'

While James was ploughing his individual furrow, his mate Ken Brown seemed equally determined, like Frank Sinatra, to do things his way. He was regularly fined for slow play and never was it more deserving. As even his best friend says: 'He was diabolically slow. When he stood over a putt you were never sure which would come first: his backstroke or darkness.' The portrait James himself paints is of a strong-minded pair, with a rebellious streak, who neither liked nor trusted those in authority, and who were rather keen to demonstrate that they would be neither intimidated nor cowed by officialdom.

Once in America, things went from bad to worse. At the gala dinner Mark James left early: he says because the room's bright lights were exacerbating his headache. Both players had failed to attend a team meeting: they say because they had been practising on the course and not seen the note shoved under their hotel door informing them it was due to take place – and when they did arrive it was to find everyone else in full uniform while they were still dressed in golf gear. Captain John Jacobs sent them off to change and yet they managed to also be late for the opening ceremony.

James wrote, just over twenty years later: 'Then we were accused of yawning and fidgeting during the national anthem. There was a definite feeling that we were being frowned upon, and we were less than enamoured with the way we were being treated.' He does not, though, deny the charge of fidgety, bored restlessness. I have spoken to a number of journalists and others who were at the ceremony and all have said that James and Brown simply made no effort to hide the disdain with which they regarded the entire process. Reading James's account at this distance it is very difficult to escape the conclusion that a deep-seated feeling of injustice has burned so deeply for so long that he has come to believe it.

James himself wrote: 'Bernard Gallacher's wife Lesley told me years later that at one stage she took me to one side and gave me a damn good talking to. If she remembers that, then I am prepared to go along with her story, but I have no recollection of it.'

I put the point to Gallacher by saying: 'James has said in his autobiography that your wife Lesley wanted to give him a good slap.'

He replied: 'Vivienne Jacklin and Lesley pinned him up against the bar and just told him to start behaving and grow up, and Mark admitted that in the book. Mark didn't feel he had done anything wrong, that was the ironic thing about it.'

Thankfully, both men went on to distinguished careers, and Ken Brown is a successful TV commentator while James has been playing the US Champions and European Seniors Tours with considerable success. James, in particular, is renowned for his dry, almost arid wit and has brightened many a press conference. More importantly, these good friends represented their country in subsequent Ryder Cups and gave all of us many better memories than The Greenbrier in 1979.

*Mark James (left) and Ken Brown, together and apart*

*He still doesn't?*

'Well, he did quite a lot wrong and was fined by the tournament committee on the strength of the captain's report. He and Ken Brown were very fortunate, I think, that they weren't banned for life.'

Even the legendarily laidback Sandy Lyle is clearly annoyed by the memory and told me: 'Whatever point they were trying to make they didn't achieve it. I think Browny himself was probably more influenced by Mark James at the time; they were the best of buddies and I can understand how Ken got on the same wavelength. It all started just leaving Heathrow. I had played in and won the European Open at Turnberry the day before we left for America so I had quite a long trek to get to Heathrow. I wasn't flying but drove for six to seven hours with my uniform on and ready for the team to leave. We were all told we had to wear our uniforms and then Mark James turned up in a pair of jeans and training shoes, which is not really what I would say was the best of starts from the team spirit point of view. And things went worse as the week went on – not turning up to dinners or not trying to turn up. You had Jacklin going into one room and Brian Barnes going into another and the two guys came out wearing ties. I don't know what was said behind the walls but that's what happened.'

After two decades James seems incapable of acknowledging, except in the most grudging way, that the events of that Ryder Cup were other than he would like to remember them. But when the whole of the world marches out of step – or rather, in this instance, recalls the events of that Ryder Cup in a very different way to you – at some point most people might question whether it is they themselves who are marching to a tune that no one else can hear. Brown hints at remorse in an interview with Laurent St John in her biography of Seve Ballesteros. He says: 'It was just a catalogue of minor incidents that would have ended if the captain had stood up and said: "Come on lads, this is a team effort."

'Did I regret it afterwards? Well, I'd have loved someone to say something at the time. At the actual time of the event I didn't really think we had done a terrible amount wrong, but when you add it all up . . .'

Captain John Jacobs was too nice a man to give them the kick up the arse they deserved but when they returned to the UK, James was fine £1500 and Brown was docked £1000 and banned from team golf for a year. Such punishments are not handed out lightly.

# 1981 (1)   The best team ever

Because the GB&I team had been widened to now encompass continental Europe, so that young, fresh, talented players like Nick Faldo, Sandy Lyle, Mark James, Howard Clark and Sam Torrance were bolstered by the likes of Seve Ballesteros, Bernhard Langer and Manuel Pinero, there was finally some substance to European optimism. Of course, every two years saw a renewed buoyancy and unrealistic expectations of success, but even the most committed 'glass half full' observer realised that, for many of the previous biennial clashes, dreams of victory were, to put it bluntly, just pissing into a hurricane. But this time there was the hope, at least, of something more substantial than simple pie-in-the-sky cockeyed optimism. Seve Ballesteros had not only won two Majors (the 1979 Open and 1980 Masters) but he had taken on the Americans in their own backyard on the US PGA Tour and beaten them there, too. In addition, he

was the most naturally gifted and exciting golfer in the world and even his peers – who by nature are conservative and not given to hyperbole – were often astounded by some of the shots he pulled off. And then, merely to prove that there are golfing gods, and that just when you least expect it they lie in wait with a sockful of wet sand to deliver to the back of your ear, the Americans turned up at Walton Heath, Surrey, with the strongest team ever assembled. And Seve Ballesteros wasn't selected for Europe.

Astonishing though it may seem now, the four players in line for the two wild-card picks – which were then made by a committee of three rather than the captain – were Mark James, who had returned home in disgrace two years earlier, Peter Oosterhuis, an experienced and successful Ryder Cupper, Tony Jacklin, who, at thirty-seven could see his best days only in the rear-view

mirror, and Ballesteros, who, along with Tom Watson, was arguably the best player in world golf. None of the four candidates had played their way onto the team by right, but in the case of Oosterhuis and Ballesteros this was because they hardly competed in Europe and only prize money earned there was considered in the Ryder Cup standings. Oosterhuis chose to make his living in America and was all the stronger for it, while Ballesteros had all but boycotted his own Tour in an argument over appearance money. The Tour was trying to ban it, arguing that all available cash should be spread among the competitors at every event. Ballesteros disagreed, pointing out that he was a star and that by his very participation, crowd numbers, television coverage and consequently revenues were greatly increased, therefore it was only reasonable that he should get a bigger slice just for turning up. His argument was bolstered by the

fact that his own Tour was continuing to pay appearance money to big-name American stars. It only baulked at the idea of coughing up for home-grown talent.

Captain John Jacobs wanted the two strongest players, Ballesteros and Oosterhuis, but the other two on the committee – Neil Coles and Bernhard Langer – felt that the Spaniard should be punished by non-selection, and that view prevailed, so Oosterhuis and James got the nod. It was like sending an FA Cup team onto the Wembley pitch without a goalkeeper.

By contrast, USA had so many star players it could have afforded to leave half of them at home and still win without breaking sweat. Of team America's twelve players, eleven were or would become Major winners – the sole exception being Bruce Lietzke who, if he'd had the application to go with his talent, would have made it a round dozen. Tom Kite and Ben Crenshaw had yet to record their Major victories but in addition to this trio, in no particular order, came Lee Trevino, Bill Rogers, Larry Nelson, Jerry Pate, Hale Irwin, Johnny Miller, Tom Watson, Ray Floyd and Jack Nicklaus. Between them they had thirty-six Majors. The Europeans had none (although Sandy Lyle, Nick Faldo and Bernhard Langer would subsequently become Major winners). The records of Nicklaus, Miller, Watson, Irwin and Floyd probably speak for themselves but of the other, perhaps lesser-known players, it is worth a few moments examining them more closely. Larry Nelson is one of the most underrated golfers there has ever been. Just a few weeks before this Ryder Cup he had taken the US PGA Championship by a convincing four strokes and two years later he would win the US Open. It is worth repeating the old adage that anyone can get lucky and win one Major but only the best take two. In addition, and perhaps even more pertinently, Nelson had played in the previous Ryder Cup with such distinction that he had been selected for all five matches for which he was eligible, and won them all. It was a streak he would continue at Walton Heath, where he won all four contests that he played and finished the week with a perfect record of played nine, won nine – a unique achievement.

Bill Rogers has subsequently disappeared from everyone's radar, but, despite the richness of talent with whom he shared a team uniform, he was the best-ranked player in the world that year and had won the Open Championship a few months before by the same comfortable four-stroke margin with which Larry Nelson had taken the US PGA. Rogers' subsequent loss of form is puzzling but if you want to compare him to anyone of recent years the most appropriate person would be David Duval.

In both cases their fall from the highest level came with bewildering speed but for a short time their flame burned as brightly as anyone's.

And then there was Jerry Pate. His only Major win, the US Open, had come five years earlier but his comparative lack of success since then was due to the persistent and perennial injuries that

About the only note of levity for the beaten home team came at the dinner that concluded proceedings. Sam Torrance and Lee Trevino – good friends who always enjoyed each other's company – had been drawn against each other in the singles, and on the first tee Trevino said: 'I'm going to beat that moustache off you.' Torrance lost 5&3 and arrived at dinner having shaved, the first time anyone could remember him with a clean upper lip since he attended junior school.

eventually forced him to quit the game. Despite that, when fit he was a match for most and Lee Trevino asked to be paired with him, saying: 'With my brains and his golf we could beat anyone.'

Despite this overwhelming firepower Europe managed to get the better of the first day, taking it 4½–3½ but after that it was one-way traffic and the United States eventually triumphed 18½-9½. When the American team had been announced, keen golfers dribbled saliva onto their Pringle sweaters at the prospect of seeing such an awesomely talented line-up in action. They were not disappointed. Out of eight fourball and foursomes matches on the second day, America won seven, and they went on to take seven out of twelve singles, with two others halved. Just occasionally super-stars live up to their billing and the 1981 Americans remain the best Ryder Cup team ever seen.

# 1981 (2)    Is that all you've got?

Some times in matchplay you couldn't hit a barn door with a telescopic rifle from 10 feet and still win, and other days you shoot the lights out and lose. Matchplay does not ask that you shoot low scores, or make a bucketful of birdies and eagles, merely that you do better than the other guy. So if he takes nine on a hole, all you have to do is get it down in eight. We therefore see real anomalies in the format, where two members of the same team could have widely contrasting days and neither get the result they deserve. Bob Bogey could have trouble finding a fairway with a compass but come up against someone even more inept and win – despite playing 18 holes in an approximate 80 strokes (and in matchplay stroke scores are often approximated because putts or holes are conceded and players do not therefore have to hole out). In contrast, Bob's team-mate Bill Birdie could have the best day of his career, hole everything he looks at and lose, by virtue of meeting someone who also plays the round of his life. The latter fate befell Sandy Lyle in his 1981 singles match against Tom Kite at Walton Heath – one of those contests that had everything.

Sandy Lyle has been a puzzling enigma ever since he first walked into our lives as a schoolboy champion. Had he been born with a few more ounces of the relentless inner drive shown by Nick Faldo he would almost certainly have won more. But it would have been at the expense of his famously easygoing charm. He's a big man, blessed with

*Sandy Lyle, on a day when even his sparkling best was not enough*

sublime talent – some believe one of the most naturally gifted golfers ever – who often seems to amble down a links course fairway, gazing out to sea with such nonchalance that it's a surprise not see him licking an ice cream cone as he goes. In their youth and early adult careers, he and Faldo were clearly destined for great things, so with almost depressing inevitability the Press built up a rivalry that assumed far greater import in the pages of newspapers than between the men themselves, and it helped that they were such a contrast in manner and style. Few have been driven to success with a more voracious appetite than Faldo. Absolutely fixated on his target of being as good as he could possibly be, he left the impression that he'd happily play Snap for money against a stutterer. Not satisfied with his impressive career, he famously rebuilt his swing in order to contend more consistently for the Major honours by which he defined every golfer, eventually taking six (three Masters and three Opens). Lyle was almost as bemused by what he could achieve on a golf course as those of us who watched, often in amazement. He wore his talent lightly and (until it deserted him) rarely questioned his swing. The problem in the latter part of

his career was that, once things started to go wrong, because he had never analysed why he could do what he did, he had no idea how to fix the broken machine. Watchers of golf in the UK tend to be fans either of Faldo, the ultimate champion, or Lyle, the ultimate golfer, and I always fell into the latter camp for the rather naïve reason that I believe the way a man behaves on life's journey is far more important than the things he achieves.

Yet despite his legendary, slightly bemused persona, Lyle is also a competitor and when he ran into form could beat just about anyone, except on this day in 1981 when he locked antlers with Tom Kite. Sandy had eight birdies but Tom Kite played the game of his life and was ten-under par, proving to Sandy that on some days even your best isn't good enough.

'That was one of them,' he agreed. 'I was six under after ten holes and was only all-square. I made another couple of birdies but got beat 3&2 in the end. There was something like seventeen birdies and two eagles in one match that didn't even go to the eighteenth. The golf was good and I enjoyed it – as far as you ever can enjoy getting beat. But you don't mind that. It's when you're playing

a lower standard of golf that you know you can normally play and you get beat by one hole – that eats away for a while. I gave it my all and had a great start but was just battered by birdies. As I was making them, he was too.

'But it turned around because a few months later I beat him 7&6 in the World Matchplay.'

That last is the measure of Sandy's competitiveness. We all remember his defeat in the Ryder Cup singles – he recalls the subsequent revenge. But he wasn't the only one to be beaten that day as America's superstars cranked up their games. Europe had ended the first day with a surprise lead, but was put firmly back in its place on day two, being hammered 7–1. Bernhard Langer and Manuel Pinero were the only pairing from the home side to scrape a point (against Ray Floyd and Hale Irwin in the morning fourballs). The singles were

Sam Torrance knew he was drawn to play Lee Trevino in the singles and offered him a lift to the course. After driving around in circles for a while, Trevino asked Torrance if he knew where he was going. 'Yeh,' Torrance replied, 'I'm going to London – I'm going to get half a point today.'

also pretty relentless one-way traffic. Bernard Gallacher fought Bill Rogers to a half, as did Bernhard Langer against Bruce Lietzke, but Europe managed only three wins out of twelve attempts. Manuel Pinero (again) showed his tenacity against Jerry Pate, Nick Faldo beat Johnny Miller and Howard Clark took the scalp of Tom Watson, but all three matches were in the second half of the draw, by which time the overall contest had long been decided.

It was now twenty-four years since we had won the Ryder Cup, the 1957 success being our only victory in almost fifty years of trying, stretching back to 1933.

Things were very serious – but about to get a whole lot better.

# 1982 (1)   Please sir, can we have some more money?

Despite the thrashing handed out by the American Dream Team at Walton Heath one year earlier, the European Tour was getting stronger with each passing year and a remarkable crop of players were vying to become the biggest fish in a small, but rapidly growing, pond. And yet the Ryder Cup once again was threatened with oblivion because the British Professional Golfers' Association was poorer than a church mouse.

The PGA was the official guardian of Samuel Ryder's trophy and event but that was because, in 1927, when Mr Ryder needed an organisation to act as custodians of the competition, the PGA was the only national organisation for professional golfers.

But then in the early 1970s came the European Tour, to which the real talents migrated, while those who were happy to remain as club and teaching pros stayed with the PGA, which became their representative body. And while the Tour was getting stronger with each passing year, and the number of events and value of prize money increased exponentially, the PGA remained dependent on member subscriptions for income and would have struggled to put on an informal barbeque for a few friends, never mind stage a major international sporting contest. So to keep the cup alive a sponsor was needed, but in one of the most ill-timed decisions ever, Sun Alliance, the insurance company that had been forking out money in support of a doomed cause since 1973, decided it had seen more lame ducks than the local wildfowl hospital and pulled out.

This left Colin Snape, executive director of the PGA with a headache. He is quoted, in Robin McMillan's excellent book *Us Against Them*, as saying: 'The Ryder Cup was finished. Sun Alliance

had been one of the last "patrons", as distinct from commercial sponsors. The chairman, Lord Aldington, was a golf nut and a friend of British prime minister, Ted Heath, and he felt that sponsoring the Ryder Cup was in Britain's national interest.'

It seems remarkable now to consider that the event that generates hundreds of millions of pounds could have been facing extinction, but decades of having sand kicked in our faces by those smart, good-looking bullies from the other side of the ocean were taking their toll. And although golf fans in the UK were still interested, after a fashion, even their stiff upper lips were beginning to wilt. British comedian Bill Bailey says: 'I am an Englishman so I crave disappointment,' and never was this philosophy more accurately reflected than in our continued willingness to turn up every other year in order to be patronised and stuffed. In America, meanwhile, you could have drawn more interest and a bigger audience with a display of aerobic crocheting. Such was the lack of interest among players that Tom Weiskopf qualified for the 1977 US team but opted instead to go hunting for an apparently rare breed of sheep.

The PGA and Colin Snape were rescued by a whisky distiller by the name of Bells, which was anxious to expand into the American market – so much so that it initially proposed to sponsor the European team only when it was playing away from home. But Snape was a canny negotiator and eventually got the company to cough up £300,000 for the next two events, which, when you consider that the Sun Alliance deal had been worth only £75,000 a pop, was pretty good going. The PGA of America still had to be persuaded but Snape had already told them the truth – that unless some sort of overt sponsorship was allowed, the contest would die. Now, of course, commercial sponsors are fighting for an opportunity to get a foot in the door and even have their proposals heard, but just over twenty years ago the whole shooting match (sorry Tom) was within months of the same extinction facing Weiskopf's sheep.

Colin Snape, in his desperation to find a backer, even approached the company that managed the careers of Tom Jones and Engelbert Humperdinck. He eventually told a meeting of the Ryder Cup committee that in six months the only offer he'd had was £80,000 in cigarette coupons that could be redeemed for cash. The committee agreed that a sponsor was needed.

# 1982 (2) Give it to Jacko

Great Britain and Ireland expected to lose and were good at it. Europe had greater self-belief, but in the two contests since Johnny Foreigner had been made eligible for team membership they had still been hammered – albeit most recently by the strongest line-up of American talent to ever pull on a cashmere sweater and pastel trousers. But the PGA of Britain was getting cute and beginning to undertake a serious analysis of what might be needed to breathe life into a moribund event.

One crucial element, it realised, was captaincy, and following on from that belated spark of genius was the recognition that the job should not necessarily be handed around among the good old boys who had done their bit as players. Okay, it had taken fifty-six years for the penny to drop but bureaucracies, especially in the UK, have a way of slowly digesting all the relevant information before eventually,

often reluctantly, making a sensible decision.

It seems remarkable that even now some people think the captain's job is overrated and consists of not much more than getting the fourball and foursomes pairings right and making sure there are enough courtesy cars. And as for the daft notion of being made captain and then trying to earn qualification as a player and combine both roles – as most recently espoused by Tom Lehman – anyone who thinks that both jobs can be done competently by one person, needs to lie down in a darkened room until they come to their senses. Any consideration of the importance of captaincy has to look at the performances of Europe in 1983 and since, when the role was transformed by a cocksure, confident, opinionated winner by the name of Tony Jacklin.

How he was offered the job remains a bit of a mystery because, although he

loved the event with a passion, he had been very angry not to be selected as a player in 1981, and Jacklin is not the sort of man to forget a slight.

Ken Schofield, a canny Scot who was the guiding, often autocratic, hand at the helm of the burgeoning European Tour, approached him. Jacklin said he wanted to think about it, and added that if he were to accept it would be on his terms, and that a number of conditions would have to be met. To Jacklin's surprise, Schofield agreed. Jacklin said, in that case I want everything to be top drawer. The players should be dressed in uniforms, provided equipment and facilities and generally treated in such a way that they feel like superstars, not some poor, embarrassing family member that no one talks about. And for good measure, he added, I want them to fly first class. Schofield said 'leave it with me' before coming back and saying that not only would they fly first class, but it

*Captain Tony Jacklin (fourth left), with Gordon J. Brand to his right*

would be on Concorde, and that their wives, girlfriends and caddies would be with them.

Every condition that Jacklin demanded was met, and he had little choice but to accept the job. He was not the first or last person to be outflanked by Schofield.

His next task was to persuade Europe's stellar player, Seve Ballesteros, to return to the fold and forgive and forget the dispute with the European Tour that had seen him also excluded from the 1981 team. Ballesteros took a bit more persuading, but after a couple of weeks he allowed Jacklin to talk him round – it probably helped that they shared the disappointment of missing the previous (non) contest. However, Jacklin didn't get everything right. He recognised early on that while he had a nucleus of world-beaters on his side, Europe still lacked the strength in depth of America. He therefore told his strong men – Ballesteros, Faldo, Langer, Lyle and Woosnam – that he would expect them to play in all five matches if necessary. Because of this he had a

conversation with one of his lesser-known players, Gordon J. Brand, on the flight to America, in which he suggested that Brand probably wouldn't compete until the final-day singles. No doubt it was well intentioned and designed to stop Brand from having his hopes of selection dashed over the first two days, but it must have been devastating to be effectively told by your captain, before even arriving at the venue, that you weren't rated too highly.

But for every decision Jacklin got wrong, he got another 19 right and he also introduced a number of innovations that were so successful they are continued even now. Among other things he launched the 'team room' where players, wives and caddies could mix and mingle with no intrusion from Press, officials or anyone else. They could swear, laugh, joke, take the mickey and bolster each other's spirits. Jacklin also insisted that players left their egos at the door, that no individual was more important than the team and that everyone should be prepared to do whatever was asked of them. It must have

been a difficult conjuring trick, convincing his 12 players that they were equals, while making it clear in his selection process for the first two days that some were more equal than others – and yet he pulled it off.

Jacklin was the son of a lorry driver and, until golf made him a millionaire, did not know too much about privilege and luxury. Nothing came easily, he worked and sweated for every success he achieved, but he was patriotic to the core and had something to prove to the Americans. Having won the Open championship in 1969, he went to Hazeltine for the following year's US Open as the holder of the claret jug, to discover that golf fans there had no idea who he was. In his first couple of rounds the addition of four men and a dog would have doubled the size of his gallery. So he won, by a remarkable seven strokes. Now he was on a mission to take the Americans again in their own backyard.

He didn't quite make it that first time but he threw down a gauntlet with which the Europeans have been slapping American faces ever since.

# 1983 (1)   I'll take care of you son

Ian Woosnam played his first Ryder Cup match at the PGA National, Palm Beach, Florida, and, like so many debutants before him, was bricking it. So wily European captain Jacklin paired him with the more experienced Sam Torrance, who had been in the previous encounter. The Scotsman played in the morning foursomes and, alongside José-Maria Cañizares, saw off Ray Floyd and Bob Gilder 4&3. Torrance was therefore the picture of avuncular charm and relaxed grace on the first tee for the afternoon fourballs, where he whispered to a visibly shaking Welshman: 'Don't worry, I'll look after you, it'll be all right' – before hitting his ball straight right and out of bounds. He went OB again on the second and then on the third put his ball into water. Woosnam smacked one down the middle at the first, made birdie and never looked back, but as he later said of his comforting partner: 'I didn't see him for

three holes.' In fairness to Torrance he did subsequently make seven birdies – which he was still anxious to point out twenty years later when I tentatively broached the subject – and his side secured a half against Ben Crenshaw and Calvin Peete.

First tee nerves, of the kind felt by Woosnam, are commonplace in the Ryder Cup and time after time even the most experienced, Major-winning players describe them as the greatest fear they have encountered on a golf course, more intense by far than setting out on the last round of a national Open championship with a chance to win. Woosie himself told the *Daily Telegraph* in 1997: 'You feel like throwing up. I always have a swift look around to check the whereabouts of the nearest bush. I mean, you don't want to be sick all over your opponents' shoes, do you?'

The point was visibly reinforced on the first morning of the 2002 contest at

The Belfry, when the opening fourball match saw Tiger Woods and Paul Azinger pitted against Darren Clarke and Thomas Bjorn. Azinger is a Ryder Cup veteran who had played in three previous matches. He's also a Major winner who would take the 1993 US PGA Championship, but, more important even than those achievements, he had overcome a personal struggle with cancer of the shoulder and said that such an experience tended to put other things – like golf – into perspective.

It was therefore surprising to see his apparent hesitancy on the first tee, where he uncharacteristically dithered over club selection, returning the iron he had selected to his bag and opting instead for a 3-wood (to the accompaniment of good-hearted cheers from the Belfry gallery). He then blocked it miles right – an appalling shot for someone of his calibre, but the overriding impression gained from watching him was that he

was relieved just to have persuaded clubhead to meet ball.

Because of that I spoke with a few more players on the subject. Lee Westwood is one of the more famously relaxed people in golf, and when I said I wanted to talk about Ryder Cup first-tee nerves his manager, Chubby Chandler, intervened: 'Wrong person to ask.' Yet Westwood said: 'Yes, I felt it. Anyone who doesn't feel nervous at the Ryder Cup, or who tells you they're not, is lying. That's the most nervous I think anybody gets: stood on the first tee at the Ryder Cup. It just becomes so difficult to get the ball on the tee.' He agreed with the impression I had gained of Azinger and said: 'Yes, he was relieved just to have hit it.'

His team-mate Luke Donald debuted at the same event and said: 'I was off in the first match and felt reasonably calm until I put the tee in the ground and then it suddenly hit me. It was fourball so we were all driving but I was first in my match and then Paul McGinley followed me. I think because there's so much hype about the first tee that it builds up and it did hit me. I put my tee in the ground and just started feeling very nervous – shaky, and I hit a horrible shot. I tried

rehearsing it a few times and saw myself hitting a good shot but when the time came I hit a horrible shot about 40 yards right.

'You can work on visualisation stuff; you can work on breathing techniques to try and calm yourself, but nothing will quite prepare you for the moment because you don't know what it will be like until you get there.'

Even the famously relaxed Sandy Lyle said: 'You have the practice rounds, working as a team, people with you and it's all very casual and nice and then the team meetings and of course the build-up – you read and hear about it so much and it's a really big thing. But come Friday morning you get on that first tee and maybe you've been drawn in the team to play first and it's quite a daunting shot, especially when they call your name out on the microphone as representing Europe. You've got to get on with it; the bell's gone and there you go. It also depends on the golf course because some of the holes can be really daunting so the hole itself can determine how you feel.'

Englishman Ian Poulter, who has overdosed on both confidence and bravura, told me about his debut in 2004 at

Oakland Hills. 'I watched everybody tee off on the Friday because I didn't play. I stood there and watched Mickelson hit it 40 yards left of the fairway, Tiger hit it 40 yards right. I didn't play until Saturday morning but no, I didn't think it was that difficult. I had to follow them on the Saturday and hit it awful, a really poor shot. It wasn't that I was really nervous but I did make a really poor swing. But it is a very daunting tee shot.'

Peter Baker said: 'People talk about these out-of-body experiences and that's what it feels like, as if it's not you, so you've just got to rely on what you've done in the past.'

Perhaps the last word should go to American Mark O'Meara, who said: 'I remember how it affected me when I made my debut with Curtis Strange at the Belfry back in 1985. I was shaking like a leaf on the first tee, as nervous standing over the ball as I had ever been in my life. And where did I hit it, I can hear you asking? Well, suffice to say that the ball rebounded off a tent some distance off the right side of the fairway. My partner wasn't real impressed.'

# 1983 (2)  Show me the Way

Rookies have often performed better than expected, and many relative unknowns (Philip Walton, Paul Broadhurst, Peter Baker, Jim Gallagher Jr, Mark McCumber and Billy Maxwell, for example) have emerged for one contest, far exceeded anyone's predictions and then disappeared, to quote Dave Hill, 'faster than a fart on a hot skillet'. Few, however, sustained a remarkable record over two Ryder Cups, which is probably why Europeans think with particular fondness of Paul Way, a short, stocky, powerful man who should have earned undisguised enmity from middle-aged bald men everywhere in view of his youth (he was twenty when he made his debut), his golf game and his head of improbably thick blond hair. He became the second youngest Ryder Cup player ever (only Nick Faldo appeared as a more callow youth but both have now been overtaken by Sergio Garcia, who debuted aged nineteen) but is statistically one of the most successful, with 6½ points out of a possible 9. Tony Jacklin famously described Way as a 'cocky little bugger', and so he could be, but an innate introversion is also there if you look closely, and may well explain his subsequent lack of success at the highest level. In Norman Dabell's book *How We Won the Ryder Cup*, Way's caddie Warren Darrell says: 'Paul's basically a shy person but at team events likes to be seen to be doing well – which he was, judging by his overall results in the two cups he played in.' It also helped that Jacklin not only put him with more experienced players (Ballesteros in 1983 and Woosnam in 1985), but kept those partnerships intact throughout the two events, giving the talented but raw youngster the chance to develop a rapport with his senior partners.

But after their first outing together, Ballesteros went to his captain and famously said that he didn't want to hold the youngster's hand. More than twenty years later, I asked Paul if he had been aware of that at the time. 'No, not really,' he said. 'I was twenty and he was twenty-five but he thought he was forty-five; that's the way he came across. But in those days Europe didn't have strength in depth so you couldn't really put all your strong players together, you had to try and partner them up in such a way that they'd help the less experienced ones.'

*How much of it do you remember now?*

'I remember most of it. I qualified in tenth place in the last counting event so I thought I would have maybe two games, three if I was really lucky. But Seve and I played practice rounds together and then Tony Jacklin said I was playing the first morning, and again in the afternoon. What I remember most now is that we were given one shirt for each day and the weather was absolutely steaming hot and when you came off the course you

*Seve and Paul Way almost agreeing the line*

were drenched, so Tony had to nip in the pro shop and buy us a bunch more shirts.

'I also remember playing against Tom Watson on the second day. He was, and still is, my hero, and that's the only time I have ever played in the same group as him – and if I remember right, we were 5-up after six holes [the Europeans eventually beat Watson and Bob Gilder 2&1]. He was every bit the man I hoped he would be, and of course Tom is an absolute gent whether he's won or lost.'

*What did you think of your captain calling you 'cocky'?*

'When you're playing well it's easy to be cocksure, but when you're struggling you go back in your shell. If I'm doing well I don't mind being out there and when I had a chance of winning, I won, and I'm proud of that but yes, I'm both cocksure and shy.'

*Does it bother you that people tend to remember and know you only for those two Ryder Cup appearances?*

'It's great to be remembered for that. Yes, people do remember those two cups more than they remember my victories, because it's a team thing and unites everyone. But I won three times,

including the PGA Championship [the European Tour flagship event, comparable to the Players' Championship in the US] and I'm proud of those wins.'

*Did you see any gamesmanship?*

'There's always lots of things going on, especially on the greens. I had a bit of a row with Calvin Peete's caddie on the first morning in '83. He was close to standing on my line so I had a word. He said: "Do you know who I am; my name's golf ball [his nickname]," as if it should mean something. I said: "No, I don't know who you are and keep away from my fucking line."

'One of the things that has stopped now – I think Sam Torrance and Curtis Strange put a stop to it in 2002 – is taking practice putts on the green after the hole has been decided. They [the Americans] were using it as a deliberate bit of gamesmanship to slow things down, take their time getting off the green and make you wait on the tee. It used to drive me nuts so I'm glad they've banned it.

'I have talked to lots of Ryder Cup players and nearly all of them have had rows at some point on the course, usually on the greens, with the other players or caddies.

'Christy O'Connor was playing Dow Finsterwald in '57 and Finsterwald had taken a hatful around about the fourth hole and Christy putted up to a few feet and Finsterwald walked off to the next tee. Christy assumed he's been given his putt but when he got to the tee Finsterwald said that he hadn't conceded it and claimed the hole. Christy said: "You shouldn't have fooking done that," and beat him 7&6.

'There's also a story that in one of the matches where Eric Brown was in charge – '69 I think – the two captains were called together because there was a danger that things were getting out of hand on the golf course. Brown nodded and agreed and then when he got back to his team, said: "Good lads, that's exactly how I want you to behave."'

Paul Way behaved properly and wasn't going to take any crap. But what we remember and appreciate more are those six days in 1983 and 1985 when he took on the best and, more often than not, beat them.

The first-morning foursomes saw the pairing for which everybody with a musical bent had hoped, Gallacher and Lyle.

# 1983 (3)   The greatest shot ever played

Not the greatest shot in the Ryder Cup but the best ever, bar none. It's 1983 in Palm Beach and a rejuvenated, up-for-it Seve Ballesteros has been magnificent all week. Captain Tony Jacklin pulled one of his motivational masterstrokes by asking Seve to partner the blond debutant Paul Way. He reckoned that the talented young man from Kent was a potential birdie machine but in order to succeed, must be paired with a senior player. Seve objected, arguing that he was not there to wet-nurse rookies or be a father figure, but Jacklin told him that it was exactly because he was the best player in the world, that he needed to take on the extra burden and that only he could do it. The best way to Seve's heart was always through flattery, and he agreed. Nevertheless, Jacklin's gamble seemed not to have paid off when the unlikely partnership went down 2&1 to Calvin Peete and Tom Kite in the opening morning foursomes. But the skipper

stuck with his men and they repaid him by beating one of the strongest American pairings, Ray Floyd and Curtis Strange, one-up in the afternoon fourballs. The next morning they halved with Gil Morgan and Jay Haas before beating Bob Gilder and Tom Watson 2&1 in the afternoon.

Then it was the singles and Ballesteros could finally relax and play his own game, man-on-man against Fuzzy Zoeller, who was suffering from a bad back, wearing a corset, eating pain-killers like sweets and hadn't played since the first day. But an old adage has it that you should beware the injured golfer. Jacklin had decided that he wanted several of his strongest players at the top of the order because, going into the last day tied at eight apiece – something the visiting team had never managed before in America – it was essential they got off to a fast start, so he put the Spanish maestro out first. In what was to become

a mantra for Ryder Cup captains in subsequent years, the skipper realised that momentum is everything and that if the blue of Europe started going up on the leaderboard it would inspire players later in the order. It seemed to work because, although he fell behind at the second hole, Seve then rattled off four consecutive birdies, all courtesy of long putts, to take a commanding lead. Zoeller, though, is made of much sterner stuff than his wisecracking, relaxed bonhomie might suggest and over the back nine he also won four consecutive holes to take a one-hole lead. Ballesteros wiped out that lead and got back to all-square with a 20-foot putt on the sixteenth green, so a match that had been punch and counter-punch all the way had two holes remaining to decide the outcome. The seventeenth was halved and the gladiators marched to the tee of the eighteenth, a 578-yard par-5 double dogleg with water all the way up

the right side and a well-bunkered green. No one had reached it in two all week – except Seve.

This was the moment he chose to hit, what he later described as: 'One of the worst drives of my life' (and the competition for that accolade, let's face it, is considerable) that dived into near impenetrable rough. Even his genius for unlikely recoveries was tested to the limit because his next shot, with a pitching wedge, could only advance the ball about 20 yards – straight into a fairway bunker, where it came to rest underneath the front lip of the hazard. Zoeller wasn't in too great shape himself, having also found rough from the tee and had no choice but to pitch out – but at least he was on the fairway quite a way ahead of his opponent, which made him odds-on to win the hole. Ballesteros was 260 yards from the flag and his only option was to advance as far as he could up the fairway with a short iron, and try to get close with his fourth shot. Except that he marched into the sand clutching a 3-wood. European supporters groaned audibly because no one else would even contemplate such a shot, let alone pull it off.

Ed Sneed, an on course commentator for ABC, later said: 'The announcers may have come to me and said: "What's Seve going to do?" And I said: "I think he's just going to take a 6- or a 7-iron and hit it out." Then he went in there with a wood, and he hits a 3-wood from 245 yards onto the fringe.'

Ben Crenshaw, in Robin McMillan's oral history of the Ryder Cup *Us Against Them*, said: 'We saw one of the greatest, most amazing shots we'd ever seen . . . when he got down in there he was in a position where you would take a 5-iron or even a 7-iron just to get it out. But here comes this 3-wood. I remember watching it on television – I don't remember exactly who I was with – but I remember we all went, "What?" And then Seve took this big cut at the ball and it popped up and ended up on the green and none of us could believe what we'd just seen. Absolutely amazing.'

It was a high, slicing shot that remains in the memory of all who saw it, even Jack Nicklaus described it as one of the best he had ever seen. To his great credit, Zoeller hit a superb 2-iron in response to about 10 feet and when the combatants holed out with two putts, both the hole and the match was halved.

But it was a half only Seve could have conjured.

Tony Jacklin's Concorde warning to Gordon J. Brand that he might not play much was proven accurate. Brand had to sit things out until the singles, where he lost by two holes to Bob Gilder. It remains his only Ryder Cup match.

# 1983 (4) Kissing the sod

Jack Nicklaus is not given to hyperbole or exaggerated gestures, which is probably just as well. because the only time anyone could remember him showing over-exuberance was in the 1970 Open championship at St Andrews. That was the year Doug Sanders famously missed a tiddler on the seventy-second hole for outright victory and had to come back next day for an eighteen-hole play-off with Nicklaus, which the Golden Bear eventually took by a score of 72 to Sanders' 73. When he holed the winning putt, Nicklaus flung his putter skyward but then, rather embarrassingly, had to cover his head as it chose to obey Newton's immutable law of gravity and plunge earthward again, almost braining the unlucky Sanders in the process. Possibly as a result of this but more likely because he simply preferred to let his golf do the talking, he spent the remainder of his career celebrating Major wins or exquisite shots with a

slightly abashed smile and gentle wave to the crowd. But emotion once again got the better of him in 1983 at Palm Beach, where he captained the home team.

That team – consisting of Ben Crenshaw, Ray Floyd, Bob Gilder, Jay Haas, Tom Kite, Gil Morgan, Calvin Peete, Craig Stadler, Curtis Strange, Lanny Wadkins, Tom Watson and Fuzzy Zoeller – was respectable but not awesome. It contained five rookies (one more than Europe) and, while built around a formidable core, names like Haas, Peete, Morgan and Gilder would not strike fear into the hearts of their opponents. Europe had its own share of lesser-lights, people like Paul Way, Brian Waites, Ken Brown, Gordon J. Brand and José-Maria Cañizares, but had a strong nucleus in the form of Seve Ballesteros, Nick Faldo, Bernard Gallacher, Bernhard Langer, Sandy Lyle, Sam Torrance and Ian Woosnam. By the end of the first day Europe had carved out a one-point lead,

but by the close of play on day two the US had fought back to level things at eight. Nicklaus was worried and annoyed and that evening told his players: 'I do not want to be remembered as the first captain of an American team to lose on American soil.' And of course, the Americans always win the singles. Well, almost. Ballesteros halved with Zoeller in most unlikely fashion before Faldo and Langer both recorded wins, over Haas and Morgan respectively. Then came three American wins to swing the pendulum back in their favour, delivered by Gilder, Crenshaw and Peete (over Brand, Lyle and Waites). Paul Way then underlined how at home he now was in this biennial event by seeing off Curtis Strange; Kite and Torrance squeezed each other to a half and Floyd was beaten by Brown. That left only two matches to be concluded, with Europe holding a one-point advantage. José-Maria Cañizares was locked in a duel

*Captain Jack Nicklaus (right) salutes Lanny Wadkins*

with one of the toughest American competitors ever, Lanny Wadkins, who had been deliberately placed near the bottom of the order of play by Nicklaus because he wanted his men of steel where the heat was most intense. The Spaniard had been three-up with seven to play and, despite a typically gutsy Wadkins fightback, was still one-up as they played eighteen.

Wadkins himself recalled: 'The second shot [of the par-5 hole] was a 3-wood over the lake. I wanted to lay up but Cañizares had already played and hit his 3-wood perfectly. I said: "Hell, I've got to hit 3-wood now." As I hit it Curtis Strange starts shouting "Get up, get up," but I said: "It's solid Curtis. It's over."'

But that was the job only half done. And if the 3-wood Seve Ballesteros had played from a bunker only a few hours earlier was the best shot ever seen in this competition, what Wadkins did wasn't too far behind in terms of execution. It was made a little easier by the fact that Cañizares had already played his third and left the ball short of the green, between a pair of bunkers and nestled in long grass. Wadkins was 72 yards from the hole, which meant he couldn't hit a

flat out shot, and when the pressure is on the last thing anyone wants to do is finesse the ball with a less than full swing because when the nerves are frayed the first thing to disappear is lightness of touch. Nevertheless, he broke European hearts with a superbly executed pitch that nestled inches from the cup for a guaranteed birdie. The unemotional, poker-faced, deadpan, unflappable Nicklaus fell to his knees and kissed the ground from which Wadkins had just played and secured an invaluable half. On television replays you can see that, as the ball reached the top of its arc in flight, lightning crackled across the tops of the trees in the background – Wadkins can even, it seems, bend Mother Nature to his will when the mood is upon him.

He said: 'When I got on the green and saw how close it was, I was like "Aghh, Aghh," and I was too dry for anything to come out. Probably the first time in my life I've ever been speechless.' And just to wrap things up, Tom Watson beat Bernard Gallacher on the seventeenth hole, so the overall result was a point win for the United States.

'A new era of Ryder Cup competition has started,' said Nicklaus, in a

statement that was more accurate than even he could have guessed. 'We will not be the favourites when we go to the Belfry in two years. This score was no fluke.'

The Europeans were devastated, having come so far, played so well, looked their opponents in the eye for the first time and felt themselves to be their equals, only to lose by the narrowest of margins. They were sitting in their team-room, feeling morose, when in marched Seve, eyes blazing, fists clenched and a smile the size of the Golden Gate Bridge plastered across his face. 'Why are you miserable?' he demanded to know. 'This is a great victory, to lose in America by just one point – we must celebrate.' And celebrate they did. They may not have beaten the mightiest golf nation in the world in its own backyard, but they had come mighty close and the contest was changed for ever.

Nicklaus is alleged to have later said of Wadkins: 'Larry has brass ones and needs a wheelbarrow to carry them around.' At the PGA dinner later the following year Wadkins was presented with a gold wheelbarrow.

# 1985 (1) Seve drives the tenth

The Belfry, the now famous course in the heart of the Midlands, has seen some of the most dramatic Ryder Cup moments of them all, but when it first opened it was not particularly well received – being described by many as too similar to the potato field from which it had recently been converted. But even in those early days it had a few dramatic holes, and none more so than the short par-4 tenth. In 1978, the Brabazon, course was unveiled to the world when it staged the Hennessy Cup, a match between Britain and the rest of Europe. Seve Ballesteros was playing Nick Faldo and when they reached the tenth the Englishman did what he was supposed to do and hit an iron from the tee, to leave a wedge shot into a green that was guarded by water. Seve, of course, rarely does what he is supposed to and reached into his bag for the driver, clearly intent on driving the green, some 310 yards distant. Nowadays, it is commonplace

for the longest hitters among the elite of the various world Tours to drive the ball in excess of 300 yards, but twenty years ago, using clubs with a persimmon head, it most emphatically was not. Once again though, the Spanish maestro was not only contemplating a shot that no one else could envisage, but he pulled it off. He launched himself at his drive as if the ball was the most hated thing in the world and almost threw himself off his feet with the ferocity of his attack. The ball flew high – very high – and eventually came to rest 8 feet from the hole. If you visit the Belfry now you can still see the plaque that was erected to celebrate Seve's astonishing shot.

So when the Ryder Cup came to town, the hole was deliberately shortened to 275 yards in the hope that more of the world's best would be emboldened enough to go for the green and create even more drama. But American captain Lee Trevino had been round too many

blocks to be suckered and instructed his team not to go for it: the risk/reward ratio was, in his view, all wrong. A mid-iron from the tee and wedge onto the green gave an excellent chance of birdie, while an attempt to go for the green offered the possibility of an eagle two, but more likely a disaster. Tony Jacklin, the home captain, issued no such instructions and left his players to make up their own minds. He then put Seve Ballesteros and Manuel Pinero out first in the opening morning foursomes against Mark O'Meara and Curtis Strange. The Americans started poorly and were four down after six holes but then rallied to win a couple so that by the time they reached the tenth hole they were only two holes adrift and clearly had momentum on their side. But Ballesteros knows more than a little about the psychology of matchplay and recognises winning a hole is important but that winning it in audacious style –

with a shot that your opponents wouldn't consider, let alone pull off – can drive a stake through their hearts. So he reached into his bag for a wood. Nobody had really doubted that it was something he would try, it only remained to be seen if his ability matched his ambition.

It should be remembered also that the Ryder Cup got Seve's competitive juices flowing like no other, because it was against the Americans. Ballesteros could start a fight at a pacifist convention and during his career had picked many – including with his own European Tour – but one of his deepest feuds (and when it comes to slights or perceived wrongs he has a long memory) was with the US PGA Tour, and the American players he felt had snubbed him. The history stretched back to 1978 when Seve, a week short of his twenty-first birthday, won the Greater Greensboro Open, overcoming a five-stroke deficit on the last day to take the title with characteristic bravado. Two days later, Tour commissioner Deane Beman, who knew box-office when he saw it, offered Seve his Tour card, which

meant he would not have to go through the rigours of qualifying school in order to play in America by right. A number of American players were so outraged by what they saw as favouritism that they immediately called for the offer to be rescinded.

Another problem was that the US Tour insisted that its members, especially Seve, played a minimum fifteen events a year, which would leave Ballesteros constantly crossing the Atlantic, or unable to support his own Tour in Europe. Things weren't improved one year later when Ballesteros took his first Major, the 1979 Open championship at Royal Lytham & St Annes, and was immediately dubbed the 'Car Park Champion' by US press and players alike because at the sixteenth hole on the final day his drive found a temporary car park, from where he made birdie. What rankled Ballesteros was that his drive – which ended up 24 yards right of the fairway – was calculated and deliberate. He knew the area would have been trampled by spectators and that in the event of his ball missing the fairway and rolling under a car, which it did, he

would get a free drop from the obstruction. Finally, it seemed that Americans, especially the press, could never get his name right. For at least two years after this Open win, whenever he appeared in the US, at least one reporter would call him 'Steve'.

So when Seve Ballesteros got to the tenth tee on the first morning, he wasn't just playing Strange and O'Meara, but seven years of perceived slights and disrespect. He drove to the back of the green, Pinero and he two-putted for a birdie three and eventually won the match 2&1.

Did you doubt it?

Seve's dislike of American reporters culminated in a memorable exchange on the practice green at St Andrews when a TV reporter opened a question with the words: 'Steve, can you tell us . . .'

Ballesteros interrupted with: 'Seve, my name is Seve.'

'Okay Steve, can you tell us . . .'

Ballesteros fixed the man with a glare and said: 'My name is Seve, your name is asshole.'

*The Belfry's famous tenth hole, immortalised by Seve*

# 1985 (2) The worst miss

The 20/20 vision we gain with hindsight is a questionable gift, but there are moments in sporting encounters that can clearly be seen to decide an event, even one that stretches over three days. They are so resonant and pregnant with meaning, that even at the time their significance is all too apparent to those both taking part and standing on the sidelines – a batsman is rattled by a bouncer, for example, and although that ball doesn't take his wicket, everyone can see that it won't be long before another does. Such a moment came on the second day of the 1985 match, when Craig Stadler stood over a putt, that could not have been more than 30 inches, for a deserved win for himself and Curtis Strange, against the European pairing of Bernhard Langer and Sandy Lyle. But to truly see how that one putt swung an entire Ryder Cup, we need to look both forward and back.

Europe got off to a bad start on the first morning, losing the opening sequence of foursomes 3–1. Only the redoubtable Ballesteros, in tandem with Manuel Pinero, managed to gain a point for the home team (2&1 against Curtis Strange and Mark O'Meara). But they fought back in the fourballs, winning two, halving one and losing one, to face a deficit of only one point at the end of the first day. On the second morning Europe won the first two fourballs – Sam Torrance and Howard Clark overcame Tom Kite and Andy North 2&1, while Ian Woosnam and Paul Way spanked Hubert Green and Fuzzy Zoeller 4&3. The American pairing of Mark O'Meara and Lanny Wadkins (damn his eyes) had inflicted a rare defeat on Seve Ballesteros, who was paired again with Pinero, by 3&2 and so, with the scores tied at 5½ points each, all eyes turned to the final match on the course.

Sandy Lyle was reigning Open champion, having lifted the claret jug only two months earlier, but if Bernhard Langer had matched his level-par 70 on the final day, he would have won by three. On paper, therefore, they were a redoubtable force. But Lyle was out of sorts and the first day he and Ken Brown had been on the receiving end of a 4&3 drubbing handed out by Lanny Wadkins and Ray Floyd – two men you would definitely not want to meet in either a dark alley or on the golf course. Lyle was annoyed because he had not been picked for the afternoon fourballs but his anger, as so often was the case with this ambling, shambling, good-natured man, was directed at himself for his poor play, rather than at others.

His nonchalant charm was entirely natural and his long-time caddy, Dave Musgrove, once wrote: 'My wages must be the best on Tour and when I stay at his house in Wentworth he brings me tea in the morning. That can't be bad, can it?'

But despite his thoroughly deserved reputation as a gentle soul, Lyle still has a great deal of professional pride, and on this morning he showed it by playing some pretty good golf. His partner Langer, it seems, always plays pretty good golf, especially in the Ryder Cup, and it was he who struck first with a birdie on the opening hole. The match then developed into one of those classic encounters in which four strong men trade blows, and where thrust is met with parry and counter-thrust – with one small distinction. The Americans were either square or ahead but from the second hole onwards the Europeans could not get their noses in front. Stadler made birdie on the thirteenth from 10 feet to increase his side's lead to two-up but Lyle struck back right away, being the only one of the four who could scratch a par on the next hole. But then, two holes later, Strange landed what seemed to be the killer blow, putting his approach shot at the 410-yard par-4 just about stone dead for a tap-in birdie that left his side dormie two – they couldn't lose. But then Sandy, bless him, took the Tiger line off the tee at the par-5 seventeenth and despite his drive hitting a spectator's umbrella he still managed to knock his next onto the green, albeit 25 feet from the cup. When he holed the little beauty for an eagle three the deficit was down to one, with one to play.

For the United States a half on the final hole would be enough to take a crucial point, while Europe had to win. Four drives were launched across the daunting water hazard at the Belfry's famed and feared eighteenth – Langer's was good, Lyle and Stadler's were safe and Strange's found a bunker. He couldn't reach the green in two and had to lay up, short of the water hazard guarding the green, and hope to get down in a chip and putt. But that's easier than it sounds because the green on this hole is one of the biggest in golf – not particularly wide but very deep, with three different tiers, and the flagstick was on the middle tier. Lyle found the bottom level and Langer was on the same tier as the flag but about 36 feet away. Hopes of an upset were raised when Stadler hit a middling approach shot, also to the bottom level, but were quickly dashed when his first putt covered almost 60 feet and came to rest just past the flagstick, no more than two-and-a-half feet away. It was, by any definition, a gimme and had he putted that close on any of the other seventeen holes the next would have been conceded without a second's thought.

Bernhard Langer wrote in his autobiography: 'Sandy and I were thinking, "Let's give it to him and then we can go," but then we said: "We know we have lost but let him putt it."'

Sandy Lyle himself says: 'The thing is that Langer missed a very holeable putt at sixteen to put it back to one-down with two to go, so we were 2-down with two to play and even getting to the eighteenth was a bonus. I'd made one of these miraculous long putts on seventeen for an eagle to go down the eighteenth because otherwise we were out. My putt was really the start of it, but then we got to the eighteenth and it looked like it was all going to be over. So he [Stadler] had a 2-foot putt and I thought: "Well, you know, you've got that to win and sometimes things can happen."

'Perhaps if it was 6 inches further away he might have taken a bit more time over it. But because it was so close

On the final day only four Americans out of twelve won their matches but, to his eternal credit, one of them was Craig Stadler.

he probably thought: "It's a straight putt, I can handle that." Because of that he might have approached it with not quite the same focus as he should have done. As it turned out it was quite a turning point, but sometimes it just works out that way in matchplay. It was also a turning point for the singles matches next day, that little half point.'

It is surprising that Stadler missed but even more surprising that his ball didn't even touch the hole, so badly did he pull it straight left, before spinning away with an anguished expression and draping his putter over his shoulder to hang down his back. For a couple of moments even Lyle and Langer were shell-shocked and looked at each other in disbelief.

The moment was pivotal – optimism and energy flowed through the European team with the crackle of electricity and the Americans took on the dejected appearance of an inflatable girlfriend with a slow puncture. The home team took the afternoon foursomes 3–1, opened a two-point gap at the end of the second day and took the singles.

# 1985 (3)  Go fly a . . .

Tom Kite may look like an accountant but you don't get to be the all-time money winner on the US Tour, which he did, without having some kind of game. In addition, he was tough as old boots and has probably never been intimidated by anyone in his life – he's from Texas and in them there parts a certain 'screw you and the horse you rode in on' attitude is compulsory. He played in seven Ryder Cups, through the thick of European resurgence, and still managed a healthy total of played twenty-eight, won fifteen, lost nine and halved four – in fact, any record in which only a third of the matches are lost is not just healthy, it's fit to run a marathon. Kite is such a tough competitor that when the Ryder Cup went to continental Europe for the first time ever in 1997, as soon as word got out that it was to be held at Valderrama in Spain it was clear to a blind man that Seve Ballesteros would be captain. The American PGA, therefore, wanted one of its own elite to go up against the Spanish hothead; a strong, hard, unblinking competitor who wouldn't lose a game of tiddlywinks against his children. They turned to Kite and made him captain.

But in 1985 he was in the side as a player, and if anyone needed proof of his matchplay pedigree they needed only to think back to the drubbing he had given Sandy Lyle in 1981, when Sandy played his socks off and would have beaten

anyone that day – except the Texan. But four years later he got a little taste of his own medicine in his singles match against Seve Ballesteros, a wonderful encounter between magnetism and proficiency in which the American produced some of his trademark excellent golf, to stand three-up with five to play. Seve was disgusted with himself, his caddy, the course, his clubs, anything that moved and, most fiercely, his opponent. He was, like the character in a P. G. Wodehouse book, 'disturbed by the uproar of butterflies in an adjoining meadow', and just about anything or anyone else. For a man of his talent and remarkable record it is worth noting that of his twelve losses in the Ryder Cup, four of them came in the singles (and another two singles were halved). He surprisingly won only twice when not in harness with another player in either foursomes or fourballs. It is also worth noting that in his own mind he has never lost a golf match, just run out of holes.

The Ryder Cup captain's strategy in his fourball and foursome pairings is important but arguably the most crucial element is getting the singles right, especially in a tight contest. At the end of the second day each captain writes the names of his team members down in numerical order from one to twelve, without seeing his opposite number's list, and they need to do one of two things. Either create a strategy of their own by, for example, 'loading' their strong players at the beginning of the sequence, to try to get some momentum going early, or guess at the opposing captain's strategy and try to outflank him. Jacklin, because his team had a two-point advantage, surmised that his opposite number, Lee Trevino, would put some of his strong players out early, in an effort to quickly eliminate the deficit and then put the rest of his strength at the bottom of the list, in case things were tight coming down the stretch. Which was exactly what Trevino did. Four of his grittiest players – Lanny Wadkins, Craig Stadler, Ray Floyd and Tom Kite – filled the first four berths.

To counteract this, Jacklin put his strongest men in the middle of the order, with Seve Ballesteros, Sandy Lyle, Bernhard Langer and Sam Torrance occupying positions four to seven, and that's how Ballesteros and Kite came to be pitted against each other in the fourth match. Unfortunately for Trevino, the first part of his masterplan didn't quite work. Manuel Piñero, to everyone's surprise and all Europeans' delight, beat Lanny Wadkins 3&1 (that'll serve you right for 1983), while Paul Way saw off Ray Floyd two-up.

Ian Woosnam had lost by the same two-hole margin to Craig Stadler, so Europe had increased its overall lead to three points and even this early in the day the point between Ballesteros and Kite was taking on huge significance – a four-point margin would almost be game over, but reducing it to two would give the Americans a real boost.

Ballesteros had started with a pair of pars but was still one down to Kite's par, birdie opening. He fell further behind at the par-5 fourth when he couldn't match his opponent's par. He reduced his deficit at the seventh with a birdie but Kite came right back with his own birdie two holes later and at the halfway stage was two-up – comfortable but offering no room for complacency. The next three holes were halved, the tenth and

European captain Tony Jacklin had persuaded the PGA to let him have three wild-card picks to finalise his team. He had argued for being allowed to pick all twelve – and presumably wanted them all to be called Ballesteros.

twelfth in pars, the eleventh in birdies. Being 2-down with six to play was bad enough, but then Seve visited a greenside bunker at the thirteenth and failed to get up and down, couldn't match Kite's par and was therefore 3-down with five to play.

It was now, of course, that he embarked on the most unlikely comeback since Lazarus sat up in bed and asked for a cup of tea, two sugars please.

After the tee shots at the fourteenth it was advantage Ballesteros, who was at the back of the green while Kite had just missed it. But the American chipped to five feet so if Ballesteros two-putted he had a good chance of taking the hole. Just to make sure, though, Seve holed it – all of 35 feet – and with a face that still looked like a smacked backside, marched purposefully to the next tee, the par-5 fifteenth. The Spaniard hit two mighty blows but could then only chip his third to about 20 feet, but he knew he needed to drain it to get another one back, so that's what he did. The sixteenth was halved in par, Seve took the Tiger line from the tee on the par-5 seventeenth and drove more than 50 yards past his opponent, who was beginning to look like a man being run over by a steamroller – which, of course, he was. Kite couldn't reach the green in two, while Ballesteros smashed a 3-wood just through the putting surface and in all likelihood would win the hole with a chip and a putt.

Then, almost as if he was deliberately trying to heighten the tension, he duffed his chip shot and came up 20 feet short before, with apparent nonchalance, sinking the putt and winning the hole. Kite should have been in shock and praying for a quick release, having played four holes in level par and losing three of them, but it is the measure of the man that he played the last hole superbly. His long drive flirted with the water hazard but his courage paid off and he was left with only a 9-iron approach. Both men found the correct tier of the green but Kite was considerably nearer so the Spaniard was putting first from over 50 feet away, but although he coasted his ball to near gimme range, it didn't drop. Kite was clearly not playing for a half because he knocked his first putt about 5 feet past but then showed his mettle again by holing the return, and when Seve did the same it was a halved hole and match.

Seve remained disgusted not to have won but he was the only man on either side who could have chiselled out that vital half – probably the best half point ever seen.

# 1985 (4)  Sam, you are the man

Quite simply, the greatest single moment in Ryder Cup history and one of the iconic, defining images of sport – Sam Torrance, arms aloft on the eighteenth green at the Belfry, having secured the point that sealed victory for Europe after almost three decades. We had been consistently beaten by toothsome, healthy, well-fed American millionaires, who not only whupped our arses every two years, but also didn't have to get out of second gear to do it. The fact that they were just so gosh-damned nice, and appeared genuinely embarrassed at the ease with which they picked our pockets and broke our hearts, made it even worse. In sport we're used to losing to Argentinians: they cheat. We're used to losing to the Germans: they're better at penalties. We're used to losing to Australians: they're just better.

But the Americans? They gave us nothing but baseball caps, Hawaiian shirts, Bermuda shorts, hamburgers and an inferiority complex the size of the Empire State Building. They looked better on a golf course than we did. They dressed more expensively, used superior equipment and trousered more money than we could even dream about. And they won all the Majors. They couldn't talk ('I played great on the backside') couldn't spell ('I just went for the center of the green') and couldn't lose. And then came the *coup de grace* – their wives. Uniformly blonde and gorgeous, they squealed in unison when their men holed a putt, flashed their dazzling white teeth at all and sundry, and tottered onto the green in stilettos for the inevitable celebratory kiss with their victorious men.

But lo, it came to pass that Great Britain and Ireland became Europe, and selected a mighty leader, the man called 'Jacko', and he rose up to smite the foreign invaders. It was 1957 when Great Britain and Ireland had last captured the trophy, and since then it had been a non-contest. The Yanks turned up, enjoyed a bit of sightseeing, stopped off at a golf course for a few days and went back home with the trophy they had brought over. Either that or our motley crew of wannabes spent three weeks travelling steerage class to the States only to be sent quickly packing with their tails between their legs. It wasn't disappointing it was ball-crushingly, heart-breakingly predictable.

And into this strolled Sir Torrance of Largs. He was not what a professional golfer should be. He was neither smooth, urbane, sophisticated nor stylish, but an everyman who liked a flutter, supped beer through his unlikely moustache and was no stranger to late nights and early-morning, hungover tee-off times. In short, he was one of us – with one tiny exception. He could play golf. He had the game to win an Open but somehow we knew he never would. Blond superheroes like Jack Nicklaus won the Open; Kansas

City kids with Huckleberry Finn gap-toothed grins called Tom Watson won the Open.

But Sam did what neither of these legends managed to do. He gave a whole nation, an entire continent, a moment of pure, unalloyed, ecstasy. After three days of unbearable tension he allowed every single one of us to leap from our armchairs, fist clenched and pumping to shout 'Yesss' at the top of our voices. We laughed while he cried. For us, it was a mixture of relief, pleasure and we're not ashamed to admit it, triumphalism. Just once we'd taken on the rich, smart, good-looking, popular kid in the playground and stuffed it right up him. And he didn't like it any more than we had.

An order had been overthrown, a universe tilted on its axis and things would never be the same again, and Sam realised that no matter how long he lived, how many more rounds of golf he played, and how many trophies he might collect, nothing would ever surpass these few seconds of joy. It was the defining moment of his career – or at least, so he thought – and it made him an instant folk hero. It was entirely appropriate that Sam, for that afternoon in the sun, should embody everything that is great in sport, and life. Our man played alongside eleven other heroes, but he did it, he sank the winning putt, and for that he has earned our undying gratitude.

For the pedants among you who insist on knowing the details, he was playing Andy North and had been behind for most his match until winning the seventeenth and pulling all-square. He hit an absolute crackerjack drive on the last hole while North dumped his in the water. By the time Sam stood over his ball on the green he could afford to three-putt and still win, but where's the drama in that? He stroked the ball – and in the days before he converted to a broom handle putter he could still stroke the ball – and long before it reached the cup he knew it was in and raised his arms in triumph, pencil stuck behind his ear, satisfied smile lost behind his facial hair. He was engulfed by Jacklin, players who had already finished, players' wives, officials and anyone else who could get close. But mostly he was engulfed by the noise coming from the throats of tens of thousands of spectators and millions more watching at home.

Sam was almost beaten to the punch by Howard Clark who, a few moments earlier had the chance to beat Mark O'Meara on the seventeenth but his short putt lipped out. And the BBC producer televising the event had anyway taken the decision to stay with Torrance and North, because the huge galleries at the eighteenth hole provided a much better theatrical backdrop for such a stirring finale. In truth, the match was not a classic and neither Torrance (one point from a possible three) nor his opponent (none from two) had been enjoying their best form. Perhaps because of this, their match was a tense affair, with neither man able to gain a significant advantage. But timing is everything in life and Sam did his best to ensure that the end could not be more dramatic. In addition, heroes don't come more heroic – and the celebrations were only just about to start.

Once the match was decided in Europe's favour a few games were still out on the course, including Ian Woosnam and Curtis Strange, with the Welshman one up as they played the sixteenth. Strange walked over to shake Woosie's hand but Woosie, who has never won a Ryder Cup singles match, said: 'Why don't we just keep going?' Strange birdied the last three holes to win by one. Woosnam later said: 'Typical. I wish I had just kept my mouth shut.' He has still never won a singles match.

# 1987 (1)   Cor! What a pair

Ryder Cup history has seen many tremendous partnerships, but surely none will ever surpass that of Seve Ballesteros and José Maria Olazábal. Time and again they conjured unlikely victories and never was their flair more amply demonstrated than at Muirfield Village in 1987, when they first appeared together and Europe claimed its maiden victory on American soil, as the amigos took three points out of four, against the best pairings the Americans could produce. The Spanish duo competed together in only four Ryder Cups, but such was their dominance that it seemed as if they had been entwined forever, and would remain so.

Before Olazábal came along Ballesteros had already played in 1979, 1983 and 1985; they partnered each other in 1987, 1989, 1991 and 1993. Olazábal missed the 1995 contest through a career-threatening back injury, but although he returned for 1997 and 1999, Ballesteros was by then well past his sell-by date as a competitive force. Nevertheless, their exploits in those four encounters were the stuff of legend and are unlikely to be surpassed. They played together fifteen times in all and won twelve of those possible fifteen points, a quite staggering record of proficiency and consistency over a seven-year period.

They didn't win every match, but such was their reputation and play, that they invariably walked onto the first tee one-up. Only two combinations beat them – in 1987 they lost 2&1 to Larry Mize and Hal Sutton in the afternoon fourballs, and in 1993 they went down 2&1 in the morning foursomes to Tom Kite and Davis Love III. However, the same afternoon they roared back to beat Kite and Love 4&3, and just to rub it in, the next morning they met the same partnership again in the foursomes and this time took them 2&1.

When they first came together at Muirfield Village, Olazábal was just twenty-one-years-old and had only made his way into the team as a captain's pick. He is more difficult to read than Seve, he tends to keep his own counsel, is fiercely protective of his privacy and is not always comfortable in the spotlight. In a world of automaton clones he is easy to spot because of his absolute determination to do things his way.

His manager, Sergio Gomez, was the junior convenor at the course where Ollie learned to play the game and has only ever had one client – but the client drives him to distraction on occasions. For example, José Maria likes a long lay-off in winter and will have nothing to do with golf in that time – no matter how lucrative the offer. For the majority of his career he has had only three major sponsorship deals, and refuses all but a small number of the Monday corporate outings that can be so lucrative. And

*The greatest pairing the Ryder Cup has ever seen, or will ever see*

during the eighteen months later in his career when he could barely walk because of foot problems (later diagnosed as a lower back disorder), he sent back several large cheques to those sponsors, on the grounds that he hadn't earned the money. His view, simply, is that he has enough cash and does not need to demean himself for more.

But it is not only financially that he ploughs his own furrow. He still lives with his parents (albeit in a spacious house) in the area of Spain where he was born and enjoys peace and solitude, which he seeks avidly. A journalist once flew from America to Ollie's home without prior arrangement in the hope of an interview. He was turned away at the gate and no amount of pleading would reverse the decision. So, although Olazábal was a Ryder Cup rookie and, by his own admission absolutely petrified of the ordeal he was about to face on the first morning of the 1987 contest, he was not the sort to be intimidated by others or allow the circumstances to overwhelm him. Mark O'Meara once said of him: 'The guy defines clutch. He's underrated with the public, but anybody out here

will tell you that he's got some brass ones.'

But you wouldn't have necessarily known that on this misty, cool morning, as he was about to launch his Ryder Cup career in the morning foursomes, against Larry Nelson and Payne Stewart. He told *Golf Digest* magazine in 1999: 'I think Seve virtually made the decision that he wanted to play with me. That made things much easier for me to start with. He was at that time one of the best players. And he took all the pressure off me. When we stood on that first tee, he said: "Don't worry about anything. You just hit the ball and try to do your best and that's it. Forget about the people and everything."'

Easier said than done. Ollie was so nervous he could hardly grip his club, so Seve nursed, encouraged and cajoled him around the course. And then, on the back nine, Seve's form disappeared in a blink and Olazábal swapped roles and carried his partner the remainder of the way. By the eighteenth they were one-up but Olazábal put their tee shot into a bunker (wayward driving would ever be his Achilles heel). Ballesteros, of

course, still managed to find the green, albeit a long way from the cup. The Americans were struggling because Payne Stewart hit a rank bad push/slice that left his partner with a hugely difficult chip that he nevertheless played to perfection. Olazábal got his long snaking putt to 5 feet and Ballesteros holed what was left for a par 4 that the Americans matched but couldn't beat. Larry Nelson was playing in his third Ryder Cup, and to this point his record was played nine, won nine. He and Stewart were the first American duo to be beaten by Ballesteros and Olazábal. They would not be the last.

Two days later, when the contest was decided, Olazábal performed an impromptu, exuberant Spanish dance on the final green that irritated some Americans, especially Paul Azinger, who considered it disrespectful. 'I have to say that my intention was not at all to upset any of the American players or the public,' said Olazábal, 'it was just one of those things.'

He didn't add: 'And they should get a life and a sense of perspective.'

# 1987 (2)  Get inside that

Muirfield Village, Ohio, was built by Jack Nicklaus and named in honour of the Scottish course over which he won his first Open championship, in 1966. So when the Ryder Cup came to town in 1987, with big Jack as American captain, looking to uphold the astonishing record of never having lost on home soil, both history and circumstances did not favour Europe. What the Americans did not know was that Europe had four particularly potent weapons. First, Tony Jacklin was captain for the third time, and the lessons he had learned from his previous two matches in charge were well learned. Second, Seve Ballesteros was on a mission, and when the Spanish maestro set himself a target he didn't often miss. Third, the stunning victory at The Belfry two years earlier ignited the whole team with a sense of self-belief – with the knowledge that they deserved to be there, on equal terms. Fourth, they had some great players who surpassed even their own expectations by coming together as a unit, having left their egos at the door. But it was close.

Europe had the best possible start, ending day one 6–2 ahead, with Ballesteros and Olazábal in particular leading the charge. On the second day the lead was increased to five points, at 10½–5½ and one match in particular stands out – the afternoon fourball encounter of Lanny Wadkins and Larry Nelson against Sandy Lyle and Bernhard Langer (they had also faced each in the morning foursomes, when Europe won 2&1, with the turning point being a Lyle 2-iron to within a few feet on the par-5 eleventh for eagle). The quality of play had been astonishingly good for two days – the highlight for the visitors to date being Nick Faldo and Ian Woosnam taking Curtis Strange and Tom Kite 5&4. The American duo was an approximate 5-under par when the game finished on the fourteenth, but the Europeans were 10-under. American captain Jack Nicklaus said: 'I can't believe the scores you guys are doing out here. I thought this was supposed to be a hard course.'

It is, but when four of the world's best are all at the top of their game, no course is safe from the onslaught. The morning had started with a half-hour frost delay and the first series of matches had been slow. In truth, any game in which Langer is involved will be slow – the word 'meticulous' only begins to describe him. Colin Montgomerie tells the story that he was once playing a practice round with the German and when asked his yardage, Monty replied: 'I've got 125 to the front and the flag's 25 on, so that's 150 yards.'

'Are you sure?' asked Langer.

Monty was nervous, so checked his figures and repeated the information.

'Where did you take your measurement from?' asked Langer.

'That sprinkler head,' [a circular disc, about eight inches in diameter] replied Monty.

Langer said: 'Was it the front or the back of the sprinkler head?'

The story is well known and no doubt apocryphal, but at the Association of Golf Writers annual dinner at the 2004 Open Championship Montgomerie told a new tale, concerning the Ryder Cup of two years before. He was due to tee-off in a practice round but couldn't find Langer anywhere and went in search of him. He eventually stumbled across him holding a couple of putters up against the clubhouse wall.

'What are you doing Bernhard?' Monty asked.

'I am checking the loft of my putters against this wall.'

'For God's sake man,' Monty said, 'how do you know that the wall is square?'

Langer looked at him in puzzlement and said: 'In Germany, all zee walls are square.'

Because of the morning delay and Langer's absolute refusal to be hurried this momentous afternoon encounter was settled almost in darkness. Over the first eleven holes it had been tight but the Europeans held a one-hole lead, which was increased to two when Langer birdied the par-3 twelfth from quite a distance. Lyle then eagled the fifteenth and the visitors were dormie. But Wadkins never gives up a cause as lost (if you were ever to shoot him it would be as well to go back and stab, poison and bludgeon him, too). To prove the point he birdied the sixteenth and seventeenth – in fact he birdied all of the last five holes – which meant that if the Americans could win the last they would snatch an immeasurably precious half. And on such moments do Ryder Cups turn. All four players hit good tee shots on the eighteenth and then Lyle, who had taken an iron from the tee for safety, and was therefore farthest away and playing first, struck another beautiful iron to about 6 feet and turned to Langer with a grin and the words: 'Get inside that and we'll be all right.' But it wasn't his turn to play. Nelson was next and he fired his approach to about 20 feet. When Wadkins played it looked for a moment as if he might even hole out, his ball pitching just a couple of feet from the flagstick. But it then rolled and ended up about 15 feet away. So now it was Langer's turn and, with Lyle's exhortation ringing in his ears he played an 8-iron that did get inside his partner's ball, to a foot from the hole. It was an extraordinary shot but somehow fitting for this day and this match.

Sandy Lyle remembers it even now: 'It was pretty close all round and was really down to the last five holes and if you meet Lanny Wadkins he will quite happily talk to you about it because he's just amazed that he birdied all five of the last holes and lost ground – that's just the way it was. I had a memorable 2-iron to the par-5 eleventh off a very tight lie. Bernhard was thinking I'd maybe play safe with a 6-iron and just get in position and I said: "No, I think I can get it onto the green," which hadn't even entered his mind. His thought pattern was "2-iron onto this green, 230-yards uphill, on a cool day?" I threw a very good 2-iron. I remember Lanny was halfway up the fairway and he looked at this thing going over his head and it flopped down about 2 feet away –

Jack Nicklaus said: 'I've seen superior golf played by the European team. We fought to the end but our best simply was not good enough today.'

*Bernhard Langer gets a helping hand from Sandy*

I think he even gave us the putt. But you could almost see him bowing, as if to say, "We are not worthy, I can't match that."

'On the last I had an 8- or 7-iron and put it to what looked to be about 5 feet, so I said: "Put it inside that." And he did and finished the match off right there. That was a good turning point, too, because it gave us an extra little advantage going into the singles next day. It was a good match.'

It was a 'good match' in the same way that Pele was 'a bit of a footballer' but Sandy never did like to exaggerate.

## 1987 (3)   Thank you Lord

Imagine this. You have played ten times in this and three previous Ryder Cups and your total number of wins is zero. Nothing, *nada*, zilch. You were at Laurel Valley in 1975 and lost in the first day foursomes, alongside Christy O'Connor, and although you and Guy Hunt did get a half the following morning, it was quickly forgotten as you were beaten in the afternoon. You then lost in the final morning singles and were not picked for the afternoon series. One Ryder Cup, four matches, one half and no wins.

Two years later at Royal Lytham & St Annes you and Tony Jacklin managed a half with Ed Sneed and Don January but the next day you were both beaten by the two Dave's, Hill and Stockton. To wrap up your second outing in this biennial competition, Hubert Green hammers you in the singles. Two Ryder Cups, seven matches, two halves and no wins.

You don't qualify for the 1979 encounter, which is probably something of a relief but when you make the 1981 team at Walton Heath you pick yourself up, dust yourself off, gird your loins and no doubt repeat a reassuring mantra that this time things will be different. They are – you come up against the strongest team ever assembled on either side of the Atlantic. But you're Irish, and in that part of the world a certain optimism, love of the craic and belief in lady luck is imbibed with your mother's milk. Only you must have been bottle-fed because things do not improve. On the first day you and Bernard Gallacher go down to Hale Irwin and Ray Floyd so you're probably not too distressed to sit things out until the singles, where you lose again, this time by 5&3, but at least it was to Jack Nicklaus, the most successful golfer the world has seen. Three Ryder Cups, nine matches, two halves and no wins.

If you're absolutely honest with yourself, missing out on the 1983 and 1985

*Finally, a win for Eamonn Darcy, in front of an enthusiastic American gallery*

encounters was probably what you needed in order to lay some gentle balm on your wounds. And so, with this legacy of bitter, heart-breaking disappointment you arrive at Muirfield Village in 1987, where Europe has an outstanding chance of victory for the first time ever in America. You sit on the sidelines for most of the first two days (clearly not one of Jacklin's chosen few), being called into action only for the second-day afternoon fourballs. The fact that you and Gordon Brand Jr lose by 3&2 to Andy Bean and Payne Stewart must, by now, have a certain inevitability to it. And before you know it, it's the final day and you're playing Ben Crenshaw in the singles, and he's so angry to go two down on the sixth that he breaks his putter and has to use a wedge or 1-iron on the greens for the rest of the round.

Crenshaw, incidentally, has the nickname 'Gentle Ben' and is known to go all misty-eyed and unnecessary just looking at photographs of a gutta percha ball, but the 'gentle' part of his name is pure irony, and was given to him (because of the temper he used to show in his youth) by a golf writer of the name Dick Collins after Crenshaw had won the city championship at the age of 15.

Crenshaw told *Golf Digest* in 1999. 'I

walked off the edge of the green and I just tapped this thing – and I've hit it much harder before – but it was certainly not at a force I ever thought would break it. But it did. It broke right in the middle of the shaft, at its stress point. Turns out it was rusted out inside, and it broke. I was absolutely stunned. Of course, the first thing you think is, "God, why now? Why, on the last day of the Ryder Cup, in a tight match?"

'I will never forget, I played the seventh hole and Jack Nicklaus came by and asked: "How're you doing?" I looked down and kind of murmured under my breath: "Well, I broke my putter."

'He said: "You did what?"

'I said: "I broke my putter on the sixth green."

'He said: "Well, with the way things are going, I don't blame you."'

Remarkably, his singles opponent in 1987 didn't learn about the broken putter until towards the end of the match – Eamonn Darcy, for it is he described above, had assumed that Crenshaw was using irons on the putting surface to try and hit the ball gently on extremely fast greens. And he wasn't doing too bad a job of it either.

Nevertheless, our unlikely hero, with an even unlikelier swing, opened up a

three-hole lead with only seven to play. Darcy's manner of hitting a golf ball has attracted similes like no other before or since – at least until Jim Furyk came along. It has been likened to a man trying to kill a snake in a phone booth, but the most satisfactory description, inevitably from David Feherty (and which also came to be applied to Furyk), has it resembling an octopus falling from a tree. Nevertheless, appearances can be deceptive, and Lee Trevino, among others, reckoned Darcy to be among the purest strikers of a golf ball, especially with an iron, that ever lived.

But he would not be human if, with his Ryder Cup record, he wasn't feeling extremely nervous over the final few holes – especially as Crenshaw came inexorably back at him. The American was given the twelfth hole courtesy of an extremely ropey Darcy three-putt and at the next he stuck his approach shot to 6 feet and holed for birdie. When he then took the fourteenth it was all-square with four to play and Darcy was, to quote Johnny Miller, in the throw-up zone. He nevertheless holed a great 25-foot putt on fifteen to match Crenshaw's birdie but immediately followed it with a bogey-four on the sixteenth, so he was now one-down with two to play.

A great approach shot to 6 feet at the seventeenth restored parity so they walked to the eighteenth all-square. And now, with the Americans staging the sort of comeback for which they are renowned (at one point they were up in seven matches, level in three and fighting back in the other two), Darcy hit a drive that was almost incredible, because it found the fairway. Crenshaw went into a water hazard on the left and after his penalty drop could find only a greenside bunker. Darcy then followed him in.

When both had splashed out Crenshaw was 6 feet away, Darcy 4½, but the American, one of the greatest putters there has ever been, rolled his ball into the hole with the leading edge of his 1-iron. He had recorded a remarkable five, so if Darcy wanted to win the match and a vital point, he had to sink his own downhill, right-to-left effort. He wasted no time, and with a short jab despatched the ball into the hole. After four Ryder Cups and eleven matches, Eamonn Darcy finally had a victory under his belt.

David Davies, golf correspondent of the *Guardian* for many years, retired in 2004 and penned a piece in which he selected his greatest players and moments. He wrote of this match: 'Eamonn Darcy holed the winning putt and turned to his team-mates as if to say: "You didn't think I could do that, did you?" The fact that they still had their heads buried in their hands suggested he was right.'

# 1987 (4)    Doing them in Jack's backyard

Europe was determined to win in America for the first time, and by the end of the second day of the 1987 contest, had made huge strides towards achieving that previously unattainable goal. The first-day morning foursomes had been shared two apiece but then Europe went loopier than a mad dog on acid and whitewashed the afternoon fourballs, to close the day leading 6–2. The United States came back the next day but still trailed overall – they took 1½ points from the foursomes and the afternoon fourballs were shared. So by the end of two days Europe led 10½–5½, which meant they needed four points to win the cup outright, three-and-a-half to retain it as holders.

American captain Jack Nicklaus had been puzzled by the home fans lack of vocal support after the end of the first day and arranged for them to be given stars and stripes flags to wave on day two, with the suggestion that a bit more

support might not go amiss. Somebody should have told him that it's difficult to hoot and holler though when your team is being roundly beaten. European fans, in contrast, were delirious and treating it like a home fixture. But Nicklaus had another ace up his sleeve, and resorted to the nuclear option of bringing out the American players' wives. Not only that, but the better halves of the US PGA officials were also dragooned into service to squeal their support. Never before have so many permed, perma-tanned and preening Dolly Parton look-alikes been assembled in one place, and if that wasn't enough to scare the living bejesus out of the European team, nothing would be.

So now, all that team Europe and their supporters had to do was wait for the *coup de grace*: because they needed only four points and with Faldo, Woosnam, Langer, Lyle, Ballesteros, Olazábal and Torrance in their team, they would be easy enough to get. Wouldn't they?

Except that of those players mentioned, only one managed to record a victory. In a tale that had become worryingly familiar – and which would reach its peak in 1999 at Brookline – those damned Yankees refused to lie

down and came out in the singles determined to prove to the world that, as the US PGA Tour says with monotonous regularity: 'These Guys are Good.' And prove it they did. The strategy of both captains yielded mixed results. Jacklin dotted his strongest players – Woosnam, Faldo, Olazábal, Lyle, Langer and Ballesteros throughout the list, while Nicklaus loaded his strength towards the bottom, an odd policy when you consider that he needed a fast start to prevent the whole shooting match being over before PGA officials from either side of the Atlantic (and their wives, presumably) could wade into their first pink gins of the day. Nevertheless, it worked, as Andy Bean beat Ian Woosnam by one hole in the first match out, but parity was quickly restored when Howard Clark saw off Dan Pohl by the same margin. But then came a run of American successes that started with Larry Mize gaining a half from Sam Torrance.

Mark Calcavecchia had so far played one match, the first-day foursomes where, with Andy Bean, he had lost one-down to Sandy Lyle and Bernhard Langer. Nick Faldo, in contrast, had forged an almost impregnable partnership with Ian Woosnam, during which

they took three-and-a-half points from a possible four. The record book, recent form and respective stature of the players all pointed to an emphatic Faldo win. He lost one-down and later wrote in his autobiography, *Life Swings*, that he simply ran out of steam – a not unusual phenomenon in the days when Europe's best half-dozen players were almost expected to beat an American dozen on their own. José Maria Olazábal also lost, in his case to Payne Stewart by 2-down. Scott Simpson saw off Manuel Rivero 2&1 and that talented pain in the backside Tom Kite despatched Sandy Lyle 3&2. This was getting serious. The home team had reduced the deficit to two points and a major turnaround was on the cards. Europe then managed to stop

Gordon Brand Jr was deeply impressed with American hospitality when he and his team-mates arrived in America. They were assigned individual limousines and fast-tracked through immigration, barely having to show their passports. But there was a sting in the tail. 'When we won it,' he said, 'the next morning there was no Danish [pastries], no papers, no coffee, nothing at all. It was like: "Get back to Britain, you bastards."'

the rot with Eamonn Darcy's unexpected but wholly deserved and heart-warming victory over Ben Crenshaw, which was followed by a halved match between Larry Nelson and Bernhard Langer. Europe, now on 13½ points needed just one more win to seal victory.

All eyes turned to the last three games on the course. In the penultimate match Ken Brown was a lost cause against the cold-hearted matchplay assassin known as Lanny Wadkins. In the final game Hal Sutton was locked in a fight-to-the-death with Gordon Brand Jr that would eventually end all-square. As if it were written, it seemed the crucial game would be between Curtis Strange and Seve Ballesteros. Curtis is an old-fashioned, courteous Virginian gentleman who thinks carefully before speaking and then delivers his thoughts in a quiet but authorative voice. Had you asked him before the match if he could win, he would probably have considered the

question with care, outlined the respective merits and skills of the two protagonists, pointed out that over eighteen holes of matchplay, any player can beat any other player on a given day and added that yes, he thought he could win, but most of all was looking forward to the match.

Seve Ballesteros would probably have looked at the questioner as if they were crazy, and said: 'Of course.'

It was said of Jack Nicklaus, and has been said of Tiger Woods, that great players simply have the capacity to make things happen when they most need it, and Seve Ballesteros was a great player (and you have no idea how much it hurts to write 'was'). By the middle of the back nine he was two up on Strange and on the fifteenth had to hole a good putt to remain that way. On the next, a par-3, he hit a beautiful shot to 6 feet, while his opponent was twice as far away, and with a putt that had consider-

ably more break. He missed, but so did Ballesteros; at least the Spaniard knew that he could not now lose, being two-up with two to play. At the seventeenth Seve drove well, Curtis did not, and followed up his poor tee shot with an approach that ran through the green. Ballesteros put his ball into the heart of the putting surface and made the coolest par to score the point that ensured an away victory for the first time ever. He barely looked at his opponent as he gave him the most cursory of handshakes before walking off the green to start the European celebrations (don't take it personally Curtis).

Never was it more fitting that this Spanish genius should be the man to make history. When I asked him what was his own greatest Ryder Cup moment, he immediately pointed to this match and, despite his many heroics throughout the years, it is difficult to disagree.

# 1989 (1)   The feud begins

In 1989 at The Belfry the US captain Ray Floyd introduced his team at the pre-match dinner as 'the twelve best golfers in the world', causing Nick Faldo to choke on his soup. He was, after all, sharing a table with, among others, Seve Ballesteros, Bernhard Langer, José Maria Olazábal, Sam Torrance and Ian Woosnam. Faldo himself had won the Masters that year, and a few months later at Augusta National would become only the second golfer behind Jack Nicklaus to defend successfully. Twenty-two years earlier in 1967 Ben Hogan had pulled a similar stunt to Floyd, but the difference was that he spoke from a position of strength and was simply a hard enough man to put voice to the thoughts of everyone in the room. Now, however, Europe was the holder of the Ryder Cup, had won the previous two contests and boasted some of the most talented players in the game, so all Floyd did was wind them up when no motivation was needed, and the man he annoyed the most was a volatile Spaniard.

*Memo to Raymond Floyd*: When you're leading a team of Americans into the Ryder Cup at The Belfry, do as you see fit, with one small proviso – under no circumstances should you piss off Seve Ballesteros.

There is virtually no one in the game of golf that Seve has not argued with at some point in his career, ranging from his own Tour, the US Tour, the Ryder Cup committee and numerous caddies, with whom he is notoriously ruthless (and in a game in which partnerships can last an entire playing career, a full season on Seve's bag without getting the sack was cause for celebration). When Dave Musgrove left Seve's employ, he said he had served his sentence. Ballesteros epitomises the view of caddies that believes they should turn up, keep up and shut up. Seve once said: 'The only time I talk on a golf course is to my caddy – and only then to complain.' So if that is his attitude towards the one person who is supposed to be an ally, imagine what he thinks of matchplay opponents – especially American ones. And in the interests of balance, much as I loved what Seve did for me and every other European golf supporter, when it came to the Ryder Cup it has been suggested that he could be a little bit naughty.

I asked his 1983 partner Paul Way if he'd ever seen any Seve gamesmanship close-up and he said: 'Not really in '83. I think he got worse when he started to struggle with his game, and I think all sportsmen are a bit like that – when you're on top and winning it's easy.'

Peter Jacobsen told me: 'I think he is probably the greatest competitor I have ever played against, but I was wise to his games and would accept them. When he would maybe clear his throat or step forward on your downswing I would just

stop my swing, he would carry on forward and I would say: "Hang on Seve, wait till I hit," to kind of put it back on him.'

In 1989 we saw the beginning of a Ballestros/Azinger feud that would rumble on for a few years, when they met in the singles. Azinger later told *Golf Digest*: 'That was the first year the USGA [the governing body of golf equipment and rules in the US and Mexico] reminded Tour players that square grooves scratching a ball didn't justify taking it out of play. We were shredding up balls with those grooves. On the second hole, my ball was shredded, and his ball also had some marks on it. I hit it to about 3½ feet, and he hit it to about 12 feet. I said: "I don't think you can take that out." The problem was, he had already thrown his ball to his caddy. So I had to go to his caddy, and I said: "I don't think you can take that out." Then Seve said: "Is this the way you want to play today?" And it was on after that. I said: "I think we should ask the referee." The referee said: "Sorry, you can't take that out."

'Then on the eighteenth hole [after Azinger had driven into the water hazard from the tee], Seve accused me of taking a bad drop. But when there's an official standing there and the player is doing something . . . the difference in that situation was that Seve had walked all the way across the fairway; he was in the right rough. Peter Kostis even said on the air: "Seve just walked all the way across the fairway and told Paul where to drop it." I won the match. Then three months later I read that Seve had accused me of taking a bad drop.

'I never set out to be controversial or anything like that, and I don't think I am. I was just passionate, like everybody else. When I played Seve, somehow I was never nervous. I was always just hyped and motivated. You know, we're both very patriotic, and occasionally we had run-ins. He'd do something that I didn't think was right, or I'd do something that he didn't think was right. Curtis Strange told me when I got paired with him: "Don't let him pull anything on you" – first thing out of Curtis' mouth. Seve and I were young. We've kind of apologised for whatever.'

The reality is that Azinger never had anything to apologise for. As a European fan I idolised Seve for the way he took the fight to the Americans, never backed off and played some of his most astonishing golf – and that's as good as golf gets – against them in this biennial match. But that shouldn't blind us to the fact that he stretched the spirit and etiquette of the game, while never, of course, breaking the rules. There is no doubt, because there are simply too many American opponents who tell the same or similar stories, that he developed a selective vocal noise during Ryder Cup week. He would never be so churlish as to cough on someone's backswing, but he would have a few clearings of his throat as they were settling over the ball, so they inevitably wondered if it would happen again as they committed to the stroke. And such was his reputation that Strange was not the only US player or captain who felt the need to advise rookies on his team not to put up with Ballesteros' nonsense.

Later, in the 1990s when Azinger was diagnosed with cancer of the shoulder, Seve was among the first to send a message of good wishes and speedy recovery. Ryder Cup enmity can be deep and wounding, but it rarely spills over outside the competition.

# 1989 (2)   Like an arrow

Christy O'Connor Jr was one of Tony Jacklin's wildcard picks and it was a selection that aroused much controversy. I remember interviewing the Irishman for a magazine profile between his selection and appearance and he said: 'By all means criticise me if I make a mess of it, but no one has the right to say it's a poor selection until we see what happens.' What happened has gone into Ryder Cup folklore. His was not the first controversial wildcard selection and will not be the last because the final piece in the Ryder Cup team puzzle is always the decision on which men will make the team at the captain's nod, rather than play their way in by right.

In America the qualification process was traditionally held over two years (it has been changed for 2006 to mirror the European one-year qualification period) so virtually as soon as one contest ended, speculation, at least on the other side of the Atlantic, began as to who would make the next team. On this side of the pond, every Tour event in a Ryder Cup year has a significant side story to the main event of who has won and lost, and it concerns the respective Ryder Cup points won by those in contention, and throughout the season as form and prize money ebbs and flows, so the team gradually takes shape. And then comes the final counting event, in which a few players are inevitably battling for the last one or two automatic places, followed by the press conference in which the captain announces his wildcard decision. Sometimes it is predictable – Langer going for Colin Montgomerie and Luke Donald in 2004, for example, but often it is the catalyst for huge debate, such as when Tony Jacklin was omitted in favour of Mark James in 1981, or the several times John Daly has been overlooked.

O'Connor Jr had played in the event once before but that was 14 years earlier, during the 1975 contest at Laurel Valley in America, where his record was played two, lost two. On the first-day fourballs he and Eamonn Darcy had gone down to Tom Weiskopf and Lou Graham 3&2, and in the following day's foursomes he partnered John O'Leary in a 5&3 defeat by Weiskopf and Johnny Miller. Now, almost a decade-and-a-half later, things weren't going much better. In his only outing before the singles (the second-day foursomes) he and Ronan Rafferty had lost to Mark Calcavecchia and Ken Green 3&2. For the singles, Tony Jacklin, in his last appearance as captain, stacked the top and bottom of the draw with his bankers. Seve Ballesteros led off, followed by Bernhard Langer and José Maria Olazábal, while Sam Torrance, Nick Faldo and Ian Woosnam filled the final three places. O'Connor was buried in the middle order and faced Fred Couples, a big-hitting US Ryder Cup

*Christy looks heavenward as the gallery erupts*

rookie who had so far played one, lost one (he and Lanny Wadkins had gone down 3&2 to Howard Clark and Mark James in the first-day fourballs, on an afternoon when Europe took a clean sweep, winning all four matches).

Both men could therefore be excused for feeling less than confident but Couples at least had the advantage of youth and distance from the tee. It is fair to say that rarely have two such contrasting players been drawn together. Couples was a raw, wild young man who would go on to win the Masters and could always propel the ball prodigious distances, while O'Connor, with his prematurely silvered hair, was the epitome of the journeyman pro: in a 19-year career he had won just three times and had only once made the top-10 in the Order of Merit. It wasn't quite a Manchester United vs Twickenham Ladies Reserves match-up, but the bookies would have given pretty heavy odds against the Irishman winning this particular duel.

And yet, despite being out-driven by 50 yards all day long, Christy just kept plugging away and by the time the match reached the eighteenth tee, they were all square, but four of the five matches behind were shaping up for American victories. Captain Jacklin had watched play on the seventeenth and when he saw Couples miss a short putt with a jerky stroke – something that haunted him for many years when he was under the cosh – he was convinced that the likeable American was about to crack. It didn't look like it however, a few minutes later when he launched a majestic drawing drive that just avoided the water, and ended up being the longest and best of the day. Jacklin though was not convinced and felt sure that Couples had pulled his drive and got away with it only because of his awesome length. O'Connor hit a safe enough tee-shot but was a huge distance from the green, estimates vary between 200 and 230 yards. There are also a few different versions about the words Jacklin whispered in O'Connor's ear before he prepared to play the most important single shot of his life. Some versions have it as: 'If you put this on the green I know that something good will happen,' while others say the words were: 'Just one more good swing for Ireland, Christy.'

Whatever the words, they worked. O'Connor launched a towering, majestic, beautiful, heart-stopping 2-iron that finished less than 4 feet from the cup. He barely had time to see it come to rest before he was engulfed by Jacklin and several other European players. Couples' nerves were shot and he half-shanked his 9-iron approach an acre right before conceding the putt, the hole and the match.

The final say in this tied, and somehow deflated contest, was had by José Maria Cañizares in the group behind, who beat Ken Green one-up and secured the point that meant Europe could not lose – but the shot that did it was Christy's 2-iron. Following on from Darcy's triumph of two years before, the legend of magnificent Irish contributions to the European cause continued.

It was remarkable to have won in 1983, but to then repeat the success two years later, for the first time on American soil, gladdened the hearts of European supporters everywhere. To wish for a third successive victory was just being greedy, so we tied the match, but still retained the trophy, as holders. It was time for a dose of reality.

The story grows that Christy's magical 2-iron O'Connor has been donated to charity auctions many times since that wonderful day.

# 1991 (1)  Wakey-wakey

As we have seen, the Ryder Cup has not always been played in a spirit of generosity, warmth, good humour and with a desire to foster European–American relations. Sometimes it has degenerated into bickering, squabbles, bitterness, acrimony and outright hostility, and on both sides of the Atlantic, players and galleries have played a part in cranking up the temperature in what is already a hot-blooded contest. European fans point the finger at noisy, vociferous away galleries and their chants of 'USA, USA' but their own battle cries of 'Europe' and 'Ole, Ole, Ole' are every bit as loud and their over-heated support two and four years before at the Belfry often over-stepped the limits of sportsmanship.

Peter Jacobsen, the ever approachable and affable American, said of the 1985 contest: 'Oh yes, that for me was the start of seeing how the Ryder Cup started to go away from what I thought the intention was, which was a friendly match between the US and Europe. I remember hearing players being booed as they were teeing off; players that had been playing in the Open championship for many years, who had been great champions and who had always received great ovations. And then in the Ryder Cup I started seeing it turning the other way and I'm glad to say that in the last couple of years it has again turned back to the way it should be – which is in good spirit and good competition.'

None of the 29 stagings of the event to date, however, could prepare us for Kiawah Island in 1991 where, from the outset, animosity ran deep and wide. This was, without a doubt, the most spiteful, nasty and bitter Ryder Cup ever held, and we can all only hope that it produced at least one positive – the desire to never again allow the competition to sink to these depths, the blame for which rests with a number of factors coming together at the same time.

First, and possibly most importantly, America was in the unique position of not having held the trophy for seven years following two European victories, one at home one away, and a tie. In a nation of its size, with the resources it has and its general obsession with sport, victory in international competition is not only expected, but demanded. Not only that but American golfers had so dominated the landscape, that their success was a foregone conclusion, particularly when it came to competing against 'Yoorop', a strange and exotic place that many US citizens couldn't point to on a map, never mind consider visiting. But things had changed. Over the previous nine years, Europeans had in all but one of them, won at least one Major a year, and three times had managed to take two. So the American audience was stirred from the apathy that had been borne of relentless,

almost unchallenged success, and was spoiling for a fight. Second, Operation Desert Storm, the original Gulf War, had finished a few months earlier and some Americans, confusing patriotism with flag-waving xenophobia, felt they were on a mission to uphold US values and commemorate the heroism of their brave boys. Third, *Golf Digest* – a magazine that is so often an oasis of common sense but this time got it entirely wrong – ludicrously dubbed the contest 'The War on the Shore' and virtually every other news outlet picked up the subtitle and ran with it. Fourth, at a pre-event dinner, the American PGA showed a film celebrating the Ryder Cup but it failed to mention that there were two teams competing and concentrated exclusively on US wins and success. It was poor taste, bad judgement and a pretty hefty insult to their guests.

To the watching Europeans it seemed that the US golf authorities still went along with Tom Kite's assessment of the Ryder Cup from a few years earlier: 'A couple of cocktail parties, we kick their butts and go home.' Nick Faldo, who had a pretty torrid time himself at Kiawah Island, subsequently wrote: 'As a sporting contest, the Ryder Cup surrendered its dignity and unique charm that September, when winning became the be-all and end-all of everything.' But it gets even worse.

The Ocean Course at Kiawah Island, South Carolina, designed by the inspired lunatic Pete Dye, had never been played in anger and had only been finished a few weeks earlier. Dye was previously best known for Sawgrass, the home of the Players' Championship (TPC) and notorious for its island green at the seventeenth. When Jerry Pate won the TPC in 1982 he threw the architect into the water before diving in himself. Ron Coffman later wrote in *Golf World*: 'There was no doubt a few professionals watching who were hoping the water was 10-feet deep and that neither could swim. Especially Dye.'

There were few permanent buildings on the Kiawah site, trailers were used as lockers so the players could change and they had to live away from the course and be driven in each day. A great deal of earth had been moved to create the mounding that was meant to resemble a Scottish links but that was where the similarity ended.

Because of its seaside location, Kiawah was usually subject to strong breezes, if not winds, so the ability to hit low shots under them was a considerable advantage. However, the greens were often elevated and therefore required a high approach shot to get close, especially as many of them resembled a hastily-constructed landfill site and were so full of bumps and hollows that putting the ball in the right place on the green was paramount in order to score well. And it was long. So foot-sloggingly, back-breakingly, soul-destroyingly long, that most players wouldn't be far enough off the tee to hit high approach shots anyway. Dan Jenkins, the Daddy of modern golf writers, once wrote of Prestwick in Scotland that you would

American captain Dave Stockton clearly had only one item on his agenda – to get the cup back. During the practice days a psychologist who had been working with the US team was riding an elevator with Stockton when it stopped and the doors opened. Seve Ballesteros was standing there and the psychologist, who knew him, exchanged a few words. When the doors closed again, a livid Stockton made it clear to the psychologist that during this week she would under no circumstances, talk with any of the Europeans.

*Pete Dye's remarkable masterpiece at Kiawah Island*

like to gather up several of its holes and mail them to your top-ten enemies. No doubt a number of golfers have thought the same of Kiawah Island. Apart from that, everyone was happy.

But before the event started, the host nation had just one more surprise in store for its guests. An American disc jockey decided to stoke the growing controversy even further by staging a stunt called 'Wake the Enemy', which involved calling the hotel rooms of every European team member at 4 a.m. to wish them well. He said: 'It was just a joke.'

# 1991 (2)   The plot thickens

When a Ryder Cup is as acrimonious and venomous as the War on the Shore, conspiracies can be seen around every corner and bogeymen lurk down every alley. It is therefore not surprising that Europe, having been woken before dawn every morning by an asinine disc jockey and insulted by their hosts with a 'history of the Ryder Cup' that barely mentioned their exploits, were looking for an opportunity to strike back, and latched onto Steve Pate's injury as an excuse.

'He's a very, very fierce competitor who will walk through a wall for you if you ask him to,' said Ben Crenshaw eight years later, when making Pate one of his wildcard picks for the contest at Brookline. He is also hugely talented and on his day capable of beating anyone in the world. He had played his way onto the US team by winning the Honda Classic and posting four other top-three finishes in 1991. David Feherty said of his selection by Crenshaw: 'He's one of those rock-solid guys who doesn't give a rat's ass. You can put him up against Sergio or Montgomerie, and it won't matter.'

Two other things stand out about the man. First, he is accident-prone and second, TV commentator Gary McCord nicknamed him 'volcano' because of his volatile temper, and the name clearly had resonance among his fellow pros because it stuck throughout his career. Even in his college days at UCLA he exploded like a firecracker so often that he became accustomed to the long, lonely walk back to the campus when he was banished from the course by the team coach. He managed to get himself fined for bad language in seven consecutive US Opens and, although his anger was always directed at himself, wise men gave him a bit of space when, as the Scots say, he 'lost the heid'.

His many accidents involved driving into the back of a flatbed truck on his way home from a golf event (that cost him a broken wrist,) a year later damaging the other wrist when he slipped on a boat during a family vacation, and being knocked over and almost trampled by a deer when he was on a bicycle in his own driveway.

But they were all in the future, and at Kiawah Island he was a hot young golfer in tremendous form and played so well in practice (67 was his highest score) that he was bound to feature strongly in captain Dave Stockton's line-up. In fact, the US skipper later said that his strongest duo was to have been Corey Pavin and Steve Pate.

But then the first of Pate's many injuries through accident occurred on the eve of the Ryder Cup. All the players were being ferried by limo to the pre-event gala dinner when the car in front of Pate's – containing the Fehertys and Faldos – suddenly braked when it appeared that it was about to accelerate through a junction. Pate's car ploughed into the back and he was thrown forward onto a drink tray set in the seat in front of him and took a heavy blow to the torso, damaging both his ribs and hip. As a consequence he

sat out most of the first two days, only getting onto the course during the second-day afternoon fourballs where, with Corey Pavin, he went down 2&1 to Colin Montgomerie and Bernhard Langer. It was after this match that the fun really started, and it mostly seemed to centre around timing.

Bernard Gallacher, the Europe captain, says he watched Pate play and thought he was 'hitting it a mile' and when each captain produced his list of players for the singles, Pate was included, and was drawn to face Seve Ballesteros, who had won three-and-a-half points from four in partnership with José Maria Olazábal, and was considered to be the toughest gladiator that Europe could field. Langer had also been impressed with Pate's play and didn't think the American's movements had been at all inhibited, before adding that, if anything, he had been stronger than his team-mate Pavin.

Then word came through that Pate had suffered a reaction to his injury and was having to withdraw from the singles, which meant that a European also had to stand down. The axe fell on David Gilford. He had endured a miserable Ryder Cup debut, being partnered with both Montgomerie and Faldo and losing

both matches. So when he drew Wayne Levi in the singles he was ecstatic and convinced that he could now prove himself. Levi was a victim of the American selection system that picked players over two years' play, and was in the team because of a hot 1990 that had now dissipated to such an extent that he could barely beat an egg, let alone Ballesteros. He had so far played once, alongside Lanny Wadkins, and both had been soundly beaten 3&1 by Mark James and Steve Richardson. So now, instead of Gilford having a crack at Levi in a contest he was sure he could win, the 'weak' American was up against Ballesteros, who most believe could have beaten any one of the opposition.

Gilford told me: 'I heard about it when I got to the course and Tony Jacklin said to me that Steve Pate was not playing and that I had been beaten heavily twice and was therefore going into the envelope. Tony Jacklin wasn't the captain but was one of Bernard Gallacher's assistants. I had been beaten twice but had played in two foursomes matches, where you're dependent on a partner. I was very upset and disappointed. I had been playing very, very well. In the two weeks before the Ryder Cup I had won the English Open and then come second in the Lancombe Trophy and I was pleased with the way I was playing. But that's the way it goes in team competitions and is one of the reasons why I'm not a great fan of them. You're relying on someone to pick you, but they have all sorts of reasons of their own.'

I asked Bernard Gallacher when he found out Pate had been withdrawn and was told that he was having breakfast with Ian (now Lord) McLaurin when he noticed there was a gap in the draw. The first I heard about it was when he [Stockton] did it. He didn't phone me up and say: "We've got a problem, can you come and see me, Steve's not going to play." As far as I was concerned, Steve Pate played on Saturday and was fine.'

*And outplayed his partner, Pavin, by all accounts?*

'Yes. He was hitting the ball miles and playing well but they decided not to play him in the singles. He was due to play Seve, and Seve was still great. He wasn't number one player in the world but was quite close to it. Woosnam was number one, Nick Faldo was number two, but Seve was inspirational and virtually unbeatable at that time. But the way the draw fell, it fell kindly for America because Seve then got to play Wayne Levi and to be honest, anyone could have beaten Levi at the time. So what happened was, Wayne Levi's been sacrificed against our best player. I loved the draw the way it was; Seve was in the middle of the draw and could affect the result, but only if he's playing one of their good players.'

*Can we be explicit about this – are you saying you seriously think the Americans decided to withdraw Pate after they saw the draw?*

'It just looked that way. They certainly didn't tell me the evening before that there was even a suspicion he wouldn't play. It just looked convenient; everything worked conveniently – if Steve Pate doesn't play he gets half a point. If he does play, chances are Seve would have beaten him. I felt very sorry for David Gilford because I couldn't prepare him for being the name in the envelope.'

*He says it was Tony Jacklin that told him he was enveloped.*

It was because I told Tony to go in. I had already spoken to David and he was upset and he doesn't remember the order of things. I had told David he was in the envelope and the reason was that it was between him and Paul Broadhurst, and Broadhurst had only played once. He won his match and I said it's only fair that he doesn't go in the envelope and you do. David was a young player and had taken two big, heavy beatings. But I had great confidence that the singles was a good time to get it back. But he was so upset that he started to cry and I had to go because it was getting quite close to the tee-off time. That's when I said to Tony Jacklin: Could you go in and try to console him, so David has forgotten that I told him first and gave him the reason why – but that's why he remembers Tony Jacklin speaking with him.'

Whether Pate did indeed suffer a

Bernard Gallacher was also angered by the jingoism at Kiawah and said: 'They were caught up in the euphoria of victory in the Gulf War and that's why it came to "War on the Shore". They were doing a lot of inspirational speeches about we've beaten Saddam Hussein and now we're going to beat you, sort of thing. I remember saying to Dan Quayle, who was vice-president at the time: "You know, we lost a lot of people in that war, too, and we were right with you."'

reaction and was unfit to play or whether his withdrawal was a tactical move by captain Stockton we shall never know. Nick Faldo, talking to *Golf International* magazine some years later, said: 'The Steve Pate thing – injury, play and then injury again. That was a question mark . . .'

The magazine asked: 'Particularly when they saw the draw before they withdrew him from the singles?' Faldo replied: 'Yeah, exactly.'

Innocent interpretations could be placed on all of these events but they left a nasty odour in the air.

# 1991 (3)   The feud resumes

As 1989 showed, Seve Ballesteros and Paul Azinger were never going to be the best of friends and if there is bad blood between golfers, matchplay in general and the Ryder Cup in particular are exactly where it is most likely to be spilled. Ballesteros remained convinced, even two years after the event, that Azinger had got a 'bad' (which means favourable to him) drop after driving into water on the final hole of their singles match at The Belfry. The fact that the American dropped where he was told to by a rules official cut no ice with the Spaniard and twenty-four months later he was still seething, but the truth is that his anger was really caused by the fact that he lost to the American. No golfer likes to lose, Ballesteros loathed it to the core of his being. Because Seve and his fellow Spaniard, Olazábal, had already proven to be a peerless combination, it was entirely natural and predictable that Europe captain Bernard Gallacher, who had succeeded Tony Jacklin, would select the duo to open the batting for the away team and be first on the course on day one in the opening series of foursomes. To counter this obvious ploy, home captain Dave Stockton picked Azinger and Chip Beck. The American pairing dovetailed beautifully and were two-up after seven holes before the galleries, a significant percentage of whom were waving blue in support of Europe, could really find their voices. In America it's called 'ham and egging' and is the essence of foursomes play, where both members of each team play the same ball and must complement each other. But that's how the bitterness and rancour kicked off, with a row over golf balls. Because it was foursomes, each team had to play the same make and compression of ball, a fact that the Americans either misunderstood or ignored.

José Maria Olazábal was the first to notice, and told his playing partner, walking off the seventh green, that he

*Paul Azinger, Seve, Jose-Maria Olazabal and Chip Beck in their bad-tempered, bickering match*

thought their opponents were switching between 100 and 90 compression balls – and if you get such a suspicion in matchplay it's fairly easy to check because once you concede a short putt you can pick up your opponent's ball and toss it back to him. Both Spaniards and their caddies were now watching Azinger and Beck the way a cuckolded husband studies his wife at a party, and on the eighth all were agreed that it had happened again, so Ballesteros asked for captain Gallacher to be called. He arrived just as the players had teed off at the ninth, which the Americans also won to go three-up, and on the tenth tee the recriminations and accusations started. At first it was Olazábal who did most of the talking, giving chapter and verse on each occasion and at which holes the Americans had changed balls. At first the accused flatly denied the charge, and then conceded that they may have been in error, but Azinger insisted they had not been cheating.

'Paul, nobody's accusing you of cheating,' said Ballesteros, 'just breaking the rules – that's a different thing.'

The problem for the Europeans was that in matchplay any protest has to be lodged, and the dispute settled, before the hole is completed. If it is not, the result stands and you have to get on with it, and

that's what happened here. Billy Foster, who was working as Seve's caddy, is quoted in the book *How We Won the Ryder Cup: The Caddies' Stories*, as saying: 'We restarted and Zinger walked past me, saying almost under his breath and sort of sneering, "Nice try."'

*Memo to Paul Azinger and Chip Beck*: When you're playing Seve Ballesteros in the Ryder Cup and want to win, do not, under any circumstances, piss him off. See under 'Floyd, Raymond'.

For many golfers, anger on the course is destructive and damaging only to themselves and because of this many people in matchplay will try to wind up their opponents. The ploys designed to irritate are as old as the hills – from forcing someone to hole every putt, no matter how short (the inference being that you think he has a dodgy putting stroke and is liable to miss one; or just for the sheer bloody-mindedness of making him play it), to deliberately walking slowly when up against a player with a naturally quick tempo and rhythm, to lingering over a few practice putts on the hole just completed, so that he has to wait on the tee when it is your honour. But the one player in the world you would not want to annoy is Seve Ballesteros. He played angry golf better

than anyone who ever lived. For most, strong emotion gets into their swing or putting stroke, making it shorter, choppier and less effective.

Except that Ballesteros could take that anger – and on this particular day he was livid with his opponents – and channel it into ever more outrageous shots of brilliance, and Olazábal did exactly the same. From three down after ten holes the Spanish duo won five of the next eight and won the match 2&1 on the seventeenth. And of course, luck, kismet, fate or the gods of golf who wait to remind you of your own frailty and deliver a steel-capped boot to your groin, conspired to pit the same players against each other in the afternoon fourballs. It would be a hard-hearted person indeed who did not feel just a smidgeon of sympathy for Paul Azinger and Chip Beck as they lost, again – on the same green, by the same margin, to the same pair of Spaniards.

Stop laughing at the back.

Azinger said of Ballesteros: 'He gets a really bad cough every Ryder Cup.'
Ballesteros said of Azinger: 'The American team is eleven nice guys and Paul Azinger.'

# 1991 (4)    Pavin goes to war

Kiawah Island in 1991 probably represents the lowest point of the competition's seventy-nine-year history in terms of losing sight of what a sporting competition should be (although Sam Torrance maintains that Brookline, nine years later, was even worse). But the gesture that absolutely beat all others for ludicrous excess was Corey Pavin appearing on the first day wearing a Desert Storm combat cap. He said it was in honour of American troops in the Gulf War – seeming to forget that European soldiers had not only been involved but in some instances been slaughtered by 'friendly' fire from their supposed allies. Pavin also overlooked the fact that, despite having been dubbed the 'War on the Shore', the Ryder Cup and a conflict in which thousands died could hardly be seen as synonymous. Matters weren't helped when the US PGA itself picked up on the war on the shore theme and gave the name to the infamous 'history of the cup' video that barely mentioned a European player or European success. And US PGA official Jim Awtrey, at a dinner held to welcome the European team, prayed to God for an American victory, in a room in which the American team was seated centre stage and the Europeans banished to the periphery. Welcome to Kiawah, boys. European Tour executive director Ken Schofield was ready to walk out and take the visiting team with him but Bernard Gallacher prevailed on him to stay.

Almost anyone who has been in the public eye for any length of time will make errors of judgement that they subsequently come to regret but in Pavin's case the mistake involved a lapse of thinking so glaringly inappropriate that it is difficult to reconcile it's being made by an intelligent man. And yet he is exactly that, and someone that European golf fans have come to detest in the Ryder Cup because he is such an indefatigable competitor – and it is difficult to pay any golfer a higher compliment.

I asked him about the Desert Storm cap and he said: 'All I was thinking about was showing solidarity for the troops who were involved in Desert Storm and what was going on overseas and I really wasn't thinking any other way about it at the time. And of course I was aware that other countries had also committed forces but what I was trying to do was simply show solidarity for our troops. After the fact I heard some grumbling and criticism from the other side of the Atlantic about "going to war" and all that stuff, and if I had known it would have been interpreted like that I wouldn't have worn the hat. I also thought it was a cool hat.'

Pavin's nickname on the US Tour is 'Bulldog' and that sums him up almost perfectly – in attitude if not appearance. He is a slight, 1-iron-thin man, who

probably has to run around in the shower to get wet and who looks considerably shorter than his 5 feet 9 inches. Never a long hitter, he had to find other ways to compete against the Tour behemoths who launched the ball impossibly long distances, and he eventually settled on three methods. First, he is one of the last of the great shot-makers, shaping the ball to move through the air in the direction, and to the degree, that he dictated. Second, he developed a remarkable short game. It does not have the flair or imagination of a Ballesteros (but then, what does?) but is remarkably effective and although he might be out-driven, from 100 yards and in, he was rarely outscored. Third, and probably most important of all, he's such a bloody-minded, hard-nosed, iron-willed fighter that he never, ever knows when he's beaten. On reflection, 'Bulldog' is not quite right and perhaps 'terrier' is better – the sort that grabs an opponent's ankle on the first tee and drags him around the course, shaking its head, snarling, snapping and being an all-round pain in the backside until he eventually prevails.

If you were on the green, and close, in two, while Pavin was lost in the woods for three, he would find a way to win the hole. If you manage to get him down, stand on his neck and don't ever let him get up because if he does, he'll go on to beat you. In short, he's exactly the guy you would want on your team. Unfortunately, for us Europeans, he was on theirs.

He was also pumped and says: 'I remember it being a big deal for me personally and for the team as a whole. There was a lot of competitiveness between the teams building up before and during the event. The atmosphere was very emotional and the fans were very emotional and it was the first time I had experienced anything as intense as that.'

*Was there too much emotion and partisanship?*

'I would say that in the grand scheme of things it was probably better for the Ryder Cup in the long run, but for that week in particular I didn't find it very attractive – especially the way the crowds reacted; it was a bit too much. The effect was that it didn't seem like a golf event. I loved the whole thing and had been trying to make the team for a long time because to me it's the ultimate competition in golf.'

It is easy to admire Pavin and respect his capacity to wring every last tiny drop of success from his golf game, and in the process get the home fans rooting for him and his team, but there is a thin line between supporting your side in its efforts to win and denigrating, abusing or insulting the other team. Pavin led the American fans, knowingly or not, to overstep the mark.

As a result of his cheerleading and Dave Stockton's myopic captaincy, in which winning was the only thing that counted and the manner of it was deemed irrelevant, the American galleries whooped, hollered, bellowed, screamed and generally went far over the top as it is possible to go. Pavin was ably supported by disappointing comments from people like Paul Azinger, who said:

In 1997 Ian Woosnam was still mad about the whole thing and knew exactly who to blame. He told the *Daily Telegraph*: 'I think Stockton was completely out of order. He went out to win and he didn't care how he did it. When the British lost in the 40s, 50s and 60s they did it with grace; when the Americans began losing they didn't like it and Stockton got the crowds too aggressively wound up. It almost turned into a riot. It wasn't golf and it wasn't a fair match.'

'American pride is back. We went over there and thumped the Iraqis. Now we've taken the cup back. I'm proud to be an American.'

Well, yes, Paul, but if you truly take pride in likening a sporting contest to a war it's time for a reality check. In 2004, Europe captain Bernard Gallacher told *The Observer* newspaper: 'It was like that World Wrestling Federation stuff on television, where you have bad guys and good guys. We were the bad guys. When the Americans apply themselves to winning something as seriously as they have the Ryder Cup, you know you have to cope with a very ruthless animal.'

Stockton was ruthless and sadly, his leading lieutenant on the course was the otherwise wholly admirable Corey Pavin – and he wore the uniform to prove it.

# 1991 (5)  With friends like these . . .

David Feherty is an Irishman with an Irish love of blarney and is one of the few genuinely funny professional golfers who have ever lived. He has a wonderfully perverse, and very honest, sense of humour that holds nothing sacred, and he can spot an inflated-ego-pricking opportunity at a 100 yards.

He was once quoted in a newspaper as saying that Colin Montgomerie's face resembled a bulldog eating a wasp and was extremely indignant to have been misrepresented. 'What I actually said', he corrected journalists the next day, 'is that he looks like a warthog licking piss off a nettle.'

Feherty also has an innate curiosity and inquiring mind, although it can lead to trouble. Some years ago while playing a practice round alongside Sam Torrance at Wentworth GC for the Volvo PGA Championship, they met an adder, Britain's only venomous snake, basking in the sun. Torrance, who spotted the reptile first, prodded it a few times to antagonise it and then called his mate over. Feherty, in the mistaken belief that he's some kind of macho hunk, went in for a closer inspection and the snake not surprisingly bit him on the finger, and he had to withdraw from the event with a digit swollen to three times its normal size. Sam Torrance insisted they play the remainder of their practice round, however, because they were in a money match against two others and winning. After the round, when he accompanied his friend to hospital, Torrance came out to be met by reporters and told them: 'He's dead.' They looked at him and said: 'Jesus Christ.' Torrance replied: 'I know. Feherty's fine but the snake's dead.'

*David Feherty and Torrance, almost joined at the hip*

Many commentators on the game of golf (Gary McCord springs to mind) think they are funny but their wisecracks – greens so fast they must have been bikini-waxed – have a well-rehearsed, glib feel to them, as if they were written the night before. Feherty has the wit and the intelligence (which he tries quite hard to hide) to be both spontaneously funny and devastatingly accurate, as when he called Colin Montgomerie 'Mrs Doubtfire'. Feherty wasn't, in fact, the first person to use the term, but when he applied it, it stuck. The caricature had just enough truth to offer hints of recognition of the figure who so often makes his morose and scowling way down fairways all over the world.

Feherty's best friend in the world is Sam Torrance, whose own wit leans much more towards the dry and understated, but it is clear that both men love each other dearly and particularly love being together on a golf course. So when Feherty made the 1991 Ryder Cup team it seemed pretty obvious that he and Torrance would be yoked together at some point. They didn't have to wait long, going out in the first day fourballs, immediately after lunch, against Lanny Wadkins, the man with barbed wire for blood when it came to matchplay, and Mark O'Meara.

Feherty wrote in *Golf* magazine, for which he is a columnist: 'I was shaking so badly that on my first two swings it was a miracle I made contact with the ball. But somehow I managed to fudge it up there about 20 feet short of the hole. During my putting stroke, everything moved except my bowels. I kind of scuffed the putt up to about 4 feet short. Sam made the half and on the way to the next tee he put a bear-like arm around my shoulder and squeezed me tight. He grinned, let me go and began to roll a cigarette as we walked to the second tee. "Just think", he said to me, "you're on the same team as Seve, Faldo, Langer, Olazábal, Woosie, Monty, and most impressive of all, me. This only happens tae a few people, so you'd better be up to enjoying it."

'He flicked open an old brass Zippo, took an enormous hit on the Old Holborn [tobacco] and blew the smoke in my face. I still love the smell of it. "So dinnae be a prick," he grinned. "Or ah'll join Wadkins and O'Meara and you can play all three of us."' In some versions of this story the words 'you useless bastard', are attached but you get the drift.

The match was a good one, and although Feherty does his best to self-deprecatingly suggest that any decent shots he hit were flukes, once he overcame his initial nerves he contributed every bit as much, if not more than his more experienced friend and partner. The Europeans were 3-down after nine holes – never a surprise when Wadkins is part of the opposition – but Feherty won eleven with a chip-in, and then took the fourteenth with a birdie two, to reduce the deficit to just one hole. In his book *David Feherty's Totally Subjective Guide to the Ryder Cup*, the Irishman writes: 'Sam almost holed his tee shot at seventeen but so did O'Meara, and all four of us puked our

Feherty should also, perhaps, be allowed the final word but with typical generosity, always quotes his source. On the last day when everything came down to the final match, between Bernhard Langer and Hale Irwin, Feherty was crouched next to Laurence Levy, a much loved and greatly missed photographer who could deliver a few apercus of his own. Levy turned to Feherty and said: 'Last time a German was under this much pressure he shot himself in a bunker.'

way up eighteen, finding more sand than a cat with diarrhea [sic]. It was the last match of the day [none of those following reached the 18th] and in the gathering gloom I ended up with a 12-footer to win the hole and half a point. The Almighty was clearly a total bastard – why me? I read it left edge, and of course, Torrance read it right edge, and I accidentally flinched it off

straight, and watched, horrified, as it cruised straight into the back of the hole.'

The friends were retained as a pair for the next morning's fourballs but lost to – you guessed it – Lanny Wadkins, this time playing alongside Hale Irwin, and if there were ever two harder matchplay opponents, it would be difficult to think of them. Feherty won his

singles match on the final day to record a creditable one-and-a-half points from a possible three. The Irishman never played in another Ryder Cup, his bowels probably couldn't have coped anyway, but this experience at Kiawah Island left him, and millions of us, irreversibly hooked.

# 1991 (6)   Do I know you?

David Gilford has played in only two Ryder Cup matches but, after his first, he must have felt like never playing in another. In the singles he was famously 'enveloped' to become the man paired with injured Steve Pate, and therefore not play. It was a bitter blow and one from which lesser men would not have recovered; but he bounced back from that huge disappointment to star four years later. He was never a dominant

world-beater but relentlessly straight, an excellent iron player and consistent rather than spectacular on the greens. If he had one weakness it was his chipping, but he is one of those players that no one else really notices until they have had their pockets picked of the tournament winner's cheque. He took six European Tour titles and was as well known for being a cattle farmer as a golf pro, and quite possibly the least

flashy, most unpretentious man in the game.

Before his singles disappointment he had two other outings, both in foursomes. On the first day he and Colin Montgomerie, also making his debut, lost to Lanny Bloody Wadkins and Hale Irwin 4&2. Gilford himself says of that match: 'The course was tough; the greens were like concrete and very difficult. In the first foursomes against

Wadkins and Irwin they were quickly four under par and in foursomes I think would have beaten any combination on that day; I don't think we stood a chance.' Foursomes play is a difficult enough discipline in which to make your debut, but to do it alongside another rookie, against one of the opposition's toughest combinations, in the atmosphere of Kiawah Island, was asking a great deal.

On the second day he had what many regarded as the ill-luck to be partnered with Nick Faldo against Paul Azinger and Mark O'Meara. Faldo was out of sorts, going through a divorce and had already been beaten twice in tandem with other partners. Gilford cut a disconsolate figure as he marched apparently on his own, with his senior partner barely looking, smiling at or talking to him, and there was considerable disquiet among the British press corps, most of which wrote that Faldo had been selfish, aloof and arrogant. It is a story that has grown with the telling, as most do, and come to be regarded as an absolute truth but it is not, and it's now time to put the legend to rest.

Faldo himself, in his autobiography, *Life Swings*, wrote in his own defence: 'I daresay I should have offered David more support and a friendly word of advice. But in the cauldron of the Ryder Cup, when you are fighting your own demons on the course, as I was, it is difficult to provide your equally despondent partner with a stout shoulder.'

His caddy, Fanny Sunesson, is quoted in the book *How we won the Ryder Cup: The Caddies' Stories* as saying: 'The main thing was, though, that the two of them just did not know each other at all . . . I think Nick had talked to him once, or we'd played with him once. I don't think that was the right situation to put them in.'

It's a view endorsed by Gilford's own caddy, Martin Gray, in the same book. 'There was a lot of bad press about Faldo blanking Gilford but it didn't really come over like that on the course,' he said. 'Gilly's a nightmare to try and get into – quiet as a mouse – and Faldo's not really an extrovert.'

In view of these three apparently supportive opinions it seemed only natural to ask Gilford himself, and he said: 'I don't think there was any of that [animosity or ill-feeling between him and Faldo] and I don't know where that came from. Early in the match against Azinger and O'Meara the momentum went with the Americans, the wrong way, and as a result we were always struggling; that's the way it goes sometimes. Faldo was what you would expect but he wasn't deliberately rude.'

So there you have it, the four people who were there on the day and are in the best position to give the definitive account agree that Faldo was simply being his usual self, that it was a case of two quiet men who never speak much anyway being paired, and they further agree that Azinger and O'Meara would probably have beaten anyone in foursomes that afternoon – they were like a runaway train as they roared to a 7&6 victory.

And then David Gilford shed a little more light onto the character of the man with whom he was paired. Having exonerated Faldo of rudeness he went on: 'Having said that, I wasn't a great fan of his. The first time I had played with him was a few weeks earlier and when we went into the scorer's hut to check our cards, out of eighteen holes he had made ten or twelve mistakes on my card, and that's no exaggeration. Everybody makes mistakes from time to time, and they have a wrong score written down, so you hand the card back and they correct it, but this, in my view, was the height of bad manners – not to mark someone's card properly.

'I honestly don't know what he was trying to say or do but I have never had that before or since with anybody. I am a great fan of what he has achieved but he's not a wonderful man.'

So they weren't the best of enemies, and the two men support each other's stories that this day at Kiawah was just one of those things – but it was hardly love at second sight either.

# 1991 (7)   Calcavecchia's collapse

Ryder Cups have often provided the defining moment of a player's career, both good and bad. It is an event where the scrutiny is more intense and the burden of expectation carried heavier than anywhere else. Some find the load too onerous and, sadly, a man for whom it all, ultimately, proved too much, was Mark Calcavecchia. He still carries the scars and has arguably been nothing like the player he was before 1991, because in that year's singles he appeared to fall apart like a cheap suit, in front of millions.

This was his third appearance in the event (and he would resurface eleven years later) and from his previous two, in 1987 and 1989, had the respectable record of won three, lost four – considering he was playing when Europe was fielding its strongest ever teams. He was also having a pretty good time at Kiawah Island: he had been picked for three of the first series of matches and had two points to show for it. And then he drew European debutant Colin Montgomerie in the singles. Monty has always worn his heart on his sleeve and sometimes is too open and honest for his own good, which does not always endear him to the people against whom he is competing. In addition, there was a rumour circulating among the American camp (subse-quently proven to be absolutely untrue) that when told of Steve Pate's car crash, Monty had replied: 'Good, I hope it killed him.' Not surprisingly therefore, the Americans were queuing up to take his scalp, and when he heard the draw, Calcavecchia must have been rubbing his hands in delighted expectation.

If any player ever defined the adjective 'streaky' it is Calcavecchia. Often it would be generous to describe his play as 'average' but when he catches fire there are few who have scorched around a golf course in more scintillating style. As a result, Montgomerie was warned that under no circumstances should he

*Colin Montgomerie misses a putt on the eighteenth – but Mark Calcavecchia did likewise*

allow the American to get off to a fast start, because few players feed on confidence and momentum like him. Fat chance. Calcavecchia was clearly having one of his better days and after nine holes was four under par and 5-up on an opponent who looked shell-shocked and forlorn. Making up a five-hole deficit on the back nine of any course against any player is a tough ask, but over Kiawah Island, against an in-form Calc – what are you, some sort of comedian? Except that, as Colin Montgomerie admitted later, the long buggy ride between ninth green and tenth tee gave him a few precious moments to gather his thoughts and give himself the proverbial kick in the derrière. Unfortunately, his little pep talk only caused him to bunker his approach shot but, miracle of miracles, he holed it from 40 yards to claw a hole back. Even then, however, his only real intention was to reduce the margin of his eventual defeat. But then he birdied the eleventh to reduce the deficit to three holes and maybe, just maybe, a most unlikely comeback was about to occur.

Except it wasn't. The next two holes were halved and then that great useless chump Monty lost the fourteenth to go four down with four to play – Calcavecchia was now dormie and to seal the victory only had to half one of the closing holes. Hold on to your hats though. What happened next constitutes one of the most dramatic sixty minutes ever seen in the Ryder Cup, and the competition is pretty intense.

The first thing that happened is that the wind had changed direction, so that as the players stood on the fifteenth tee, it was blowing quite hard left-to-right. For the entirety of his career that is the direction in which Calcavecchia has shaped his shots and he was too damned old now to learn how to hit a draw when he most needed one. To describe the shot he hit as a slice would be generous in the extreme – it was more like a wild, ballooning, banana of a ball that started right and just kept going righter to the extent that it finished up on a beach. Several strokes later he made his shell-shocked way to the green where he holed out for a triple-bogey seven, which was beaten by Monty's less than textbook double-bogey six. So now it was three down with three to play but still no need to panic. Unfortunately for Calcavecchia, it was not the fact that he lost the hole that bothered him – he could still win comfortably – but the fact that he

butchered it like a cow's carcass. On the next hole he was again farther right than General Franco, and a routine Monty par reduced the deficit to 2-down with two to play.

Unfortunately, one of those two was Pete Dye's trademark Kiawah Island hole, a long, brutal par-3, with a green angled away from the players and a sea of water between tee and green. It was over 200 yards long and some of the competitors needed a wood to get home. Fortunately for Calcavecchia it was Monty's honour and, with a 2-iron in hand he smacked his ball straight into the water, a stupid, careless mistake. If Calcavecchia was relieved he didn't show it, because he then hit a stone-cold shank that never looked like finding dry land. The two moved ahead to the dropping zone where Monty put his ball to the back of the green and his opponent also found the putting surface, considerably nearer. Monty played first and got his ball close enough to be given the second putt. So sure was he that Calc would two-putt for victory that he gave

Calcavecchia had finished 7, 6, 6, 6 or eight over par in four holes. Monty himself had had a double-bogey, par, double-bogey, par ending and won all four holes.

his glove and ball marker to his caddy and his pessimism seemed justified as the American rolled his first putt up to 2½ feet. Monty even considered conceding the putt, but the tradition in matchplay is that if it's to win, you need to make it.

It never even touched the hole: one-down with one to play.

Monty played the eighteenth in exemplary fashion with driver and 2-iron to 20 feet. Not surprisingly the now wan Calcavecchia was way right again, and eventually got on the green in three and faced a 10-foot putt for victory. To his credit he nearly made it but it failed to drop, and the match was halved. A

distraught Calcavecchia was led away by Payne Stewart and later had to receive medical treatment for breathing problems. He was in tears and utterly inconsolable.

For Monty, it was the end of the first chapter of a remarkable Ryder Cup career.

# 1991 (8)    The greatest finish ever

With all the animosity and hyperbole that had been on show, and all the figurative blood that had been spilled over three days of intense competition, it is perhaps fitting that Kiawah Island produced the most astonishing finish ever seen, coming down to the last putt, on the last green, of the last match. It became one of, if not the, defining moment of a competition that has grown in significance over the last 20 years to become the third-most-watched sports event in the world, headed only

by football's World Cup and the Olympics – and they take place over several weeks, not three days. The estimated worldwide audience for the 2002 Ryder Cup was one billion people, or a sixth of the world's population; on this final day at Kiawah it would be several hundred millions and everyone who watched got their money's worth.

The home team had taken an early lead, starting strongly in the morning foursomes and then being slightly pegged back in the afternoon fourballs,

so by the end of the first day they led 4½–3½. In almost every regard that day's play was reversed on the Saturday, with the United States having the advantage in the fourballs and Europe stronger in foursomes, so that by close of play everything was locked up, eight points apiece.

No prisoners were taken and no time off allowed for good behaviour – of which there was precious little in evidence. American captain Dave Stockton loaded his best players – Mark O'Meara, Fred Couples, Lanny Wadkins

and Hale Irwin – at the bottom of the draw, while Gallacher sprinkled his throughout the list. He did, however, pull one masterstroke by asking an out-of-form and out-of-sorts Nick Faldo to lead off, and the Englishman, his confidence boosted by the faith put in him, took the first point of the day when he beat Raymond Floyd two-up. Then Feherty beat Payne Stewart, Montgomerie and Calcavecchia halved, Azinger beat Olazábal, Pavin beat Richardson, Ballesteros beat Levi (of course), Beck beat Woosnam, Broadhurst beat O'Meara, Couples beat Torrance and Wadkins beat James. All of this, combined with the half point each team received for the Gilford/Pate envelope pairing, meant that with the last two players left standing on the course, the United States needed just half a point to reach the magic 14½ needed for overall victory, while Europe had to win the final match to tie and retain the cup as holders.

That, however, was beginning to look unlikely because Irwin had got himself two-up with four to play, and there was no way that he would suffer a Calcavecchia-like collapse. This is a man renowned for his sheer grinding, relentless approach on a golf course. He is a good, if not long driver of the ball, one of the best long iron players ever seen and an extremely competent putter – he doesn't hole too many bombs but rarely puts himself under pressure with a knee-knocking second putt either. To some, the term 'grinder' is an insult, but in Irwin's case it is a compliment as he epitomises all-round quality and rarely beats himself. He also enjoys a reputation as being particularly at home on the most difficult courses, as anyone who lifts three US Open Championships must be – no one sets up a Major championship course to be as tough (sometimes stupidly so) as the USGA.

His opponent was Bernhard Langer, who could match Irwin for both the quality of his play but more pertinently, in steel, guts, grit, backbone and any other adjective you care to apply that signifies determination. Both had been sent out as last man because their respective captains wanted emotionless golfing automatons, or the nearest human equivalent, where they were most needed, and it was apparent that this was a contest that could go right down to the wire. Irwin played competently, but it was a Langer missed putt from four feet on the fourteenth that put the American two up with four to play. But the German came right back on fifteen and holed a nerve-testing 7-footer for par to win the hole. He did the same again on the sixteenth but this time his opponent followed him in – one-up with two to play. At the fearsome seventeenth Langer hit just through the green and Irwin, obliged to hit a wood, did the same, before his ball apparently flew into the gallery and then rolled down to within a few feet of the hole. Unfortunately for him, it wasn't his ball: some joker in the gallery had thrown a ball across the putting surface in the mistaken belief that it would be funny. Both men had similar downhill putts towards the water. Langer got his ball to within 6 feet, but Irwin had a rush of blood and charged his ball 10 feet past. He missed the one coming back and so, for the third time in three holes Bernhard stood over a knee-knocker. He bent over his (then regulation length) putter

A week after this devastating loss, Langer won the Mercedes German Masters. It is difficult to think of any other golfer in the world who could come back so well from such an experience.

*The anguish is evident – and yet a week later Langer won in Germany*

and fastened his hands in that peculiar style that he virtually patented – left hand at the bottom of the grip, right hand at the top, and the former anchored in place by the thumb and fingers of the latter. He holed it to take the match to the eighteenth all-square.

Langer drove well but Irwin hooked into the gallery and was lucky enough to see his ball rebound onto the fairway. By now, every other player and caddy was following the match, along with every golf official who ever lived, or so it seemed, and at times there appeared to be more people inside than outside the gallery ropes. Seve Ballesteros, in particular, was marching along, pumping his fist and exhorting the away fans to chant 'Europe, Europe'. On his decisive approach shot Irwin, barely able to hold a club, missed the green, chipped poorly and two-putted for a bogey. All Langer – who was safely on the edge 30 feet away – had to do was two-putt to win the hole, match and tie.

And then he jabbed his first effort 6 feet past. He and caddy Pete Coleman stalked the putt for ever and both could see a spike mark on the line but there was nothing they could do about it. The whole world held its breath as Langer settled over the ball, swung the putter back and through and then screwed up his face in anguish as the ball slid past on the right. He and Irwin embraced, the Americans went apeshit and the Ryder Cup went back across the Atlantic.

The Americans had started the week by declaring their intention to 'kick butt' and they had. But thankfully this magnificent final act played out between two decent men had done just enough to remind us all that the event itself is more important than who wins or loses it in any given year.

# 1993 (1)  Sign here please

With all the shenanigans from 1991 still fresh in everyone's memory, it is good to report that in 1993 captains Bernard Gallacher and Tom Watson went to great lengths to ensure the nasty atmosphere of Kiawah Island was forgotten – or at least not repeated – amid some spectacular golf. If America was looking for a peacemaker it could not have chosen more wisely than Watson, who is as hard-nosed a competitor as ever walked onto a golf course, and yet the epitome of gentlemanly conduct. He loves and respects the game but not in a dewy-eyed, sentimental or maudlin way, and he had been distressed by what he saw on TV of the Kiawah Island contest. Rather, he sees that tradition,

*Captain Tom Watson gives the world's most powerful man some advice*

history and heritage have created a legacy of (almost) exemplary behaviour and a code of conduct, and set of rules, that should never be breached. Watson the golfer can be a wayward driver but has a stunning short game, and it was this combination that led to the description a 'Watson par', which essentially meant: drive deep into trees, hack out sideways, fire an iron to 20 feet and bang in the putt. If he had a motto for matchplay it would be 'Hard but fair'. Few people in golf are more respected than Watson and it is almost certainly the reason he was chosen to lead an American team that was trying to consign the ill-temper of the previous encounter into the bin marked 'gone and forgotten'. He began well enough, saying that the contest was not a war, but that each team would do its damndest to beat the other, and then hopefully retire for a libation or three when it was all over, irrespective of the outcome. But if anyone who heard him say so was deluded enough to think that meant he would be happy to lose, they didn't know their man. He even steered his team through a minor diplomatic incident before they left home for the Belfry. President Clinton, a keen golfer, wanted to meet the US players, but

many showed a distinct reluctance to shake the hand of a man they perceived as a Democrat draft-dodger who wanted to tax them into oblivion. Watson responded with the words: 'It doesn't matter who the president is, if you're invited to the White House, you go.' And go they did.

Sadly, all the diplomacy was nearly undone at the gala dinner on the eve of the competition. Watson recognised that the official functions both teams have to endure, and meeting the requests of Press and public can be almost as tiring as thirty-six holes a day, so he forbade his team from signing autographs until the end of the week. The guests at the gala dinner had paid £150 each for the privilege and one of the reasons was to be close to the players and grab a much-desired autograph on the official menu. Watson, however, was adamant that if menus were handed in they would all be signed at the celebration dinner at the end of the week but not before. It was a decision that upset many, but it also broke the tradition of each team member signing the dinner menu for the other team. Sam Torrance wandered across to Watson for an autograph, was politely but firmly refused, and was considerably upset, feeling that part of

the special bond between players had been broken. The Press latched onto it and, never able to resist an opportunity to pour petrol over a smouldering flame, duly wrote up the incident as 'The Battle of the Belfry'. Watson spent a considerable part of the next day apologising – although he really had no need – but common sense, thankfully, soon broke out again, and European captain Bernard Gallacher put it into perspective by saying: 'If that's going to be the major incident of the week, that'll be fine.' The controversy was created by one man's hurt feelings and quickly disappeared, although it demonstrated in the clearest terms just how big an event the Ryder Cup had become. When such a trivial moment can become front-page news and a man respected throughout golf for his integrity be told by a tabloid headline: 'Tom Watson, you're a disgrace', it is a measure of the importance that people attach to a golf competition that a few short years earlier had been moribund.

> Expressing his reluctance to meet with president Clinton before leaving America, Paul Azinger, with his customary eloquence, said: 'I don't want to shake hands with no draft dodger.'

Either that or it merely proves that there is no level to which British tabloid papers will not stoop.

Unfortunately, it was not only Sam Torrance's feelings that were hurt but his big toe as well. A few weeks earlier he had stumbled into a plant pot in the middle of the night while looking for a loo in an unfamiliar hotel room, coincidentally at the Belfry. He thought it had improved but in fact it had become infected and by the end of his first morning foursomes match, when he and Mark James were beaten comfortably by Corey Pavin and Lanny Wadkins, he was clearly in discomfort. He took no further part in the contest and Bernard Gallacher had to reluctantly tell Watson that Torrance would be 'enveloped' for the singles and the Americans had to come up with a name of their own.

Lanny Wadkins had won two points from a possible three and had Ryder Cup credentials to burn but, because he was a wild card pick and hadn't played his way onto the team by right he volunteered to stand down. It was a selfless gesture that united his team-mates in their desire to 'win one for Lanny' – so even when he didn't play the sod still managed to motivate the rest of his team.

Torrance, incidentally, later described his enforced withdrawal as his worst ever experience in the Ryder Cup.

Ill-health proved to be leitmotif of this Ryder Cup. Debutant Peter Baker, who putted the lights out all week and won three points from four in his only appearance in the event, had spent most of the night before the competition started at a local hospital where his daughter had been admitted as an emer-gency with suspected meningitis. Baker played at the insistence of his wife and in the afternoon fourballs holed a difficult 25-foot downhill putt to ensure that he and Ian Woosnam beat Lee Janzen and Jim Gallagher Jr one up.

And then at the end of the first day, Davis Love's wife, Robin, was thought to have gone into premature labour. She had walked the course to watch her husband and Tom Kite beat Seve Ballesteros and Jose Maria Olazabal in the morning foursomes, and walked a few more holes in the afternoon before they lost to the same duo in the fourballs (by 2&1 and 4&3 respectively). Thankfully she recovered, but it meant that the Loves, along with the Bakers, Torrances, and probably a few other couples, had at least one fretful night during the week.

# 1993 (2)  The mighty are fallen

The Brabazon Course at the Belfry has been roundly criticised by some and lauded by others and it is neither as good nor bad as these commentators would suggest. There is no doubt that it first hosted the Ryder Cup when it was too young but sadly the competition is no longer taken to the best venues, simply those prepared to pay the most money. But whatever your views on the course there is little disagreement that it has two great matchplay holes: the tenth and eighteenth. The tenth is a short par-4 guarded by water at the front and with a narrow approach between trees. Conventional players (that is, Americans) hit a mid-iron from the tee and try to make their birdie with an accurate wedge approach shot. The bold go for the green with a wood.

The eighteenth is a long par-4 played to a fairway angled right-to-left and away from the tee. Reach that and you turn through 90 degrees to a massive, three-tiered green with water in front. The best chance of getting close is to hit a long, raking draw (if you are right-handed) from the tee to get as near to the second stretch of water as possible. It is the classic risk/reward drive – execute the shot perfectly and you set up a birdie chance, misjudge it a fraction and your ball, and hopes of victory, are heading for the bottom of the lake. And for those not talented or bold enough to hit the long draw needed and have to play in a straight line from the tee, a bunker awaits on the far side of the fairway, from which it is almost impossible to reach the green.

The tenth hole became the scene for many home heroics and the Europeans, spear-headed inevitably by Seve Ballesteros, seemed always to be up for the challenge and prepared to risk all in search of a birdie or eagle. Where the Americans, often because of captain's instructions and sometimes at their own choosing, invariably opted for the safer, conventional route, the team in blue seemed always to have at least one member of each pairing with the nerve and ability to drive the green.

In view of their remarkable record to date, it was no surprise that Captain Bernard Gallacher put Seve Ballesteros and Jose Maria Olazabal together again in the first morning's foursomes, a format in which they had never been beaten in six matches. But this pairing was not the formidable force of old, and Ballesteros in particular was in terrible form. Coming into the event he had no victories for the season and had only twice finished in the top ten. He was tied second in the first tournament he played, the Dubai Desert Classic, and managed the same result in the Canon European Masters a few weeks before the Ryder Cup teams were announced. Other than that, he had only one top-twenty all year, when he

*Even the greatest meet their match eventually*

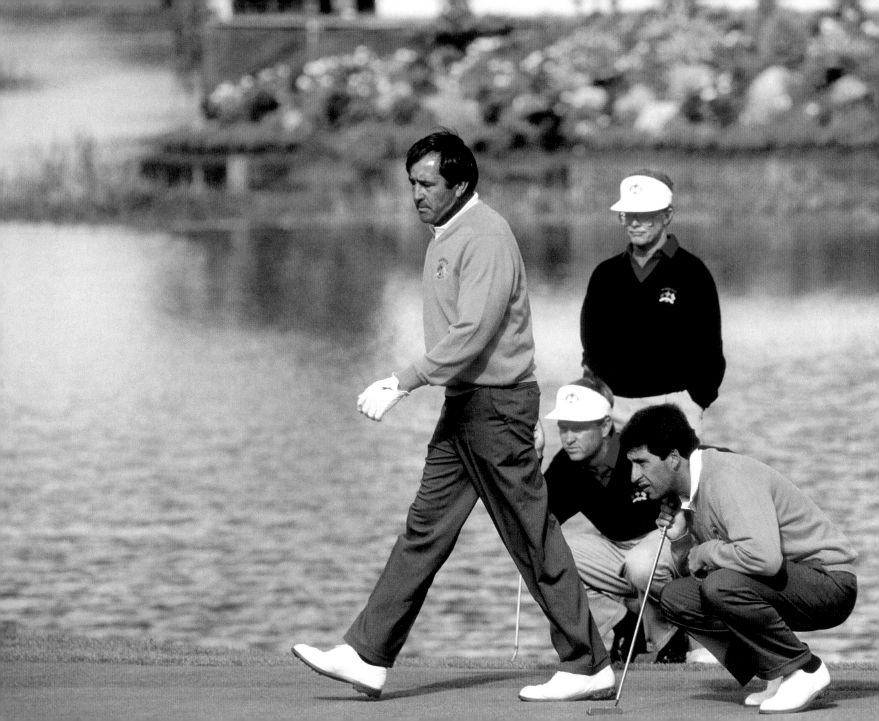

was tied thirteenth in the GA European Open – but at least that result was ten days before the Belfry. Olazabal, in contrast, had nine top-ten finishes in Europe but he also could not make the team on merit and both Spaniards had to rely on being two of captain Gallacher's wild-card picks (the other was Swede Joakim Haeggman) simply to make the team.

But this was the Ryder Cup, at the Belfry, and these were the two greatest matchplay competitors their country, and in all probability their continent and the world, had ever produced. So when, on that first morning, they drew the very strong American pairing of Tom Kite and Davis Love, we licked our lips in anticipation. Kite is a metronomic money machine who finds the fairway, finds the green and holes the putt with such relentless, niggling accuracy that he will break your heart. But even that description does him a disservice because he is also capable of superb scoring when his putter runs hot. His partner, Davis Love, is one of life's gentler souls, renowned for the considerable distance he hits the ball off the tee. He nevertheless goes quietly about his business and seems to have been a virtually permanent fixture in

the world's top-ten since the rankings were first compiled. If he has a weakness it is a fallibility with the putter, and a tendency to under-perform in the very biggest events, such as Majors, hinting at a personality that lacks a *soupcon* of the killer instinct required at the very peak of the game – and he was making his Ryder Cup debut. Nevertheless, they were a formidable foursomes pairing, with Kite's steadiness complemented by Love's birdie-making flair. In addition, of course, Kite and Ballesteros had a little history from previous encounters that always gave their meetings an added frisson. Having said that, all the Americans wanted to beat Seve particularly badly because he had a knack of getting in their faces and up their noses in equal measure. The match was considerably late getting underway because of fog, which had not helped rookie Love's nerves – and for an indication of quite how nauseous his Ryder Cup debut made Love feel, read the first chapter of John Feinstein's excellent *A Good Walk Spoiled*. In it, he also reveals that Love had been given several packets of cough lozenges by American players' wives, to offer to Balleteros, should he develop his usual throat-clearing antics.

Thankfully they were superfluous to requirements.

The match was a tight, tense affair in which the Americans took an early lead on the second hole that they did not relinquish, but neither could they put daylight between them and their opponents. The turning point came at the notorious tenth, which Ballesteros and Olazabal had made famous so often in the past. But this day and this Ballesteros were different. His driving all season had been terrible and already this morning he had found parts of the course from the tee that no one else had ever seen and to describe his driving as poor would be like saying that Bill Gates is quite well off. He dithered and debated with his partner endlessly over club selection and it was clear that he no longer had faith in his ability with a wood. Eventually, to surprised gasps, he took an iron from his bag and nurdled it down the fairway. Kite immediately grasped both the significance of the moment and his 3-wood, with which he lashed his ball to within 6 feet – it was as fine a moment of 'Take that you woosies!' bravura that the hole has seen. Olazabal put the European ball to about 10 feet before Seve – proud, noble unrepentant beast that he is – rolled in the putt for birdie. But then Love, taking a cue from his more experienced partner, slotted his putt home for the eagle that put his team two-up.

The Americans went on to record a 2&1 victory and the seemingly invincible Spanish duo lost at the seventh time of asking, their first ever foursomes match. But what the result also did was give the US team fresh heart and belief. The Belfry was their bogey course, and in particular the tenth and eighteenth were their bogey holes. The ghost was about to be laid to rest.

# 1993 (3)    Italian scapegoat

Because of a two-and-a-half-hour fog delay in the morning, one of the afternoon fourballs did not finish on the first day. It involved Nick Faldo and Colin Montgomerie against Paul Azinger and Fred Couples, and therefore pitted four of the most talented match players in the world against each other. Two heavyweight boxers standing toe-to-toe could not define an enthralling contest more eloquently. All-square at the halfway stage, the Americans went one-up at the sixteenth but their advantage was immediately nullified when Faldo, by now virtually playing in the dark, nailed a mid-iron to 4 feet at the next and holed for birdie. But the light was too poor for them to continue and all four had to reassemble on the eighteenth tee at 8 o'clock the next morning – not the sort of prospect on which you want to retire to bed. Monty found rough from the tee and all he could do was hit his second into the lake, joining the ball of Fred Couples, who had taken one shot fewer to find a watery grave. This left only Faldo and Azinger standing, with the American having hit the superior drive – one he described as his best ever. As a result he also hit his second considerably closer, to less than 20 feet, while Faldo was more than twice that distance away.

The Englishman then failed to appreciate how much early-morning dew there was on the grass and left his first putt 10 feet short, after which Azinger almost nailed his winning birdie but had to settle for par. It left Faldo with a knee-knocking, very missable putt to halve both the hole and the match and he knew exactly how vital it was. Miss, and the first day's scores would be tied at four apiece, hole it and Europe would have a crucial one point lead at 4.5–3.5.

He bolted it straight in the cup, looked around and said: 'Anyone for breakfast?'

Well, he is an Englishman.

The slender one-point advantage Europe held after the first day was maintained into the singles. Europe took the second-morning foursomes 3–1 but America came back with the same result in the afternoon fourballs to leave everything in the balance going into the final day. The near-parity was retained throughout a tense set of matches that started with two halves, between Lanny Wadkins and Sam Torrance, and Fred Couples and Ian Woosnam. Chip Beck then raised the visitors' morale by beating Barry Lane by one hole, having been three down with seven to play. The US euphoria was short-lived, however, because in the blink of an eye, or so it seemed, Montgomerie beat Janzen and Joakim Haeggman beat John Cook by the same one-up score, while Peter Baker took Corey Pavin by two holes. Europe led by 12.5–8.5 and needed just two points from the remaining six matches to cross the winning line. However, out in the country Seve Ballesteros was being thrashed convincingly by Jim Gallagher Jr – or rather, was beating himself with his continuing inability to find the short grass from the tee, and Tom Kite was doing a demolition of Bernhard Langer, eventually running out a comfortable 5&3 victor. The news for Europe got worse when Payne Stewart took a point off Mark James, by 3&2. Ray Floyd also had a firm grip around the throat of José Maria Olazàbal (and eventually won two-up) so the entire contest revolved around two matches. The last pair out, Faldo and Azinger, were locked in a tight duel that could go either way and Davis Love was behind to the Italian rookie Costantino Rocca, who had been surprised to be in such a vital position, so far down the running order – especially as he had played only once and been beaten. But he showed real grit and when he holed a monster putt on the fourteenth from off the green to go one-up he gave home fans a huge boost. As they played the seventeenth the Italian was still one hole up and when he safely found the par-5 green with a superb 3-iron to 15 feet, he was cruising. A two-putt par or one-putt birdie would be enough to settle the match there and then. But the putt was downhill and fast and his initial bold effort, which almost went into the hole, just kept rolling once it went past, and eventually settled five feet away. For those of us watching it was almost unbearable, for Rocca it must have been a body blow. Barely able to hold his putter he stroked the ball wide and in an instant his match was all-square with one to play.

Love hit a tremendous drive down the last and Costantino did not. His approach shot barely cleared the water in front of the green so he was obliged to chip up and ran the ball 15 feet past the hole, with Love already on the green in two, 7 feet short. The Italian had another putt, almost exactly the same as the one he had recently charged on 17, but if he could hole it for an improbable par four his opponent's effort for the win would suddenly seem twice as long to him and three times as difficult. Sadly, Rocca missed and Love took the match and the vital point the Americans needed to retain the Ryder Cup. Rocca was wrongly vilified by many British tabloid papers, which seemed far less interested in reporting that Englishman Barry Lane had also

In his singles match against Azinger, Faldo made a hole-in-one at the fourteenth en route to another half. It is one of only four aces ever scored in the Ryder Cup and Europeans have scored them all. The other three came from Peter Butler on the sixteenth at Muirfield in 1973, and Costantino Rocca on the sixth and Howard Clark on the eleventh at Oak Hill in 1995.

*Constantino Rocca misses and is about to find himself wrongly vilified*

lost, and from a much stronger position against a much less-fancied opponent in Chip Beck. The criticism Rocca faced would have broken a lesser man but thankfully we would see him in the competition again, in very different circumstances.

The European skipper Bernard Gallacher called on Seve Ballesteros and asked him to find Costantino and offer whatever encouragement he could. Ten minutes later Gallacher saw a dry-eyed Rocca and asked: 'Where's Seve?'

'He's over there,' Rocca replied: 'I had to leave him, he's crying his eyes out.'

# 1995 (1)    Take that

It took nearly six hours to complete because none of the four combatants has ever sought or been offered the title of 'Quickest Golfer in a Starring Role' but the Saturday afternoon fourball in which Nick Faldo and Bernhard Langer played against Corey Pavin and Loren Roberts was a classic encounter in which four men at the top of their game went at it like bare-knuckle prizefighters. The golf was sublime and it seemed almost pre-destined that this one would go until the final bell, and require a particular bit of magic to be decided, especially as the overall contest was so finely balanced. Victory for the USA would open up a two-point lead going into the singles – not insurmountable but daunting enough for the visitors – while a European win would send the teams into the final day locked at eight each.

Loren Roberts is one of those quiet, undemonstrative characters who steadily goes about his business almost without notice, until one day you look up the statistics and realise he is one of the most consistent golfers of all time, having notched up eight career victories and been inside the top-100 on the US money list for seventeen consecutive seasons. He earned the cheesy nickname 'Boss of the Moss' for his touch on the greens and is considered among his peers to be one of the best putters who ever lived. Surprisingly for a man of his ability, this was his only Ryder Cup appearance but he would be forgiven for thinking it was, as Seve Ballesteros would say: 'A piss of cake.'

On the first-afternoon fourballs he and Jeff Maggert had slaughtered Sam Torrance and Costantino Rocca 6&5 and in the Saturday foursomes he partnered Peter Jacobsen to a one-hole victory over Ian Woosnam and Philip Walton. So now here he was in the afternoon four-balls, having proven himself to be the perfect partner in either format – rather

like one of his opponents, Bernhard Langer – because of his ability to keep the ball in play and make the putts when they were needed.

In Faldo and Langer he was facing Europe's most prolific points scorer and most respected player respectively, who would amass eight Majors between them. Pavin and Roberts would have one – the US Open title that Pavin had taken just three months before this Ryder Cup, with a stunning 4-wood to the final green at Shinnecock Hills. And in this contest it was the bantamweight Pavin, one of the grittiest match players ever, who had the final word, chipping in on the eighteenth to send US to bed with a vital two-point lead, instead of one.

He told me: 'That match was the most intense that I have been involved in and obviously chipping in was pretty exciting.'

*You seem to have done a lot of that in the Ryder Cup?*

'Really? All I remember is Seve and José Maria chipping in a few times. It's just amazing, though, what can seem to happen in matchplay, especially in this event. When I did chip in on that Saturday afternoon I couldn't really react the way I wanted to because Nick still had a putt so it was, for me, a very subdued reaction. But I made eye contact with Bernhard, with whom I'm fairly good friends and I sort of shrugged in a kind of "sorry about that" way. He smiled and nodded "great shot" and I don't think anyone around the green picked up on it or saw it but it remains my neatest recollection of the whole week.'

Even team-mate Peter Jacobsen, who wasn't involved in the match, describes it as his most exciting Ryder Cup moment. 'I would say my most memorable was Corey Pavin in '95 at Oak Hill when he chipped in against Faldo,' Jacobsen said. 'I was on the practice range and we were watching it on the big jumbo screen and I remember Corey's face didn't change but everyone else went crazy.'

Pavin continues: 'That's exactly to me what the Ryder Cup is all about; intense competition against and with people you respect and like. I played Bernhard Langer four times and it's wonderful to play against him because we respect each other's games and friendship.'

But respect and friendship only go so far when you're trying to beat someone's brains out on a golf course although Pavin, despite his justly deserved reputation as one of the hardest competitors you will ever meet, clearly values the friendships he has built up with some of the Europeans, and would never let gamesmanship get in the way of the sport he loves – he wants to win, but in the right way. This may seem strange in view of my criticism of his Desert Storm antics at Kiawah, but that was an instance of being misguided, not malicious.

On the first morning at Oak Hill he and Tom Lehman had drawn Europe's strongest pairing, Nick Faldo and Colin Montgomerie, and on the second hole there was one of those incidents that can assume far greater importance than they deserve. Faldo told Lehman his putt was good but the American didn't hear properly and asked him to repeat it. Faldo did and still couldn't be heard properly and then said, with an irritated gesture:

> Dan Stojack, caddy to Loren Roberts, was rumoured to have bet on Europe to win. Roberts said he heard three different versions from his caddy, who later denied the accusation to *Sports Illustrated*, and that it put him in a position where he 'couldn't do anything but let him go'. Roberts used another caddy for the remainder of the year.

'When I say it's good, it's good.' Lehman was making his debut in the event and was determined not to back off and replied to the effect of: 'If you spoke clearly so that I could understand you there wouldn't be a problem,' and Corey quickly jumped in, reminding his partner that neither man was trying to antagonise the other, and that it was a simple misunderstanding.

Now, in the most crucial match of the 1995 Ryder Cup, the inexorable, slow screw of tension was winding things up so tight that on the fourteenth hole, according to Tim Rosaforte's book *Heartbreak Hill: Anatomy of a Ryder Cup*, Roberts called team-mate Peter Jacobsen over and said, simply: 'I'm dying.' Jacobsen told him to breathe deep and said that, with four holes to go, it was like having eight more shots on the driving range.

He was probably helped by Pavin making his fourth birdie of the day to take the United States into a one-hole lead that lasted only until the next green, where Faldo made his own birdie to tie things up again, which is how it remained until the eighteenth. Faldo and Roberts found the fairway, although the Englishman had hit his drive out of the neck of the club and lost considerable distance, while Langer and Pavin were in the right rough. Faldo played first and struck a towering 3-iron to less than 20 feet but Pavin caught a good lie in the rough, lashed a 4-iron with everything he had and finished up through the green. Roberts hit a weak 5-iron to the middle of the green 60 feet away but lagged the putt up close enough to allow Pavin to chip without fear of the consequences. It came off exactly as he saw it, pitching three feet left of the hole before rolling in. Despite the fact that his team-mates were going crazy with excitement, Pavin showed virtually no emotion because the shot didn't seal victory, simply gave them a chance as Faldo still had to putt. Sadly, it was anti-climactic because it was never on line.

# 1995 (2) Jacobsen goes bizarre

As we have seen throughout the history of the Ryder Cup, tension does strange things to even the most battle-hardened veterans, but one of the oddest incidents ever involved Peter Jacobsen, one of the most likeable men ever to have his name embroidered on his golf bag, who was making his second appearance in the event, a decade after the first. In 1985 he had lost two of his three matches and now in the first-afternoon fourballs he was making his 1995 debut as he and Brad Faxon took on the unlikely pairing of David Gilford and Seve Ballesteros. Jacobsen is a tall, easygoing man with the heart of a clown, who never quite takes anything too seriously. He is well-known for his ability to imitate the swings of other golfers and for fronting an occa-sional, semi-shambolic band called Jake and the Flounders. He was once asked what turned him on and replied: 'Big galleries, small score, long drives, short rough, fat pay cheques and skinny trees.'

But his flippancy disguises the depth of his competitive instinct and he had also said, just a few months before this Ryder Cup: 'What I've learned is that I want to be remembered as a golfer. To do that, I've got to go out and win tournaments.'

He had done that in 1995 and now faced the most intimidating opponent, in Ballesteros, the Ryder Cup has ever produced. But the Spaniard, who had for so long been the inspiration for Europe, was in woeful form, enduring the desperate slump no one would wish on their worst enemy and from which, ten years later, only he seems to think he will emerge. Gilford had endured a miserable Ryder Cup at Kiawah Island four years before and was anxious to make amends. Legend has it that Gilford virtually carried Ballesteros that day and legend is not far wrong. Seve had said to his partner on the first tee: 'You're the best player out there', and it seemed as if Gilford was trying to

justify the faith put in him – and making a pretty good job of it. A mental image remains of Ballesteros hugging his partner with such enthusiasm at one point that Gilford's hat was knocked sideways and when the Spaniard raised his arm, the way a manager will lift the hand of a triumphant boxer, Gilford pulled off the difficult trick of looking hugely embarrassed and spectacularly pleased at the same time – a point I put to him.

'That's probably right,' David confirmed. 'Seve is the way he is, full of energy and optimism and self-belief and it was great to play with him. He is so enthusiastic and he wants to win so much that it's difficult not to be swept along with it. But I played well, solid rather than spectacular; it was wet and windy and cold and not very nice, and the course was playing like a US Open set-up, so one-under was a good score. There was a par-5 where I holed a good

*Peter Jacobsen (front) and Brad Faxon consult*

putt from outside them, and instead of being all-square we were two-up with only about five to play.'

But the match was actually settled far earlier, on the seventh hole, when Peter Jacobsen had one of those brains-out moments that affect all of us on occasion but in our case the humiliation is not witnessed by several hundred million viewers. He drove well but his partner, Faxon, pushed his tee shot right into a bunch of weeping willow trees. He discovered it had found a ditch, or water hazard, so took a penalty drop, fired a low driller under the branches of the trees and watched his ball come up about 20 yards short of the green. It was a stroke that made Jacobsen, standing in the fairway ready to play, think: 'Wow, what a tremendous shot.'

The Europeans were also having their problems, with Ballesteros already having run up too many strokes to be a factor in deciding the hole. Faxon then chipped onto the green, to about 15 feet, on the same line as Jacobsen, so he asked his partner if he wanted him to putt first to show him the line. He duly holed out for a five but Jacobsen was unaware he had taken a penalty drop from the stream, assumed he had holed

for a four, picked up his own ball marker and walked off.

Even now the memory is burned deep and he explained: 'Brad hadn't said anything to me about what he lay, I assumed he laid three and putted in for a four. And I thought "great four" because the crowd gave him a roar and he pumped his fist. I putted up to about two feet from the hole. They had just instituted a rule saying you could practice putts between holes as long as you're not holding up the group behind. We were playing with Seve and Gilford and Seve has a tendency to slow things down a bit and we were real slow. And I remember Torrance and James, Maggert and Love were in the group behind us [in fact it was Torrance and Rocca against Maggert and Roberts] and it started to rain, so up go the umbrellas, and they're standing in the fairway behind us. Gilford had a 10-footer for birdie and they were kind of prancing around the hole and I remember Mike [Cowan, his caddy] saying to me: "Let's get out of here." I agreed and said: "I'd like to putt but let's go." So I bent down and picked my coin up, walked over and I still hadn't talked to Brad. I said: "Great four," and he goes: "Oh that was a five." And he

didn't know that I'd picked my coin up and I said: "Oh my God, you made five?" Lanny our captain was great and when we got off that hole he said: "Hey, don't worry about it."'

But Jacobsen couldn't stop berating himself for acting in such a way. He described his actions as bone-headed but more telling than the incident itself was the fact that he felt so bad for letting down both Faxon and the rest of the American team, that he played poorly for the rest of the match and didn't make another birdie.

Ordinarily, with Ballesteros having no idea where his ball would go, or if he would then be able to find it, this wouldn't be too much of a problem, because it effectively meant that Faxon and Gilford were playing each other. But of course, Seve being Seve, he then struck with two killer blows of his own that gave impetus to the European momentum and put the American duo

Peter Jacobsen is still troubled by his aberration that day and says: 'It was miscommunication on my part. In fact it's one of those things where Brad and I look at each other to this day and go: "Can you believe that happened?" It was bizarre.'

to a disadvantage from which they would not recover.

At the ninth hole Seve's tee shot clipped a tree branch, losing considerable distance, so he had to hit a 3-wood second shot, followed by a 7-iron that found the green before he holed the putt for a most unlikely, yet typical Ballesteros par. At the next, a par-3, he found the green and holed for birdie so the demoralised Americans were now two-down with eight to play.

Seve then decided that nurturing, guiding and shepherding Gilford around the course was much more profitable than trying to make birdies himself so he consulted the Englishman on virtually every shot and showed him where to hit the ball, especially on the sort of delicate chips around the green that are the Spaniard's bread and butter. At least, that's how it looked. In truth Gilford is too much his own man to play second fiddle and may well have quietly appeared to listen while deciding to play his own game. But whatever the reason, the pairing worked to win Europe its only point of the session, which would prove to be of inestimable importance as the three days of competition wore on.

# 1995 (3)   Yorkshire grit

Howard Clark is, in many ways, a typical European Ryder Cup player. He earned a good living, won a few events but was never going to be mentioned in the same breath as the greats and never take any of the truly significant prizes the game has to offer. But when it came to the Ryder Cup he became a different man – fierce and aggressive, yes, but touched with genius and a capacity to play at an entirely different level. He was not, to put it mildly, the most easygoing or relaxed golfer in the world, especially when things were going wrong, and to spend time as his caddy (and many people did) was regarded as just a step up from having electrodes attached to your genitals and being asked questions to which you do not know the answers. He was every bit as harsh on himself.

In Ryder Cup partnerships with great mates Mark James and Sam Torrance he thrived, but it is Clark's record in singles play that is particularly impressive. This was to be the last of his six appearances in the event and his overall record read, played fifteen, won seven, lost seven and halved one. But of those seven wins, four came in singles (and the other three in fourballs – he played four times in foursomes and lost them all). And if his well-deserved reputation as the sort of opponent you would rather avoid in

singles matchplay was to be enhanced, now was the time to do it because Europe needed a stirring final day, starting it two points in arrears.

It wasn't insurmountable but was unlikely for a number of reasons. Players like Per-Ulrik Johansson, Costantino Rocca, David Gilford and Philip Walton hardly put the fear of God into opponents, Europe had only won once in America in fourteen previous attempts, a couple of their banker players – Seve Ballesteros and Nick Faldo – were in woeful form and the United States always win the singles. Apart from that, we weren't worried at all.

Captain Bernard Gallacher, serving his third consecutive term in charge and yet to taste victory as Tony Jacklin's successor, then made the sort of decision that is feted if it comes off but leaves you damned for all eternity if it goes wrong.

In a move subsequently copied by Sam Torrance, he loaded his best players at the top of the draw, reasoning that they needed to get off to a fast start. Perceived wisdom until then was that you should either hold back some of your aces until the end, needing your men of titanium where the furnace temperature is hottest, or sprinkle them throughout your line-up, so that the other side

doesn't get the all-important momentum by seeing a leader-board dominated by its own colour. The one exception to this policy was the hopelessly out-of-form Seve Ballesteros, who was first man out. Some suggested that his positioning was because Gallacher wanted him finished early, so that he could act as on-course cheerleader for the rest of his team-mates as they reached the critical stages of their own match.

Another school of thought believed that if he could somehow pull off a miracle it would galvanise the rest of Europe. But in reality Gallacher probably just decided that he would be a sacrifice. Any one of the Americans could beat Ballesteros in his current form, and American captain Lanny Wadkins was bound to have one of his strongest players going out first, so why not let him have the point against Seve, rather than a stronger European player? Seve did lose, by 4&3 to American hard man Tom Lehman but if it weren't for his short-game genius it would have been a far more crushing defeat. His opponent subsequently said, in the book *Us Against Them*: 'He showed a lot of heart in the way he hit it all over the park but managed to stay in the match for a long time. His short game

was phenomenal. It was a pretty amazing performance.'

Nevertheless, the first point on the board was in the red of America but then Gallacher's players responded to his bold tactics and started delivering some points of their own. And none was timelier than that of Howard Clark who, in the second match against Peter Jacobsen, was doing his own impersonation of Seve Ballesteros. In truth his form was woeful and he couldn't have hit a 2-acre green from 100 yards – he actually hit only six all day in regulation. But his short game was little shy of miraculous and he was chipping stiff or holing from off the green all day long.

Jacobsen remembers: 'He played badly and chipped-in from everywhere. You could argue that he was the best kind of matchplay player to have on your team because every time I had

When Clark walked off the eighteenth green after a most unlikely win – in which he didn't get his nose in front until the sixteenth hole – he was still clutching the ball with which he'd made his ace. He wrote on it 'Hole-in-one, 1995 Ryder Cup' and put in his pocket with the words: 'Shows what you have to do to win out here.'

*Howard Clark misses another green but was otherwise inspired that day*

anticipation of a birdie or a par or a win he would do something fantastic. I think he maybe only hit a half a dozen greens that day but we both shot one under par for the round, I believe, and he beat me one-up. Those things happen.'

It was one of those classic matchplay encounters, with Jacobsen playing steady, efficient, fairways and greens golf, while Clark was scrambling like mad just to stay in it. A Jacobsen birdie at the tenth put him one-up so he had the honour at the par-3 eleventh and duly despatched a 6-iron to the heart of the green, about 20 feet away – a good chance for another birdie to at least maintain, if not increase his lead. Clark, also using a 6-iron, turned away in disgust as soon as the ball left the club-face because he knew he had pulled it left. But the left-to-right breeze grabbed the ball, dragged it back on line and dumped it onto the shoulder of a bunker, from where it kicked right and rolled into the hole.

Jacobsen laughed and warmly congratulated his opponent, when he could have been forgiven for muttering 'jammy bastard'. Clark eventually took the match by one hole on the final green and was soon followed by a number of other Europeans.

# 1995 (4)   Nick of time

If Howard Clark's hole-in-one started the European resurgence, it was Nick Faldo who reinforced it most emphatically. Faldo, who has been named as captain for 2008, is Britain's most successful Ryder Cup golfer and has stamped his talent and competitiveness on the event more times than it is possible to recount. He has played in more matches (eleven) and scored more points (twenty-five) than any other GB&I or European player. In the process he has formed stirring partnerships with Colin Montgomerie and Ian Woosnam and been involved in some of the greatest matches of the last three decades. His finest moment of all came here, against the man who beat him in an 18-hole playoff for the 1988 US Open, Curtis Strange.

The men were similar, building their careers on doing everything well but leading the statistics in few, if any, categories. Neither was the longest hitter but both were straight, excellent iron players and good putters who were occasionally very good. Both were grinders; the sort of remorselessly dogged, persistent hangers-in who often wore down opponents. If you

*Faldo in tears, such was the significance of the putt*

keep making pars, the other guy thinks he has to make birdies to beat you, and in striving for something a little bit better, often deliver something considerably worse. If Faldo had an edge it was possibly in his short game but trying to predict the outcome of their match was too close to call because both were surviving on guile, experience and bloody-mindedness rather than the quality of their play.

Faldo had played three matches in tandem with Colin Montgomerie and won only one, while Strange had had two outings and lost them both, causing him to fend off a lot of questions about a situation that was not of his own making – being selected by his skipper despite being in poor form. Oddly, for men with their experience and ability, both had to rely on being selected as wild-card picks, as neither had played his way onto the team on merit. But until much more recently, captains rarely gambled with rookies in their wild-card picks and more often than not went back to seasoned veterans who have been there, done that, and bought the T-shirt. Sadly, both men were running on fumes and the memory of what great competitors they used to be. Strange had not only

been a wild-card pick but captain Wadkins had selected him from outside the world top-50, creating a storm of controversy in America that had still not dissipated, especially with his 0–2 record of the first two days.

Faldo, meanwhile, was in woeful form of his own, unable to buy a putt and, as it transpired, playing out the final moments of his marriage. Whether it was this off-course turmoil that was affecting his form or whether he was playing like a dog because that's the way it goes sometimes, is impossible to say, but his marital problems couldn't have helped.

The match was more a war of attrition than anything else, with Strange taking an early one-hole lead, being pegged back, regaining the narrowest advantage again on the eleventh and keeping it until the penultimate hole. In truth, both golfers were now in a state of some anxiety and Faldo has subsequently said that as he reached the seventeenth, one-down, it was becoming increasingly obvious that this match had become a crucial turning point of the whole day and it was imperative that he got something from it. Both men made a hash of the hole, but Strange missed an 8-foot putt while

Faldo, on a similar line, got a good read from the American, changed his mind about the line, and holed from a foot nearer, to bring their contest all-square with one to play.

Faldo, with the honour, drove into the left rough, from where he had no chance of reaching the green so poked the ball forward, hoping to leave himself a comfortable distance for his third. Strange, to his credit, found the middle of the fairway but then left his long iron approach short in the rough guarding the front of the green before Faldo hit a three-quarter wedge from 93 yards to 5 feet. It sounds almost humdrum for a golfer of his quality but in his book *Life Swings*, he writes: 'For the very first time in my career my legs completely went. From the waist down I turned to rubber as though I had been hit by a haymaker from Mike Tyson.' Strange pitched to 8 feet but then missed the putt, leaving Faldo with the

American captain Larry Wadkins was so distressed to lose that at the closing ceremony he stood up to speak and no sounds came out. His opposite number, Bernard Gallacher, put his arm around Wadkins and said: 'Let me help.'

sort of 4-footer to win the hole and the match that all pro golfers hate – left-to-right and downhill.

Psychologically, most golfers would rather face a 10-foot putt at a time of crisis than one of 3 to 6 feet. The shorter ones are expected to be holed, and usually are, but enough of them will have been missed over a career to leave scars, and the niggling, nagging voice in the back of the mind that says: 'Don't screw this up'. Johnny Miller once shanked a pitch shot to the eighteenth green at Pebble Beach and said that for the rest of his career he never stood over a less than full wedge shot without a demonic inner voice saying: 'Now you're not going to shank this, are you?' He never did, but it always flashed through his mind that he might. So it is with missed 4-footers, and now Nick Faldo, one of the most driven, dedicated, focused golfers who ever lived, found his knees knocking over the consequences of a short putt for victory. He made it, and the first of his team-mates to reach him was a tearful Seve Ballesteros, who almost hugged the life out of the Englishman and said: 'You are a great champion.' And so he is.

Faldo subsequently said that of all his many Ryder Cup experiences, this was the sweetest but that's because it was the toughest, and brought out the best of a man who has done pretty much everything there is to do in golf.

Spare a thought, though, for Curtis Strange, who bogied the final three holes and was unfairly pilloried, particularly by the US press. He didn't ask to be selected but when he was, knuckled down and gave of his best, and no one should be asked for more. If there is blame to allocate, it should rest on the shoulders of captain Lanny Wadkins who did a great deal more right in the Ryder Cup than he did wrong.

# 1995 (5)   Walton comes of age

European supporters, having watched the agonisingly tense match between Nick Faldo and Curtis Strange, could have been forgiven for wanting a quiet lie down, but there was still golf being played and a Ryder Cup to be won. With two matches still to be decided everything was in the balance with Europe leading 13½ to 12½. The United States, as holders, only needed a tie to retain the trophy, so a win and a half from the last two games would give them the 14 points total they so desperately craved. In one of the matches former university college team-mates Phil Mickelson and Per-Ulrik Johansson were playing out a strangely lifeless match which the American would take 2&1, but the other game, between Philip Walton and Jay Haas, had all the hallmarks of one that would go to the wire and make or break a career or reputation – which is not to say that it was a classic feast of splendid golf. Wayne Grady once said of losing to

Greg Norman, on a final day when both were in contention but played equally badly: 'I played crap and he played crap but he out-crapped me.' Sometimes, it matters not how you do it but simply that you do – and so it was for Philip Walton in 1995 at Oak Hill.

It started well and got better. Hiding his considerable nerves under an apparently nonchalant façade, Walton glided into a two-hole lead and then hit one of the shots of the week at the par-3 fifteenth. Because he was so pumped with adrenaline he took a 6-iron to cover the 186 yards to the flagstick and, in American parlance, 'pured' it to 6 feet and holed the putt to go three-up with three to play. All he had to do now was halve one of the remaining three holes to win the cup for Europe – stroll in the park. Yet, anyone who has watched any big-time sporting occasion, and especially top flight golf, knows that anything can, and usually does, happen as soon as

you begin to entertain the thought that all is wrapped up. Walton played the sixteenth in textbook fashion, and lost. He drove up the left side, put his approach into the middle of the green and watched (with presumably well-disguised pleasure) as Haas found the greenside bunker on the right. The American then holed his bunker shot, Walton missed his putt and was suddenly only two-up with two to play. The Irishman Walton would not be human if he didn't start thinking to himself: 'Dear God, please don't let me lose from here.' Golf psychologists spend a great deal of time getting their protégés to concentrate on the good, and positive, at the expense of negative thoughts. Classically, an amateur stands on the tee thinking of all the trouble – the bunkers, water, rough and trees – he wants to avoid, while the pro concentrates only on the place where he wants his ball to finish. The pro also has a lengthy reper-

*Constantino Rocca gives Philip Walton a hand with the celebrations*

toire of positive thoughts, such as the memory of great shots he has hit in the past, with which to bolster his ego when even the act of breathing suddenly assumes a degree of difficulty not previously encountered.

Unfortunately, in Philip's case, none of it seemed to be helping. Both men drove into trees to the right of the seventeenth but Haas hit a career shot, starting a long iron low under the branches before his ball travelled 200 yards, coming to rest 15 feet from the hole. Not only that, it was below the flagstick, so he had an easier, uphill putt. Walton responded with an iron of his own that came up a touch short but then played an exquisite chip to about four feet. Neither putt even touched the side of the hole, so Haas with par beat Walton's bogey to reduce the deficit again. Now only one-up with one to play and even the commentators were having difficulty breathing now – and the two central attractions weren't about to lessen the pressure on their own or anyone else's nerves.

Haas had the honour and hit a woeful drive, a pop-up, skied shot that went considerably further up than forward, but nevertheless still managed to find trees on the left. Door ajar and all Walton had to do was push gently against it, but what he actually did was almost slam it back in his own face with a terribly weak, slappy slice that finished in the right rough. He had a considerable time to consider what to do next because Haas was in such a horrible place that for a while he had to seriously study the terrain just to see if he had any shot at all. He eventually hit a deliberate hook to near the spot from where Faldo had hit his superb wedge shot a few minutes before, although it now felt a lifetime away. Walton, from a reasonable lie, lashed a metal wood but it came down in the long grass guarding the front of the green where Strange had so recently been. Haas, considered by his peers to be one of the best wedge players in the game, hit his approach from 97 yards; it barely made the green and then backspin sucked it straight back off again.

Walton's ball, meanwhile, was so far buried in the rough that he all but trod on it while searching – suddenly looking down and seeing it between his feet. He was now faced with the sort of greenside shot that the USGA, in its infinite stupidity, likes to create for US Opens, but which European Tour pros who remain on their side of the Atlantic almost never play. It involved hitting a ball buried in thick, clinging rough, to a rock-hard, undulating green just a few feet away, and even for the very best involved a degree of hit and hope. Luckily for Walton, earlier in the week he'd had a lesson on exactly this type of shot from team-mate Ian Woosnam. Walton dropped the clubhead onto the back of the ball, and watched first in fear and then relief as it just cleared the fringe, dropped onto the green and rolled to about 12 feet. When Haas failed to hole out the Irishman had two putts for victory and decided, because he was shaking so much, to take them both.

For only the second time ever the Ryder Cup had been won in America by the visiting team, and now it was heading off to continental Europe.

United States captain Lanny Wadkins said to Phil Mickelson, as his singles match with Per-Ulrik Johansson was getting tight: 'You asked to be in this position, I put you in this position so you had better get your ass in gear.'
Mickelson won.

# 1997 (1)    Seve shows his dark side

Seve Ballesteros had been such a guiding light for Europeans on the golf course that it was inevitable that he would one day captain his side. By 1997, his game had gone further south than Scott of the Antarctic so there was no point considering his selection as a player, even for the motivational value. And as soon as the announcement was made that the competition would be visiting continental Europe, and specifically Spain, for the first time, it seemed pre-ordained that Seve would be captain and that he would not even countenance the possibility of losing. Yet long before the Ryder Cup started, there were to be two major rows at which he was the centre; one involving the team he would lead, and the other concentrating on the venue where he would lead them.

Valderrama, in southern Spain, is owned by a diminutive South American multi-millionaire named Jaime (Jimmy to friends) Ortiz-Patino. It was designed by Robert Trent Jones Snr. and originally called Sotogrande New, before being renamed Las Aves and finally settling on Valderrama. Jimmy, as I would like to call him but would never dare, acquired the property in 1985 and from the outset spent considerable money and time bringing it up to the standard of a Ryder Cup venue – although nowadays that is a fairly worthless currency because if you have enough money, you can get the Ryder Cup, as it has proved with Celtic Manor in Wales, which was awarded the biennial event for 2010 on the proviso that it construct at least nine new holes.

But Ortiz-Patino did not have a new, relatively untried layout but one that has consistently been voted the best in continental Europe, and which plays host to the European Tour season-ending finale, the Volvo Masters. He was also, of course, prepared to spend however much money the Ryder Cup Committee demanded to present his golfing lovechild in whatever state was required.

His relationship with the Ryder Cup had begun forty years earlier. Dai Rees sacked his caddy at the Italian Open and Patino offered to carry his bag. In payment Rees, who was GB&I captain that year, gave him some Ryder Cup tickets – they did things much more informally then – and Patino was hooked.

Yet even concerning the venue, Seve, who seemed determined to micromanage every aspect of the competition, created an enormous row. He accused the European Tour of taking bribes to favour Valderrama but didn't say that one of the courses it beat in the bidding war was designed and run by his own management company.

Even this spat faded to insignificance, however, compared to the almighty row that Seve generated over team selection. Previous captains had

enjoyed three wild-card picks and, while Seve probably thought that he should have twelve, he was reduced to two, which immediately left him with a dilemma. Nick Faldo wasn't playing well enough to earn a place on merit but Ballesteros wanted him – especially after seeing his pivotal match with Curtis Strange at Oak Hill two years earlier. But Seve also wanted his inspirational partner José Maria Olazábal who, to everyone's delight, was recovering from the ill health that had kept him out of the game for the best part of two years, almost unable to walk. So far, so good. Seve's problems were exacerbated, though, by the likeable, endlessly flaky Swede Jesper Parnevik, who so often seems to march to the beat of a drummer only he can hear.

Because he chose to play virtually full time in America, his earnings there did not count towards Ryder Cup points (the selection process has subsequently been altered to give 'world' players a better chance of qualification), so he also could not earn a place on merit. When the final counting event of the European season was concluded, the man in tenth place, and therefore occupying the final all-exempt berth, was fellow Spaniard

Miguel Angel Martin – but in this case any fraternal feelings Seve may have had for the man, born of their shared nationality, counted for nought. Martin's problem was that he had qualified due to his excellent early-season form, but then suffered a wrist injury that kept him away from the game for several months. The captain wanted Faldo, Parnevik and Olazábal and would have moved heaven and earth to get them. Olazábal was eleventh on the points list so Seve simply excluded Martin to make way for his pal.

Although Martin said he would be ready to play and could provide doctors' letters and medical evidence to prove it, Ballesteros insisted that he play some weeks before the event began, so that his injured wrist could be monitored, and when Martin refused, calling his captain's demand 'barbarous', he was dropped. Ballesteros, perhaps revealing far more about his state of mind than he suspected, said: 'He was not welcome before, do you think he will be welcome now?' And when he heard that Martin was prepared to sue to keep his place he added: 'That little man? He can't stop the Ryder Cup. Lawyers can only do so much. He's like a machine-gunner shooting in all directions. He is trying to be a hero for a week.

We would be out of our minds to change the decision.'

Finally, in a remarkable example of the pot calling the kettle black, he added: 'He has only been thinking of himself.'

Almost everyone in golf supported Martin and felt that he was being treated shamefully, but few were prepared to stick their heads above the parapet and say so. Ignacio Garrido, who also played his way onto the 1997 team, is a friend of Martin's, which possibly explains why he was prepared to say: 'It's the most unfair decision I have heard in the history of golf. I cannot like Seve's attitude on this and if he comes and asks me my opinion I will say: "You are crazy."

'They are not giving Miguel Angel a chance, and anyone in his position would try to do the same. It's very unfair what they are doing, and I don't think it ends here.'

But, despite a great deal of huffing and puffing, it did end there. Martin was excluded and then patronised by being named thirteenth member of the team – he was even given the full uniform and dragged along to the opening ceremony to pose for 'official' photographs. Seve tried to suggest that

*The 1997 European team, with Miguel Angel Martin (far right, standing)*

the decision was made solely by the Ryder Cup Committee but he, we and everyone else knew it was not. Even Mitchel Platts, the urbane spokesman for the European Tour who chooses his words with great care, said: 'Following close consultation between the Ryder Cup Committee and Severiano Ballesteros, Martin has been informed he would be replaced.'

Seve was prepared to do just about anything to get the team he wanted. The fact that he was allowed to remains one of the most regrettable episodes in Ryder Cup history.

# 1997 (2)    Here, there and everywhere

If we thought that Seve's approach to captaincy was a little too 'hands on' in the months leading up to the event, we hadn't seen anything yet because once the two teams arrived at Valderrama the proud, determined man was ubiquitous. He was even seen at 3 a.m. on the eve of the event walking round the swimming pool trying to work out his pairings, and when inspiration failed to arrive he got his deputy, Miguel-Angel Jiménez, out of bed to help. It was impossible to move on the course without the risk of being run over by his golf buggy – which some assumed had been supercharged – because he seemed to be everywhere,

watching every match, mentally playing every stroke and, in a number of cases, giving his team advice on how to execute a particularly difficult shot. However, Seve's team did not always welcome or appreciate his advice.

Colin Montgomerie, for example, resented his intrusion at the notorious par-5 seventeenth (which Seve had re-designed, to pretty general disapproval). Monty and Darren Clarke were paired in the second series of fourballs against Fred Couples and Davis Love III. Having urged Clarke to go for the green in two, and watched as he dumped his ball in the pond guarding the green, Seve then

tried to advise Monty on the best way of playing his third, and was told: 'I'm as nervous as hell, Seve, leave me alone.' Later that afternoon Monty was paired with Bernhard Langer, both of whom missed the fairway on the last. Seve explained to Langer how he could manoeuvre a low draw over one branch and under another and turned to Monty to further illustrate what a comparatively simple shot it was. While he was still explaining, Langer, always a man to follow his own counsel rather than the advice of others, chipped out sideways to the fairway. Less fortunate was rookie Thomas Björn, who was about to play a

*A bemused Tom Kite watches Seve offer advice to anyone he can find*

shot in a practice round when Seve drove up, took the club out of his hand, gave him another and drove off. The final words, though, should probably rest with Jesper Parnevik. When he was in trouble against Mark O'Meara in his singles match (which he lost 5&4), Seve came bustling over to offer a few words and was met with the response: 'Get the fuck away from me.' He took the hint.

In his redesign of the notorious par-5 seventeenth hole, Seve had grown a strip of rough across the fairway at the point where the longest drivers – men like Tiger Woods, Davis Love and Fred Couples – would be hoping to land, and grown the rough flanking the fairway so that anything missing the short grass was going to be more comprehensively lost than Lord Lucan. But his most controversial changes were at the green, which sloped from back to front towards a large pond, so Ballesteros had a wee collar of rough removed and the grass shaved with a cut-throat razor so that anything hit fractionally hard from above the hole would not stop until it reached the water – something Tiger Woods learned when he putted into the pond. At the 2004 Volvo Masters, seven years after this match Darren Clarke came to the hole in a share of the lead.

He hit three wedges onto the green, all of which rolled down the severe slope into the water. He wound up with an eleven, which dropped him from first to twenty-fifth place in a matter of minutes.

But the players of both teams had more to worry about than one rogue hole. The Andalusia region of Spain in which Valderrama is situated had experienced about a year's worth of rain in the week immediately preceding this Ryder Cup, so the course was long, heavy underfoot and demanding, and even during the competition there was overnight rain and the daytime conditions were grey, cool and damp. It is, in fact, quite remarkable that play was possible at all, and it is difficult to think of another course anywhere in the world that would have stood up to such a deluge and still been playable – a testament to Jaime Ortiz-Patino's millions. When he was asked before the event if his course would be ready he replied: 'Don't worry, I have a golden rule here. I have the gold, I make the rules.'

Play eventually got underway, several hours later than scheduled, and the pride of Europe was faced with probably the most daunting American side since the 'Dream Team' of 1981. Captain Tom Kite had Fred Couples, Davis Love, Tiger Woods, Justin Leonard, Phil Mickelson, Mark O'Meara, Lee Janzen, Brad Faxon, Jeff Maggert, Scott Hoch, Jim Furyk and Tom Lehman – and to date only three of them, Maggert, Hoch and Faxon have failed to lift a Major. In contrast, only four of the European side had won one of the big four – Nick Faldo, José Maria Olazábal, Bernhard Langer and Ian Woosnam. They were lined up alongside Per-Ulrik Johansson, Costantino Rocca, Thomas Björn, Darren Clarke, Jesper Parnevik, Lee Westwood, Ignacio Garrido and Colin Montgomerie. But as we have seen so many times, the strongest-looking team does not always prosper, and that is exactly what happened as Europe – aided just a little by a bit more Seve manoeuvring – got off to a flying start.

For many years the format had

One explanation for Seve's ubiquitous presence is that he was familiar with a number of underground tunnels and passages around Valderrama – information that was not given to his opposite number, Tom Kite. Those damned Europeans will do anything to win.

involved foursomes in the morning and fourballs after lunch, and, for some inexplicable reason, Europe always did better in the fourballs. So Seve demanded that they be played first so that his team would get a fast start, and made such a fuss about it that he once again got his own way.

In 1999, Ben Crenshaw was asked by *Golf Digest*: 'Looking back, did Seve Ballesteros snooker Tom Kite in 1997 when he convinced him to flip-flop the foursomes and four balls the first morning?'

Crenshaw replied: 'You'd have to ask Tom. I've never discussed it with Tom. It was a departure from the usual format, but I don't know how it happened.'

When asked if it was evidence of gamesmanship from Ballesteros he said: 'Well, one could draw that conclusion. I don't know whether it had an effect, but it possibly did. But it was, shall we say, slightly odd.'

The benefits were not immediately apparent, however, as the first sequence of matches were shared two apiece. Europe perversely did better in the four-

somes, winning two and halving one, but in the second series of fourballs they moved into top gear, taking three-and-a-half of the available four points. When they also had the best of the foursomes as well, they went to bed after two days leading by 10½ to 5½. No team had ever overtaken a deficit of greater than two points in singles and even the Americans, notorious for their fightbacks on the final day, could not have felt confident, because they needed to win nine of twelve matches to take the Ryder Cup back home. It was an impossible task.

# 1997 (3)  Tiger is tamed

As usual though, when we pundits, reporters and fans decided that the final day of the 1997 Ryder Cup was to be a triumphal procession for Seve and the boys, no one thought to tell the Americans and they came out of the traps like greyhounds with fireworks

tied to their tails. As the day progressed, us watching Europeans began to know the meaning of real fear as we saw the stars-and-stripes brigade knock over the best we had to offer. The pattern was set early in the opening match between Fred Couples

and Ian Woosnam which was, coincidentally, the third consecutive time they had met in Ryder Cup singles – the two previous matches being halved. But despite his justified reputation as one of the nicest, most laidback characters in golf, Couples is a competitor

and when he's on song and determined you'd get more sympathy out of a pox-clinic nurse. So it was this day. Woosnam started with a double-bogey but thereafter played well – unfortunately his opponent was on one of those hot streaks of form that Freddie has almost patented, and by the eleventh hole was an estimated seven under par and handed Woosie the joint biggest spanking ever seen in Ryder Cup 18-hole singles, 8&7 (American captain Tom Kite had beaten Howard Clark by the same margin eight years earlier). The comeback had started but was only just getting going.

As previous (and subsequent) Ryder Cups have demonstrated, momentum is everything and for the first two days it had almost all been with the Europeans – partly because they played well but also because the several delays, interruptions and late starts for bad weather and poor light meant that the Americans never had a chance to regroup and rethink tactics. As soon as one set of matches was completed the players were off again, so the European snowball just kept gathering pace. But in a last throw of the dice, Tom Kite had loaded his strong players at the top of the draw, knowing that if he didn't get

some red on the leaderboard early on, the contest would be effectively over, while the fat lady was still waiting for her cue. It worked remarkably well, although not quite as everyone predicted. A couple of early European points gave heart to the home team, but then Justin Leonard halved with Thomas Björn before three American wins on the bounce – from Phil Mickelson, Mark O'Meara, and Lee Janzen, over Darren Clarke, Jesper Parnevik and José Maria Olazábal respectively – shifted momentum back to the visitors. It was then emphasised by Tom Lehman, who racked up another point, this time at the expense of Ignacio Garrido. Theirs was, in fact, the last match on the course but Lehman was so dominant in his 7&6 thrashing of the Spaniard that they finished well before many of the other matches.

But the undoubted European highpoint concerned the third match, between a tall, lithe, handsome athlete who was already a superstar and multi-millionaire, and a portly, forty-year-old former box maker. Tiger Woods had been hailed as a phenomenon since he appeared as a toddler on Bob Hope's TV show, won the US Amateur an unprecedented three consecutive times

while still a teenager and announced himself into the professional ranks in emphatic style by winning the Masters in April by a crushing twelve strokes. He became world number one for a week in June of 1997, and then returned to the top of the pile in July for a nine-week stretch. He combined awesome, prodigious length from the tee with an immaculate short game, and in any list of players you would have take a putt if your life depended on it, he would feature strongly. He was currently world number two and the biggest star in the golfing firmament.

His opponent, Costantino Rocca, was a smiling, portly, genial Italian – the first of his nationality to play in the Ryder Cup – who came from a modest background and who woke every morning to count his blessings and thank God for the talent to play golf, without which he would have been consigned to a lifetime of blue-collar labour. He is a proud, emotional man who had been devastated on his Ryder Cup debut in 1993 to lose his singles against Davis Love, having been one up with two to play.

Four years later and Rocca was smiling again. He started the match strongly and was four-up at the turn, helped by the fact that his opponent started to press, and in his anxiety to overcome the early deficit, became over-aggressive and made a few mistakes. He was not, however, playing poorly, it was just that the Italian was playing better.

Over the back nine there were two turning points. At the eleventh Woods made birdie that Rocca failed to match, to reduce his arrears, but the Italian grabbed all-important halves at the next two holes. But Rocca struck the most telling blow at the sixteenth, a short par-4. Because just about every fairway is lined with cork trees, driving straight at Valderrama is an essential skill, and if any reminder were needed, Ballesteros arrived to tell his man: 'Whatever you do – don't miss right.' Inevitably, Rocca then hit it to star-board while his opponent was the fairway. Again Seve proffered advice but Rocca followed his own counsel.

He said later: 'It was a bad situation. It would have been very easy to lose sixteen, seventeen and then maybe eighteen and the game would have been halved. Seve suggested I try and chip it out or hit it into the bunker on the left-side. But I don't like long bunker shots. The Ryder Cup is different – you can sometimes make special shots in matchplay. That day was special, so I went for the 1-iron. I played the perfect shot. After I hit it, Seve said: "Okay – that is your own shot – you definitely play that sort of shot better than me!"'

Woods did not recover and Rocca went on to beat him 4&2, for the crucial point that guaranteed European victory. Seve had won the cup in his homeland and few would begrudge him either the opportunity or the honour. Special mention should be made of Denmark's Thomas Björn, who recovered from four down to half his match against Justin Leonard, but the star of the last day was a relatively inconspicuous Italian. The Americans had almost pulled off the trademark singles resurgence that every European dreads, but in the end came up just short. Surely, it was time for an end to such dramatic finales?

In a post-match press conference José Maria Olazábal tried to express what it meant for him and his countrymen to win the Ryder Cup, in Spain, with Seve Ballesteros as captain. He began by saying: 'A year ago I could not walk' and was then unable to speak for a full minute. His team-mates and everyone else in the room applauded until he was able to regain his composure.

# 1999 (1)    Faldo relegated to the waste bin

Brookline in Massachusetts would go down in history as producing the most astonishing final day of them all, but long before that day arrived the European team was riven by debate, discussion and drama, as the old habit of fighting ourselves before we could square up to the Yanks resurfaced.

Mark James was the surprise appointment, in some quarters at least, as European captain and many commented on his remarkable rehabilitation from being fined for his behaviour in his second match exactly twenty years earlier, when he and Ken Brown had almost been sent home in disgrace. But now he was the man in charge and continued to make the job of journalists easier with his penchant for memorable one-liners, such as, in reference to some of the gaudy uniforms that had been inflicted on US teams: 'The only thing I fear about the Americans is their dress sense.'

As ever, a huge amount of speculation centred on who he would pick as his wild-card choices, and in particular whether or not Britain's most successful golfer of all time, Nick Faldo, would get the nod, especially as it was known that he and James were not exactly the best of friends.

Bad blood had first been spilled at Woburn in 1994 when Faldo, who subsequently announced that he intended to play almost full-time in America, criticised some European Tour venues as being sub-standard, which was not by any means stretching the truth. James responded by saying he should have taken his comments to the Tour itself, or its players' committee, rather than the press, and suggested that the man from Welwyn Garden City was being just a tad hypocritical as he appeared to be happy playing lesser courses if the inducement – in the form of appear-

ance money – was lucrative enough. It is a charge Faldo denied, although he then spends almost a page in his autobiography, discussing the incident, mounting a robust defence of appearance money. Faldo also gives perhaps a greater insight into his mindset than he might have intended by writing of the incident: 'Mark Roe [another European Tour pro] was encouraged to join the "knock Nick Faldo" club. If it had been someone of *equal status* [my italics] – Seve or Monty say – I would have listened to his opinions.'

In golf, the commonly accepted criteria of ability is Major championships, and in the history of the game, only eleven players have won more of them than Faldo, and presumably, by his reckoning, are the only people of 'equal status' who can legitimately dispute his opinions on golf. As six of them are dead, that leaves five people in the world who can challenge his views.

With logic like that it is probably just as well that he chose a life as a professional sportsman.

In his own book *Into the Bear Pit*, James is unstinting in his admiration for what Faldo has achieved, while acknowledging that the pair are hardly soul mates, and writes that an in-form Faldo would unquestionably have been in the team.

Unfortunately, the six-time Major champion was in anything but good form. In the days before the final counting event for the Ryder Cup points table, the BMW International Open, Faldo asked James if he was in the frame to be a captain's pick and was told that, even if he won, it was unlikely he would be selected – James' thinking all along was that one particularly good or bad week would not influence his final decision. Faldo was clearly surprised and upset to receive such an honest response, so much so that he asked the same question the next morning, just to be absolutely clear about the answer. Later the same day Faldo told a press conference how disillusioned he was and again in *Life Swings*, writes: 'Having been a permanent fixture in the team since my debut in 1977, I was both crestfallen and

angry. I had achieved sufficient top-twenty finishes in the US that season to suggest I could put some European points on the board in Brookline. I made my thoughts public and went on to say that when it came to the Ryder Cup contest itself. I trusted James would have learned the meaning of the word "motivation".'

In fact the US PGA Tour's own website does not support his assertion about his results in America. In twelve events he had missed the cut in five and been disqualified in another, and apart from an eighth place in the Canadian Open, he had finished tied 33, T55, T49, T41, T44. Hardly world-beating form.

And then, just before the teams flew to Brookline, Faldo was quoted as saying that Colin Montgomerie played almost exclusively in Europe because he was happy there, the king in his own backyard, but if he wanted to seriously challenge for Majors he should consider spending more time in America. It was a reasonable observation but hyped up to the extent that Faldo felt obliged to call Monty and explain his comments, which Montgomerie told him was not necessary.

But what it boiled down to was that

Faldo had done nothing like enough to play his way into the side on merit but believed that his previous experience and American results justified his inclusion. James was always of the opinion that reputation counted for little, and that form was everything, a view with which it is difficult to disagree because otherwise Jack Nicklaus, Billy Casper and Tom Watson would presumably be picked for America to this very day.

The whole row erupted again publicly when, in the practice days before the matches started, Faldo sent a letter of good luck to the European team that, under the circumstances of his wounded pride, was magnanimous. James did not reveal it to his team (although most had heard about it on the grapevine), despite having pinned similar messages from Ian Woosnam and Seve Ballesteros on the team room notice board. He wrote in *Into the Bear Pit*: 'I took one look at it and could not believe Faldo had sent it. Not only had he had a serious barney with me relatively recently, but he had also slagged off Monty just before we came to Boston.' James says he consulted the views of a 'few other people' and that they all agreed with him that the letter should be binned.

*Captain Mark James might have been forgiven for thinking the drama was over*

But whatever James thought of Faldo himself, it wasn't up to him to decide what Faldo could, or could not, communicate to his fellow professionals. But what the whole sorry episode demonstrated above all else, is that once emotion – particularly antipathy and anger – enter a relationship, logic and adult behaviour tend to depart.

# 1999 (2)  Can we play golf now?

But at last the phoney war of selection headaches, inter-European rivalry and unseemly spats was over and the competition proper could begin. Well, almost. Mark James had, to almost universal approval, picked Jesper Parnevik as one of his wild-card selections and, to almost equally universal bewilderment, Scotsman Andrew Coltart as the other. Parnevik is the son of Sweden's most famous comedian and if he had ever had to overcome shyness and timidity as a youngster, it was a battle he had emphatically won. He continued to plough his own very individual furrow across the fairways of America so the majority of his earnings did not convert to Ryder Cup points, but he was nevertheless one of Europe's most successful golfers. In the most competitive Tour in the world he had managed four top-ten finishes, including a win at the Greater Grensboro Chrysler Classic and in eighteen events had made the cut in all but one, the Masters. In the view of many he's as mad as a box of frogs, with a penchant for eating volcanic lava and dressing like a blind man in the dark, but he could play golf and was an undoubted asset.

Coltart was a different matter. Too talented to be dismissed as a journeyman, he nevertheless had only one Tour title to his name (the 1998 Qatar Masters, he would subsequently add the Great North Open in 2001) but over the season had made a sustained push to play his way onto the team on merit. In twenty-four events he had never failed to make a cut, itself a considerable achievement, and among those results he posted six top-tens, the best of which was a tied second at the Estoril Open. Coltart is an engaging, open, honest and witty man who freely admits that he would play golf for the pure love of the game and is as determined as they come. But he finished twelfth in the final points table, a place behind the tall, blond and disgustingly good-looking Robert Karlsson, so it was a surprise, to

put it mildly, when Mark James leapfrogged the Swede and chose the Scot. If the eleventh-placed man had been overlooked in place of someone with Ryder Cup experience such as Bernhard Langer, who was also ignored, it would be understandable, but to neglect one rookie in order to select another smacked strongly of James' idiosyncratic brand of logic. He justified it, however, by saying that, in the two months before making his decision, Coltart had shown greater consistency, which isn't exactly supported by the stats.

But then, as if to reinforce his deter-mination to go his own way, having created a slew of headlines by picking Coltart, James then benched him until the singles, a fate that befell two other rookies, Frenchman Jean Van de Velde and another flaky Swede, Jarmo Sandelin. In fact, rookies were the bedrock of the European team, which contained no fewer than seven, an improbably large number. In addition to the three already mentioned, Paul Lawrie, Padraig Harrington, Miguel-Angel Jiménez and Sergio Garcia were joined by the more experienced Darren Clarke, Colin Montgomerie, Lee Westwood, José Maria Olazábal and

Parnevik. The Americans, by contrast, had only newcomer, David Duval, who was joined by the formidable line-up of Jim Furyk, Tom Lehman, Justin Leonard. Davis Love, Mark O'Meara, Jeff Maggert, Phil Mickelson, Steve Pate, Payne Stewart, Hal Sutton and Tiger Woods. Once again, team USA was over-riding favourite and, having lost the previous two contests by one point each time, determined to 'whup ass' and few doubted they would.

Cue Europe ending the first day with a 6–2 lead.

But before examining that surprise score in a little more detail, it is neces-sary to point out that American preparations had not been entirely unruffled either. In their case it centred around money, or lack of it. History dictated that no one was paid for repre-senting his country in the Ryder Cup, and until now players on both teams were more than willing to play for the honour (and the fact that appearing in the event significantly strengthened their hand when regular contracts and appearance money were under negotia-tion). Their case for remuneration was hardly strengthened by the fact that one of the most vocal in his demands was Tiger Woods, already richer than

Croesius, with more than enough dosh to spend in several lifetimes.

But although it is easy to be critical of those who wanted to be paid (and I think their position was untenable) they felt that someone was making hundreds of millions of pound on the back of their talent, and that a little of it should find its way back to them. A meeting was arranged between the US PGA and the players with a chance of selection and a deal eventually agreed that team members and their captain would receive $200,000 each, to be donated to both a university and charity of their choice.

Tony Jacklin disagrees that James was in the wrong in handling his rookies. If anything, he believes he wasn't ruthless enough. 'I never had any bones about telling someone that they wouldn't be playing until the singles,' he said. 'I did it with Gordon Brand in 1983. As captain, your responsibility is to win the cup. Mark's mistake was in putting those guys – Jarmo Sandelin, Jean Van de Velde and Andrew Coltart – out early on. He should have put them out last. What you need on the last day is points on the board early on. Get the job done as soon as you can.'

Oh, and there was the matter of the fans, most of whom had travelled from nearby Boston, a city with a reputation for being almost as hard-nosed and in your face as New York – which Bostonians considered an insult because, in their view, they were much, much tougher. American xenophobia was shown at its asinine worst, which is about as bad as it gets, when two Americans, who were caddies in the European team, were described by some of their countrymen as 'unpatriotic' because they worked for European players. Although Jerry Higginbotham (Sergio Garcia) saw the fuss as the nonsense it was, the furore caused Lance Ten Broeck (Jesper Parnevik) to seriously consider whether or not to participate. From the outset the galleries heckled and booed the Europeans, and particularly targeted Colin Montgomerie, with delicate comments such as: 'Nice tits Mrs Doubtfire.' The abuse he suffered became so bad that his father was obliged to walk off the course. Sports fans can be obnoxious but none more so than Americans deprived of their God-given right to win. They weren't, therefore, too pleased at the end-of-first-day score that showed their team already facing a four-point deficit.

# 1999 (3)   The greatest fightback

No less an authority than Sir Michael Bonallack, a former captain and secretary of the Royal & Ancient Golf Club, who usually picks his words with the same care he might use if shaving himself for a surgical procedure 'down below', was moved to call Brookline on the last day of this contest, 'a bear pit'. When someone with his diplomacy and tact is so forthright, we know something must have gone badly awry.

The atmosphere on that final singles day was certainly more Colisseum than Carnoustie and it has gone into golfing history as one of the more disgraceful scenes ever witnessed. But just for a moment, put away your Union Jack boxer shorts, cover up the 'England for Ever' tattoo and imagine this. We're playing the Ryder Cup on home soil, having only won it twice in the last seven attempts. We go into the final day singles trailing by four crucial points but then our fabulous, committed, gifted players stage the most unlikely comeback since Tom Finney won the Tour de France on a tricycle. Or something.

Imagine how you would feel if one by one we knock over the best golfers in the world, winning seven of the first eight matches out, but then things start to look ropey. Justin Leonard is four-up with seven to play against José Maria Olazábal but the Spanish genius begins to peg him back. He goes par, par, birdie, birdie to eliminate the deficit and they reach the seventeenth green, where virtually the entire European team is camped, along with wives, caddies, officials and bottle-washers. Leonard has hit the better approach and is about 20 feet away with a good birdie chance, while Ollie has a 45-foot putt to negotiate. Ollie takes his time, lines it up and lets the putter go to send the ball straight into the cup for an outrageous third birdie in a row.

Now, if that had happened, do you not think it possible that Seve might have led a charge of delirious Europeans across the green, forgetting that Leonard still had a putt for the half – because that is exactly what happened, except, of course, the roles have been reversed.

No, it remains as distressing now as it was then, no matter what the circumstances. The Americans forgot who they were, where they were, and what they were playing for. But at least it's given us moral superiority for a few years.

And to offer further insight into the actions of Team America, Olazábal himself said: 'I have to say if it would have been just the opposite, we might have reacted the same way. We're all human beings; we have our emotions. The Ryder Cup brings them to the highest level possible.'

And this Ryder Cup was like no other before or since. Following on from the examples of Tony Jacklin and Bernard Gallacher, Mark James knew he didn't have the strength in depth of the Americans, so he felt obliged to push his strongest team members to the limit. In consequence he put three pairings out four times each over the first two days. They were Colin Montgomerie and Paul Lawrie (2½ points); Sergio Garcia and Jesper Parnevik (3½ points); and Darren Clarke and Lee Westwood (2 points). Miguel-Angel Jiménez had two four-somes outings with Padraig Harrington (1.5 points) and two fourball partnerships with José Maria Olazábal (1.5 points), so the strategy worked to the extent that, after two days, Europe had a commanding lead of 10–6, the biggest advantage they had ever enjoyed going into the last twenty-four hours.

There was just one tiny problem, three of James' players – Coltart, Van de Velde

and Sandelin, all rookies, hadn't hit a shot in anger and were now about to step into probably the most raucous, intimidating arena any of them would ever face. In contrast, of course, seven of the team had played 36 holes on each of the previous two days. James led with two of his strong men, Westwood and Clarke, and then tried to hide his untried novices in third, fourth and fifth places in the running order. It didn't work and all five went down to a pretty convincing beating to, respectively, Tom Lehman 3&2, Hal Sutton 4&2, Phil Mickelson 4&3, Davis Love 6&5 and Tiger Woods 3&2. In the first eight matches the US won seven, with only Padraig Harrington managing to stem the red onslaught when he beat Mark O'Meara by one hole.

Further European success went to Colin Montgomerie, who beat Payne Stewart by the same margin, and Paul Lawrie, who took Jeff Maggert 4&3. But those were two of the last three matches on the course and were dead rubbers because America had already won a thrilling, scintillating victory. Stewart, incidentally, felt obliged to apologise to Monty for the behaviour of the crowd, which was little short of intimidating and which caused the Scotsman to back off putts at least three times.

*Bedlam as Justin Leonard – at the front of the green – holes an unlikely putt*

So what can account for such an exhilarating, if frightening, last day resurgence, when America had been, to all intents and purposes, dead and buried? Some credit must rest with captain Ben Crenshaw. Facing the media at the end of the second day he looked broken, but then gathered all the defiance of which he was capable and said that he knew it looked pretty black but he believed, with absolute conviction, that it wasn't over and something special was about to happen. The journalists duly recorded his words while no doubt thinking: 'Yeh, right, and I'm going back to my hotel to sleep with Kim Basinger'. However, twenty-four hours later they were less incredulous. Crenshaw also invited George W. Bush, at the time governor of Texas, to the team room on that fateful evening, where the governor read from a letter written by William Barret Travis, commander of the Alamo when it was laid siege to in 1836 by Santa Anna's Mexican troops.

'The enemy has demanded a surrender,' Bush read. 'I have answered the demand with a cannon shot and our flag still waves proudly from the walls. I shall never surrender nor retreat. I call on you in the name of liberty, of patriotism, and of everything dear to the American character, to come to our aid with all dispatch. If this call is neglected, I am determined to sustain myself as long as possible and die like a soldier who never forgets what is due to his own honour and that of his country. Victory or death.'

Nothing like drawing an analogy between a bloody military conflict and a golf match. Hopefully at some point in the future when the European team has its back to the wall we can expect Her Majesty the Queen to be rolled out in order to recite some of Churchill's more stirring speeches from World War II. Nevertheless, golfing history must record that this was a truly magnificent performance from an American side that had been skewered and turned on a spit for two days before rising up to remind us, in the most emphatic style, that they always win the singles.

# 2001 A sense of perspective

After the shenanigans at Brookline, when the Americans allowed exuberance to overcome reason as they trampled all over the seventeenth green, all agreed that a measure of calm and decorum needed to be reinstated. And then tragedy struck on 11 September 2001 as terrorists hijacked three aircraft and flew them into public buildings in America with a loss of over three thousand lives. Even now it is almost impossible for many of us to understand the enormity of the event. Outrage and appalled horror was the widespread Western reaction and European team captain Sam Torrance, like millions of others, says all he could do for two days was watch television, awestruck and sickened by what he saw. During that time he says that the Ryder Cup, for which he had probably devoted 50 per cent of his waking thoughts over the previous twelve months, did not enter his mind once, and it is easy to believe him.

But slowly we all came to appreciate that for the rest of us life, or a semblance of it, went on, and that decisions would have to be taken about leading those lives – and that one of those decisions involved the Ryder Cup, which was due to start just over two weeks after the terrorists had struck. Much frantic activity went on behind the scenes, involving the Professional Golfers' Associations of all nations involved – players, captains, officials and anyone else who had an investment in staging the event.

Things in America were still chaotic, with all domestic and most international flights cancelled in the immediate aftermath of the atrocity and even when they resumed, it was unlikely there would be a rush for seats. Several American players said they would feel uncomfortable boarding a plane anywhere for some time to come. Some, of course, argued that the contest should

take place as planned, and that to cancel it would merely be 'giving in' to terrorism – which was frankly a load of hogwash. Anyone who knows America and its people, let alone the nations represented on the eastern side of the Atlantic, understands that they do not back away when threatened or run away from a fight. How they respond might be open to criticism but that they *will* respond is never in doubt.

So the correct decision, to postpone the thirty-fourth Ryder Cup, was made and we all entered a strange kind of limbo. For two years in the case of America, and one year in Europe, we had seen players accumulate the points they would need to make the team, or hope to do well enough to catch the respective captain's eye and make it as a wild-card pick. In Europe Thomas Björn, Darren Clarke, Niclas Fasth, Pierre Fulke, Padraig Harrington, Bernhard Langer, Paul McGinley, Colin

Montgomerie, Phillip Price and Lee Westwood had all gathered the necessary, and they were joined by wild cards Sergio Garcia and Jesper Parnevik, both world-class players who spent most of their time in America. The team for which they were selected was a reasonable mixture of seasoned campaigners alongside four rookies – Fasth, Fulke, McGinley and Price. America had one debutant fewer and once again looked the stronger side on paper; they certainly featured higher, on average, in the official world rankings. Paul Azinger and Scott Verplank were picked by captain Curtis Strange, and they joined Mark Calcavecchia, Stewart Cink, David Duval, Jim Furyk, Scott Hoch, Davis Love, Phil Mickelson, Hal Sutton, David Toms and Tiger Woods. The composition of the team reminded us, however, that within the wider tragedy of September 11, golf was still painfully aware of its own heartbreak.

Two years earlier, a month after the America triumph at Brookline, forty-two-year-old Payne Stewart died when the private jet on which he and four others were travelling lost cabin pressure. In his youth Stewart had been cocksure, sometimes arrogant and acerbic, but through his late twenties and into his thirties he matured into the gentlest, most generous and wittiest of souls. He won two US Opens and the US PGA championship but no event set his pulse racing like the Ryder Cup. Fiercely patriotic and proud of his homeland, he played it in exactly the right spirit of hard but friendly and fair-minded competition. He liked nothing better than winning but was graciousness personified in defeat, as he had shown at Brookline by losing to Colin Montgomerie in the singles, while remonstrating with the noisier elements of the crowd who were barracking his opponent. He liked nothing more than to have, on those occasions when the two teams shared the same hotel, Bruce Springsteen's *Born in the USA* blaring out of his room, at a volume that would rattle the window panes, just to get one up on the Europeans. I once interviewed him in the locker room during a US Open and it was an impossible task. Seemingly every player who strolled by, from nations all over the world, wanted to stop and shake his hand or exchange a few words, and all walked away with a smile. The few who didn't pause because they could see he was busy had gone only a few paces before they were stopped in their tracks by Stewart shouting their names and leaping up to give them a hug or pat on the back. He was absolutely irrepressible but he brightened my life, and those of many other people, on that and many other days. His loss to golf and the wider world is still felt.

And now Payne's erstwhile teammates and opponents had to wait a year before they could resume the contest he loved so much. Rightly, and largely at the insistence of the two captains, Curtis Strange and Sam Torrance, it was decided that the two teams would remain the same and that players would be neither discarded nor included according to their form in 2002. It is difficult to talk about 'good' emerging from the rubble of the Twin

Jesper Parnevik was in New York on September 11 when terrorists struck. A year later he was at the Belfry for the delayed contest when a mild earthquake struck the Midlands of Britain in the middle of the night. He fled his hotel room, stark naked, believing for a few moments that the unthinkable was happening to him again.

Towers in Manhattan, but the September 11 attack did, if nothing else, give us a sense of perspective and helped dispel the animosity that had built up in the wake of Brookline.

But a huge amount of credit also goes to Strange and Torrance, friends, rivals and opponents over many years. Both could be outspoken and opinionated, but they were also blessed with the innate decency and sensitivity needed to steer the competition through the most difficult phase of its history. Neither put a foot wrong in word or deed and the Ryder Cup could not have been blessed with two more able stewards when it needed them most.

# 2002 (1)  Sam plays a blinder

After the glory of 1985, when he holed the winning putt and seven other appearances as a Ryder Cup player, it was destined that Sam Torrance would one day captain the side, and his chance came in 2002. Throughout a long, emotional and difficult build-up, during which several players had lost the form that got them into the side, the man from Largs on the west coast of Scotland exuded a quiet confidence that seeped its way through both his team and the watching millions. It was as if he knew a secret that the rest of us didn't, but the truth was, as he later conceded, underneath was turmoil, with a million and one demands on his time and decisions to be made. Nevertheless, throughout it all he retained a sincere belief that his players would come through, and they, and we, fed off his calm certainty. But there was one part of the job that absolutely terrified him – making formal speeches.

Give the man a pint of beer and a crowded room of golfers, journalists or friends and he would have no problem getting to his hind legs and, in all probability, entertaining them for hours, but the idea of representing his continent and speaking to millions filled him with dread and as the countdown inexorably rolled on, his anxiety started to reach panic attack proportions. As he points out in his autobiography *Sam*, this was not just a heightened anxiety or case of jitters but a genuine phobia.

Like many people with a lack of academic qualifications (he left school at thirteen because he knew he wanted to be a golf pro), it seemed that he doubted his ability to communicate, or rather, believed that the process of talking to several hundred million was different to addressing just one. Torrance is nothing

*Captain Torrance still with a beady eye on the world's press*

if not thorough, though, so he applied his common sense to assessing the problem, and then finding a solution. The second part came with the help of David Purdie, a keen amateur golfer and professor of medicine. Torrance heard him speak at a Sunningdale Golf Club dinner and was immediately struck by his timing, wit and erudition, so he approached the professor and asked for his help, which was gladly given.

Over many, many months they worked together on content and style but always with the intention that, although some of the words may have been professor Purdie's, the voice, literally and metaphorically, would be Sam's. And it was he himself who came up with the mantra that was to be repeated by European team members during the week of competition that came to summarise their whole philosophy – *carpe diem*, or 'seize the day'. The work paid off and Sam sailed through every formal speech he had to make, being sincere, articulate, warm and wise.

But in all probability the most important of all his tasks was selecting the partnerships for the first two days and order of play for the singles. His task was not made easier by the fact that Jesper Parnevik, Paul McGinley,

Lee Westwood and Phillip Price, in particular, were showing nothing like the form that had earned them their places a year before. Torrance's first decision, therefore, was to break up the pairing of Lee Westwood and Darren Clarke, who are friends, stable-mates in the same management company and who had taken two from four points at Brookline. Clarke was paired with the Dane Thomas Björn and in the first morning fourballs they beat the strong American duo of Paul Azinger and Tiger Woods by one hole in a momentous match. Woods alone made seven birdies as he and Azinger compiled an approximate 63 that was one stroke too many. An even more inspired pairing was a struggling Lee Westwood with the Spanish genius Sergio Garcia, and they dovetailed perfectly to see off David Duval and Davis Love 4&3. Magnificent Colin Montgomerie, alongside Mr Dependable, Bernhard Langer, took care of Scott Hoch and Jim Furyk by the same margin, before America finally got a point on the board when Phil Mickelson and David Toms beat Padraig Harrington and Niclas Fasth by one hole. Fourballs, however, is the format in which Europe always seem to excel, so it was a great

surprise when the US came back in the afternoon fourballs to take 2½ points and end the day trailing by one, at 3½ to 4½. Europe had played well but had also benefitted from the home advantage that allowed them to set up the course in their own favour. In particular, Torrance had the speed of the greens slowed down, in contrast to the lightning-fast putting surfaces the Americans faced on their home Tour every week, and fairways narrowed at around 280 yards, which nullified the extra driving distance achieved by some of the away team – most notably Tiger Woods, Phil Mickelson and Davis Love.

America came back even harder the next day. The morning foursomes were shared but they again took 2½ points in the afternoon, to finish the second series of matches all-square at eight points apiece going into the last-day singles.

Torrance blooded his three players yet to appear – Price, Fulke and Parnevik –

To help overcome his fear of public speaking, Sam Torrance practised for hour after hour in the garage at home. He says he learnt his speeches so well that he could probably still recite them verbatim even now.

but all lost. The first two were beaten 2&1 in the foursomes by Mickelson and Toms while the still out-of-form Parnevik, alongside Nicholas Fasth, went down by one hole to Mark Calcavecchia and David Duval. The golf had been at its usual, inspired Ryder Cup level of excellence – how many times have we seen players hole out from off the green in this competition – and now we waited to see what the singles line-up would be, and it was here that Sam Torrance pulled his masterstroke. His top players, headed by Colin Montgomerie, were all stacked in the first half of the draw. When American captain Curtis Strange saw the list he blanched, the shock was visible on his face. And then realisation dawned as he recognised that, to quote Del Boy in *Only Fools and Horses*: 'As Macbeth said to Hamlet in a *Midsummer Night's Dream*, Rodney, we've been done-up like a kipper.'

It was a bold, some would say foolhardy, decision that was intended to get that much needed momentum running in Europe's favour from the outset. Strange, by contrast, had his battle-hardened veterans – Azinger, Furyk, Love, Mickelson and Woods – occupying the final five berths where, in a tight match, the outcome would be decided. Or so we thought.

# 2002 (2)  Monty gives it everything

The label of 'Best Player Never to Win a Major' has been a millstone around the neck for many golfers, because it is widely assumed that the four Major championships are the only true measure of greatness. Because of this, many believe that Colin Montgomerie's career will always be judged lacking for its absence of a Major, but I beg to differ. Legions of players with only a fraction of Monty's talent have at least one Major to their name but would never come near equalling his seven successive Order of Merit titles (with an eighth added in 2005) and Ryder Cup pedigree. To be the best golfer in Europe for close to a decade is an achievement unlikely to be equalled.

But if those OM wins are his career, the Ryder Cup is his passion. He had been a shoe-in for his side six times since making his debut in 1991 at the Kiawah Island bloodbath where he made an almost instant impact by halving with Mark Calcavecchia in the singles, having been four-down with four to play. Admittedly that result owed as much if not more to his opponent's collapse than to any particular heroics on Monty's part, but it gave the Scotsman a taste of

success in an event in which he was determined to savour more. As the teams gathered for the 2002 contest he had a history of played twenty-three, won twelve, lost seven and halved four, and any record in which wins outnumber losses by almost two-to-one is more than respectable. But he improved it significantly in the first two days at the Belfry, adding another 3½ points from four matches. More remarkably still, three times in partnership with Bernhard Langer and once with Padraig Harrington, he hadn't been behind in a single game.

The Belfry crowds had cheered his every move but it wasn't always thus, because Monty is not, it has to be said, the most popular player in the game, at least among the fans. His greatest strength, and weakness, is that he wears his heart on his sleeve. He appears to have hypersensitive eyesight and hearing and if he hit a bad shot he would scowl his way to the ball, looking as if the business of playing golf for a living was the most burdensome responsibility imaginable. The image of him that so often comes through the television screen is, in consequence, that of a surly prima donna who should have been counting his blessings, but who would more likely be tearing a strip off some hapless spectator or photographer for daring to breathe.

Journalists, however, mostly respect and like him for a number of reasons, chief among which is his inherent decency. Also (with a few exceptions), they have learnt that, if you give him a couple of minutes to regain his equilibrium after a bad round, he will talk (and talk, and talk) until you have exhausted your supply of questions. What's more, he does not trot out the usual platitudes but listens to the question, thinks about it, and tries to give a considered response. He is an intelligent man, with a lot of passion and capable of far too much honesty for his own good. He is also sensitive to slights and criticisms, and when wounded tends to lash out, so journalists (scumbags the lot of 'em) have learnt that he often provides excellent copy. He was particularly prone to barracking when he played in America, so the Ryder Cup offered him the perfect stage on which to make a telling riposte.

Scott Hoch, his unfortunate opponent on that singles day in 2002, is also a controversial character but in his case the enmity he arouses comes equally from just about everyone. Some years ago an anonymous straw poll among his fellow pros on the US Tour revealed him to be the most disliked person among their fraternity. He famously passed up the chance to play in the Open almost every year (and couldn't even remember the names of the courses he had played in the championship), had described the Old Course at St Andrews as a 'cow pasture' and said of his experience there in the 2000 Open: 'I can't remember if I tried real hard every shot or not. But I remember making triple-bogey to miss the cut.' Among professional golfers and fans, playing badly is accepted (and in John Daly's case, often appears to be compulsory), not trying never is. Hoch is also on record, with some justification, as saying that media and galleries, with their intensive partisanship, had taken a lot of fun out of the Ryder Cup and that he would rather play in the Presidents Cup, the alternate year format that pitches America against the rest of the world excluding Europe. He was though, to some extent, like Monty, a victim of his own candour, best summed up by his captain, Curtis Strange, who said: 'If you don't want the truth, don't ask Scott Hoch a question.' The impression I have always had, is that he is a man comfortable in his own

*The only time Scott Hoch would lead Monty all day*

skin, who dares give voice to many of the thoughts of his fellow players, but he lacks either the tact or hypocrisy needed to dissemble or disguise his feelings. He is, in short, the type of dinner guest who will criticise the food if that is his opinion and his opinion is sought. He was also one of the most consistent players in the world, particularly with an iron in his hand. Sadly for him, he had already butted antlers twice with Monty and Langer in this Ryder Cup, and lost twice (he and Jim Furyk went down in the first-day fourballs 4&3, while in partnership with Scott Verplank in the second-day foursomes he escaped with a one-hole loss).

Torrance's gamble of top-loading his strong players at the front of the draw would only work if Europe got off to a fast start, and the roar that greeted Monty as he emerged for battle was deafening. He later told *Golf Digest*: 'On the first tee in 2002 I was gulping like mad. I know I'd been there before, but this was different. The match was tied, and the scene was set. I was off first – which was a shock to most people, including me – leading the team, if you like. The electricity was unbelievable. It was all building up around me. It was massive. I'd love to recreate it, but I never will. It was a one-off.'

Monty was a champion that day from start to finish and the hapless Hoch never stood a chance. The tone was set on that very first hole when Colin trundled in a 20-footer, as he had been doing for the previous two days, to establish a lead that was never threatened. He was at his imperious best and the quiet half-smile and air of invincibility he had carried all week were like impenetrable armour. By the time they reached the 190-yard par-3 fourteenth, Monty was four-up and cruising and, showing the mercy that a good vet would direct towards an ailing dog, finished his opponent off quickly and painlessly with yet another birdie, for a 5&4 victory. Hoch was magnanimous in defeat, with the warmth of his congratulations much more than the minimal smile and handshake usually expected on such occasions.

It was Monty's finest hour, or so we thought.

# 2002 (3)  Tell them who I beat

If I may mix my metaphors, underdogs don't come much lower in the pecking order than Phillip Price when matched against Phil Mickelson. Price is a quiet, modest man of whom the unkind would say he has much to be modest about, as he had hardly set the world of golf aflame in a twelve-year career. His maiden victory came in the 1994 Portugese Open and his second was the 2001 Algarve Open de Portugal, a win that was largely responsible for him making the Ryder Cup team, in the final automatic spot.

That year he recorded three other top-ten finishes, all towards the beginning of the season and his was a situation in which he was fast out of the blocks, and then hung on for the last few months to see if enough people would overtake him to snatch his Ryder Cup place away. They didn't – just. That would be bad enough but because of the year's delay, by the time the sides assembled at the Belfry, Price's scoring ability seemed not only to have flown south, but to have taken up permanent residence many thousands of miles away.

So poor was his form that many called for him to be dropped, but captain Torrance would have none of it. In the seven events Price played leading up to the Belfry, he had missed three cuts, retired once after an opening 75, and finished tied 41, T65 and T71. He was ranked 119th in the world and in his only outing over the first two days, he and Pierre Fulke lost to Phil Mickelson and David Toms. And then the draw for the singles was announced and he was matched against Mickelson again, the number two player in the world. Not too many of us rushed to the bookmaker to get £100 on Price winning.

Oh we of little faith. The people who play golf for a living on the European and US Tours are, by definition, the elite – the 0.01 per cent of the millions of golfers worldwide. Just to get on Tour takes remarkable skill, perseverance and self-belief, and to stay there, successfully, for more than a decade, sets you apart from many of your contemporaries and wannabes. Price does not have the natural flair, talent, shot-making or scoring abilities of some, but what he does have is a core of steel and the sort of resilience and bloody-mindedness that makes people walk single-handedly to the North Pole, losing toes and fingers on the way, but never once giving thought to the idea of retreat. If you went into battle, Price is exactly the kind of man you would want at your shoulder. He didn't look like a warrior – a thirty-five-year-old, tall, slim, prematurely greying man whose manner suggested he should have been a dentist or accountant – but then Jack Nicklaus didn't intimidate too many people by his appearance alone. Much fun was had at Price's expense because in

1994, the year of his maiden Tour victory, the town of his birth in south Wales (which even most Britons would struggle to find on a map) named him the 'Pontypridd Man of the Year'.

We should have known better than to poke (albeit affectionate) fun. Two years later his fellow team-mate Lee Westwood said of him: 'He is a steady player who makes very few mistakes. Phil is a great driver of the ball and his putting has improved dramatically since he has become a regular on the US PGA Tour – and it wasn't bad before that. Phil is a very consistent player and when he gets into contention he rarely lets you down. Few people gave Phil a chance when he went to play Phil Mickelson in the final day's singles matches of the last Ryder Cup. We did as a team, but none of the critics gave him a hope.'

Let us examine why. He was playing one of the most naturally gifted and best-known golfers in the world. Where Price makes his quiet, unassuming and apparently apologetic way down the fairway, Phil Mickelson buckles his swash, unleashes an unfeasibly long drive into a hopelessly thick clump of rough, performs a miracle escape with a lob wedge and holes the putt for birdie.

American galleries, in particular, love him as much for the reckless, go-for-broke style of his play as his enormous grin (in which he seems to display far more than the legally allowed maximum number of teeth), and willingness to stand patiently for hours, signing autographs and posing for pictures. His only weakness is his reckless determination to take on any challenge and, as Peter Dobereiner once said of Arnold Palmer: 'He had everything but a brake pedal,' and that is why the fans adore him.

During a ten-year career he had won twenty times, made enough money to make Bill Gates envious and was a genuine superstar of the game. By the time 2002 rolled around he was a veteran of three previous Ryder Cups in which, during fifteen outings he had the none-too-shabby record of won eight, lost four and halved three. Here at the Belfry he had taken 2½ points from a possible four and he and David Toms were the only American pairing to not be beaten by Colin Montgomerie and Bernhard Langer. This was then, a huge mismatch and as things turned out it was a no-contest.

Price annihilated him.

He jumped into an early one-hole lead, but that's nothing in matchplay and Mickelson continued on his serene, smiling way. The turning point was the par-4 sixth hole, not long, but requiring a drive that has to be threaded onto a narrow fairway between two large lakes. The American found the short grass with ease and then delivered what he must have believed was the *coup de grace*, by firing an iron to within 3 feet – virtual kick-in range for a putter of his quality. Price, in contrast, was in horrible shape. Having pulled his drive left, he watched with some anxiety as it headed for the water but, thankfully, it pulled up just short. It had, however, crossed the margin of the hazard, so Price's first difficulty was that he could not ground his club as he addressed the ball. But that was only a small part of his problems.

In order to take his stance he had to stand on the grass bank leading down

It has become a tradition at European team celebrations for Lee Westwood to introduce his fellow team members – a duty he happily takes on and performs with considerable wit and not a few insults. Throughout his long and affectionate build-up in the introduction of Price, the Welshman repeatedly tugged his sleeve, saying: 'Don't forget to tell them who I beat.' No need to worry Phillip, we never will.

*Philip Price (right) having just delivered the coup de grace on the sixteenth green*

to the lake, so that his feet were a considerable distance below the ball, and there was no way he could get the sort of flat-footed stance he would have liked for balance. He had to grip the club further down the handle than usual and guard carefully against hooking the shot as having the ball above your feet promotes a flatter swing, which leads to a right-to-left ball flight. He took up position with an 8-iron and hit the best shot of his career, one that flew straight and eventually settled onto the green about a foot further away than Mickelson. It was a career-defining moment. A few minutes later Price rolled in the putt for the most unlikely of birdies and attention turned to a clearly rattled Mickelson. His putt not only failed to drop, it didn't even touch the side of the hole. It would be another ten holes before Price ended his man with a downhill 25-foot putt on the sixteenth for a 3&2 victory but the contest was settled on the sixth, and both men, and all of us watching, knew it.

# 2002 (4)  An early bath

What is it about the Irish? They seem to have produced the goods under the cosh more consistently than any nation with such a tiny population has a right to expect. Christy O'Connor's career best 2-iron at The Belfry in 1989 to beat Fred Couples is a case in point. Only two years earlier Eamonn Darcy had ended one of the most miserable Ryder Cup records of all (it stands at played eleven, lost eight, halved two and won one), by beating Ben Crenshaw in a nail-biter at Muirfield Village. And in 1995, Philip Walton held his nerve (just) to take an invaluable point from Jay Haas at Oak Hill and set up a European victory in America for only the second time.

So when, in 2002, captain Sam Torrance pulled his masterstroke and loaded the front half of the draw with his top players, and they produced to such effect that the scoreboard was lit up with a sea of European blue, it fell to Paul McGinley, in his match against Jim Furyk, to have the chance to seal victory. A few minutes earlier it looked as if Niclas Fasth of Sweden would be the man to be touched by history, but Paul Azinger holed from the bunker left of the eighteenth green to halve his match and keep American hopes alive. If that wasn't enough, Jim Furyk not only found the same bunker but damned near repeated the effort. But he missed by a fraction.

'If I'm honest,' said McGinley, 'I don't really know [how I took the putter head back]. I was unbelievably nervous and all I could hear was my caddy, J.P. [Fitzgerald], saying: "Remember the putt, remember the putt."'

This may seem rather strange advice – rather like a driving instructor telling his pupil not to crash the car – but the caddy was reminding his man that he had faced the same putt two years earlier in the Benson & Hedges International, and canned it to finish second outright. But that was then and, with all due respects to B&H – purveyors of fine addiction sticks – their tournament cannot come close to matching the final-day singles of a tight, tense Ryder Cup.

McGinley's manager, the rotund, amiable but ever-pragmatic Chubby Chandler, saw his man stand over the single most important shot of his career, one that could make him a folk hero or burn a scar so deep into his psyche that he would never recover, and thought: 'Lucky bastard.' Having been a pro golfer himself, Chandler knew that getting on Tour was tough, making a Ryder Cup team immeasurably so but having the opportunity to win the whole damned shooting match came down, in the end,

to pure randomness and the fickle finger of fate.

On this day, the digit was pointing four-square at a short, stocky Irishman with a grin that would blind at twenty paces. But dear God, what if he should miss? Every adult and most of the children who have ever picked up a golf club have, at some time or other, stood over a putt and said to themselves: 'This for the Open,' or the Masters, or the Ryder Cup. But deep down we pray that it never happens (rather safe in the knowledge that it will not) because we know that we could not cope, and the reason for that is pressure. It is an overused word, but that doesn't mean it does not exist, and what defines pressure is context. Put a four-inch beam between two chairs in your garden and even the most unathletic of us could wobble across. Put the same beam above Niagara Falls or a pit of snakes and we wouldn't even make it on our hands and knees or dragging ourselves on our belly.

Those who compete at the highest level in any sporting arena are not different from the rest of us, they learn in exactly the same way, by repetition and by gradually testing themselves in ever more demanding situations. Few win at the first opportunity, they need to

taste and experience the greater intensity that bigger events bring before becoming accustomed enough to the situation to be able to still function.

But all of them, as they climb the ladder to greater success, find different plateaus and wonder how they will cope at this new, rarified atmosphere where oxygen is in such short supply. They find a way and then move on again, to the next level, and then the next. McGinley, on the eighteenth green at The Belfry on that September afternoon, was confronted by one last challenge, but it was bigger, more important and carried a far greater burden of expectancy and hope than anything with which he had dealt before. In terms of pressure, the needle just went off the dial.

Sam Torrance could eventually be picked out among the throng. He was wearing an enormous grin and tears were rolling down his cheeks. It was said before the competition began that there were two certainties regarding Torrance's captaincy – that he would be dignified and magnanimous in defeat, and cry like a baby in victory.

No one deserved it more.

Oh, did I mention that admirable and talented player as he is, if McGinley has one weakness, it is that he doesn't hole anywhere near enough putts in the 10- to 20-foot range? He seems to be a good putter, with a smooth stroke, but somehow, where a player like Tiger Woods seems to almost will the ball into the hole from that crucial range, McGinley's efforts seem to consistently slide past, earning him the sort of 'Good, but no coconut' back handed compliment we all remember from school.

But now there was no hiding place, no chance of a retake and no looking back. Approximately 10 feet of closely mown grass stood between McGinley and immortality. I swear that every single one of the tens of thousands around the green that day held their breath as the Irishman pulled the putter head back and sent the ball on its way. Less than three seconds later when it dropped into the hole, slap bang in the middle, they exhaled in unison in a single, deafening roar of pleasure and, it has to be said, relief. Colin Montgomerie later commented: 'The noise around that green was indescribable. Those cheers will ring in his ears for ever more.'

McGinley himself has added: 'I still get an adrenaline rush whenever I think about it. It's a wonderful thing to be remembered for and I feel blessed that I had the chance. I mean, the chances of it happening to anyone are very slim and the chances of it being so dramatic are even slimmer.'

McGinley, his team-mates, captain Torrance, officials (even journalists) and every other European supporter went nuts and the cheers, instead of lessening, seemed to gather strength and roll out over the Belfry in wave after wave of increasing intensity and noise. It was wonderful, joyous pandemonium and in the middle of it all Paul McGinley leapt into the lake. As you do.

# 2004 (1) A tale of two captains

The relative importance of Ryder Cup captaincy has been debated widely down the years. One school of thought suggests that, apart from making the pairings and deciding the order of play for the singles, captaincy is a simple matter of PR and keeping the boys happy – a little like the astronaut whose sole job is to feed the monkey that is flying the spacecraft. Others, including me, believe captaincy to be of vital importance. And to support our argument, we simply say 'Sutton and Langer' because, in 2004, Bernhard Langer got almost everything right, while his counterpart, Hal Sutton, got pretty

much everything wrong and turned out to be the most disastrous captain since the bloke on the bridge of the Titanic said: 'Do you want more ice with that gin and tonic?'

He was jokingly referred to as Barney Rubble because of his appearance, but the sad fact is that Fred Flinstone's best mate would have made a better job of captaincy (hell, Wilma and Betty too) because in just about every imaginable way Sutton got it wrong.

A couple of days before the contest started I had a conversation with another journalist and we both couldn't believe the rumours that Sutton was planning to pair Phil Mickelson and Tiger Woods because they were so clearly out of form and, despite what they may say, they are clearly not bosom buddies. Phil would try and get along with anyone but Woods has a long memory for slights and hasn't forgotten the perceived disparaging remarks that Mickelson made about Nike equipment (as played by Tiger) a few years back. In addition, Woods knows that head-to-head he's got the measure of Lefty and that's how he wants to keep it.

This was far from a marriage made in heaven, but Sutton had the idea of putting them together the day he was appointed, two years previously, and wasn't going to budge. But there's having convictions and then there's bone-headed obstinacy. Because of that decision, the US team was stuffed at the end of the first day.

In Sam Torrance's autobiography he said of his pairings in 2002: 'And as it turned out, practically none of the pairings I had in my head came to fruition. Some of the players I thought certain of participating in all five series never did, as they became tired or lost form. The need for flexibility became obvious. It had always been obvious.'

Well yes, to everyone in the world except Hal Sutton. And then, when his cream-of-the-crop dynamic duo were hosed in the morning, largely because they couldn't find a fairway between them with a compass, road map and global satellite positioning, he put them out again in the afternoon in foursomes, the format where, above all else, you need to gel with your partner and not give away holes to par.

Monty spoke for the whole Europe team when he said that beating this supposed dream ticket in the morning was the equivalent of getting two points so, of course, Sutton sent them out again, when it didn't take a student of body language to appreciate that this had been a bad idea once, and would be a disastrous notion twice. It was a decision and a day from which America did not recover, but it wasn't Sutton's only mistake.

Phil Mickelson, in a widely criticised move, had changed his equipment supplier two weeks before the contest began. With three weeks to go he was playing Titleist balls, seven days later Callaway, and then on the Tuesday of Ryder Cup week, Sutton gave him a box of Nike (the type Tiger uses) and said: 'You'd better get used to these.' No argument, no discussion. And to be honest, do you think he would have behaved in the same high-handed way to Tiger? I doubt it very much, for the simple reason that Woods would have told him to go to hell. But not Phil – he's too nice.

Sutton then, in his press interviews at the end of the first day, conceded that, with Mickelson using new equipment that he hadn't yet adjusted to, perhaps it was a mistake to ask him to play twice. 'But it's not going to give us any grief in the morning because he's going to be cheering instead of playing,' Sutton said. Trouble is, at this stage he hadn't bothered to tell Mickelson and the world's

*Tiger Woods (left) and Phil Mickelson were never natural bedfellows*

press were the first people to know that Phil was dropped.

Sutton made it a point of honour, a boast even, that his players would not find out if they were playing, or who they would be paired with, until the last minute – and this despite Mickelson asking him that very question, three times, during the practice days. If you want his own words on the subject, they are: 'I told them last night that I wasn't going to set the pairings for the practice rounds. Don't read anything into anybody you're playing with. Be prepared to beat the other two guys by yourself and if I give you a little help, then that's a bonus.' Great motivation, Hal.

Jim Furyk said of his skipper, early in the week: 'He has a formula for what he wants to do. Not all of it [pairings] has been conveyed yet. We're getting bits and pieces every day. And he's letting us be individuals as well as being part of a team.' Except a team needs time to become a team.

An American columnist for the Golf Channel in the States, wrote – two days before the competition started: 'Sutton, for all his speeches and pep talks, is finding it within himself to leave his troops to themselves in search of their own self-motivation. In other words, keep 'em guessing but keep 'em focused. And at all times, keep a belief in "the plan."'

Just one problem: his only plan was to pair two of his players in the worst form of their life (twice), keep his own team in the dark and . . . err . . . that's it.

He didn't work out a strategy for the singles, and simply turned his team out in the order in which they had qualified, with the two wild cards tacked onto the end of the list – as if the number of points they had amassed in getting to Oakland Hills was any indicator of form once they arrived. Granted, he was not helped by his players, who collectively froze, nor by the US selection system that counts over two years instead of one, so Tiger Woods, Jim Furyk, David Toms, Davis Love, Kenny Perry – and, to a large extent, Chad Campbell – were in the team for what they did in 2002 and 2003.

And this may seem rather harsh on Hal Sutton but he mismanaged and let down his players and seemed to think that they should gel as a team because he told them they had to. No. People get on better with some than others, it's human nature and is a phenomenon that was first recognised quite a while ago. As captain a significant part of your job was to recognise this basic truth when you made your pairings. In consequence of the fact that you didn't, we had the most one-sided event in recent memory. The crowds behaved beautifully, the course looked magnificent but we were all deprived of the kind of sporting spectacle we have come to expect from the Ryder Cup. It only visits us every two years and because of that it should be special, and memorable for the right reasons. Okay, his players spectacularly failed to deliver, but they weren't helped by their captain.

Billy Casper had some interesting thoughts when I asked him about the contest almost a year later. 'Our guys in the United States are all individuals,' he said. 'They play for so much money that they go for the flag every time and if they get lightning in a bottle they win a million dollars, and if they don't, they win anything from $50,000 to $400,000. They don't know that you don't go for the flag all the time. You have to know how to play matchplay with a partner. I watch it all the time. In the last three matches I watched how the Americans don't understand fully how to play. They won't get away from how they play every week.'

# 2004 (2)   Young guns go for it

As has been demonstrated so many times over the years in the Ryder Cup, and hopefully in this book, moments have moment. Craig Stadler's missed putt at the Belfry in 1985, or Seve Ballesteros driving the tenth green of the same course and many more instances have had far greater significance than the point or half they earned at the time. Major championships can turn on a made or missed putt, a good or bad bounce or any of the thousands of things that can affect players and their golf balls over several days' play across an arena that covers about 120 acres. Sometimes it is only in retrospect that we see the significance of a moment, but on other occasions it is immediately apparent that a seismic shift has occurred, that deep below the earth's crust tectonic plates have moved, grated and resettled, and that something of fundamental importance has taken place. Well, okay then, a little hyperbole – but instants can have a

decisive impact. So it was at Oakland Hills in 2004 in the second-morning fourballs.

Europe had familiarly arrived in America as underdogs because, once again, we all used the wrong criteria by which to compare the combatants. These were the world rankings, in which team USA were so far ahead that they couldn't even see their opponents in their rear-view mirrors, and Majors won (USA twelve, Europe zero). What these headline figures overlooked was not only that the European selection system was better, but that almost every member of the European side was in pretty nifty form, as they proved immediately the contest got underway.

Colin Montgomerie and Padraig Harrington started by seeing off the US 'Dream Team' of Tiger Woods and Phil Mickelson in the first day's fourballs, 2&1. They were ably supported and the only Americans to gain even half a point

that morning were Chris Riley and Stewart Cink, who squeezed Paul McGinley and Luke Donald to a draw. It didn't improve too much in the afternoon foursomes. Woods and Mickelson lost by one hole to Darren Clarke and Lee Westwood, Kenny Perry and Stewart Cink were beaten 2&1 by Sergio Garcia and Luke Donald, while Davis Love and Fred Funk went down 4&2 against good old Monty and Harrington. The pairing of Chris DiMarco and Jay Haas, which beat Miguel-Angel Jiménez and Thomas Levet 3&2, enjoyed the only American success. This wasn't a bad day for America, it was a desperate, dismal, shocking day. By close of play the visitors had opened up a lead of 6½–1½ points and it was almost beyond comprehension that only one American pairing out of eight, on home soil, had notched up a win. Their own supporters weren't even cheering them because, in one of his shrewdest moves, European captain

Bernhard Langer had sent his men out on a charm offensive. During the practice rounds the visiting team members were instructed to engage the galleries, wave, smile, give autographs and pose for pictures until their smile muscles and writing hands were numbed by the effort. It worked to such effect that when the competition got underway American fans weren't sure whether to cheer for 'their boys', applaud those gosh-darned nice guys from 'Yoorop' or keep quiet. Largely they kept quiet. Also, as someone pointed out, it is difficult to cheer your team when they're making bogies by the hatful and being roundly beaten.

All successful sportsmen (and women) are fighters, however, and fewer fight harder than a cornered American. The Ryder Cup has shown us time and time again, but most recently and dramatically five years before at Brookline, that to write them off before all mathematical chance has been exhausted is foolish, so we all expected a fightback, and it duly came.

In the second-morning fourballs Chris DiMarco was showing the considerable tenacity of which he is capable as he and Jay Haas grabbed a vital half point from one of the strongest European combinations, Sergio Garcia and Lee Westwood. But even before that heartening outcome, Tiger Woods and Chris Riley were even more impressive in seeing off Darren Clarke and Ian Poulter by 4&3. Their match had actually started behind that of DiMarco but so emphatic was the win that it finished considerably earlier. A similar thing happened in the fourth match, in which Stewart Cink and Davis Love overcame Colin Montgomerie and Padraig Harrington 3&2. This meant that only one game was left on the course and it involved three rookies. For Europe, big-hitting Paul Casey, alongside modest David Howell, were undergoing their Ryder Cup baptism against fellow Ryder Cup virgin Chad Campbell and man of steel Jim Furyk. Unlike Casey and Howell, Campbell had started on the first morning and been heavily beaten, but with Europe having slept on a dominant lead after the first day, it now faced the prospect of America taking 3½ from 4 points and lunching in a mood of euphoria.

Howell, an unassuming, quiet, self-effacing man, who is only starting to convince himself quite how good he is, knew the importance of the match from the outset and said: 'When we got out there today, it was clear the atmosphere was going to be totally different and it was also clear that things weren't really going our way as they were.'

To begin with there were few dramas in a tight, slightly nervy contest. But then Howell hit to about six feet on the sixth for a one-up advantage that should have been doubled on the eighth when Casey, one of the hottest players in golf when he catches fire, binned a curling 30-footer for another birdie. Furyk, though, does not know the meaning of 'concession', 'lost' or 'abandoned cause' and replied with a 15-foot birdie putt of his own to halve the hole. He was only postponing things though, because Casey then replied on the tenth with a similar length effort to give Europe a two-hole advantage and remind the Americans who was boss. Well, not quite. Furyk contrived to make four birdies in the next five holes, which was just as well because his talented, but

Paul Casey, who lives in the USA, has subsequently earned American wrath for quite reasonably saying that when the Ryder Cup comes around he 'properly hates' Americans. As ever the tabloid press created a raging inferno from a tiny spark.

*David Howell (front) helps Paul Casey line up a putt*

out-of-form partner, Chad Campbell, was just making up the numbers. Howell and Casey were virtually playing Furyk on his own, but such was his determination and skill that even their combined firepower could not give them an edge and the match was level through fifteen. As so often happens, though, just as the contest approached crescendo, the formerly dormant – some might say moribund – Campbell suddenly sprang to life at the sixteenth and banged in a 35-footer from the back of the green to put the Americans one-up with two to play. For the young European rookies it was officially time to panic.

The seventeenth hole is a devilish par-3, its 203 yards playing so difficult that no one from either team had birdied it in 14 attempts. Enter David Howell, who hit a 6-iron to five feet that later earned him the accolade from his own European Tour of Shot of the Year. He drained the putt and the protagonists marched to the eighteenth all-square.

Paul Casey likes the limelight. He has great belief in his own ability, which he enjoys displaying to golf galleries the world over. In his view he didn't quite catch his drive on the final hole and it 'only' flew 300 yards, straight down the middle – which is just as well because Howell was nowhere. Casey then fired at the green, but found the wrong level of the putting surface and surveyed almost the same horrendous putt that had been faced by Sergio Garcia minutes earlier. European captain Bernhard Langer had seen the earlier putt and warned Casey that it did not break half as much as it appeared. Forewarned, he got the line pretty much right but forgot about speed, knocking it at least 4 feet past. But of all the aspects of golf at which he excels – and Casey is a long hitter – it is his putting that is most envied. He holed out for the vital win and Europe had stopped the American comeback in its tracks. Casey had the pleasure of driving the final nail into the coffin, but it was Howell's 6-iron on the seventeenth which gave him the hammer.

Bring on the singles.

# 2004 (3) Monty brings home the bacon

Whether or not you believe that Leo rising in Uranus will affect your fortunes for good or bad, there is no doubt that some things are written in the stars. In sport it is remarkable how often the spotlight falls on the best players in the biggest arenas, in the most important competitions, who then deliver a career-defining performance. Those of us who gain pleasure from watching sports people of any discipline may enjoy statistics or athleticism or brawn or guile, but ultimately it is the romance that gets to us. We are enthralled by the contest between the reigning king and the up-and-coming contender; the explosive genius of a gifted young pretender against the accumulated skill of the champion. Or how about the perennial under-achiever or team that one day rises from the mediocrity that has dogged the length of its career to snatch a victory as welcome as it is unexpected?

The opportunity for greatest drama, excitement and fairy-tale stories come on the most significant occasions – and in golf, few are more significant than those that contest Samuel Ryder's trophy. Colin Montgomerie will not win a Major but, like Seve Ballesteros before him, he has holed the winning putt in a Ryder Cup and, with the exception of Seve, never was it more fitting that player and moment should meet in the same place.

Despite being an automatic member of the six previous European teams, courtesy of his seven European Tour Order of Merit wins, by the time the qualification period for the 2004 sides had expired, Monty was not in the team by right and frankly, didn't deserve to be. Those of us looking for evidence that he would be selected were having to search his list of top-ten finishes to bolster our faith, where previously he had won with apparent ease at least once every season.

A large part of the explanation for his dip in form was that he was in the process of a harrowing divorce, not of his own choosing, that involved him living apart from his beloved children. As ever, he spoke freely of the anguish this involved but there were just a few glimmers that as the playing year drew to its conclusion his game was, if not back to his imperious best, at least moving on from its appalling worst.

But to get into the side Monty had to rely on the captain, Bernhard Langer, selecting him, so he continued to drop both subtle and overt hints throughout the year that he was willing, ready and eager to play. He even managed to joke at his own expense that, as he was now single, he'd only need one seat on the flight to America and was, therefore, a cheaper option. It worked, and Langer announced that his wild cards were Major champion in waiting Luke Donald, and grizzled veteran Monty. It

was a risky decision for the captain to make and he was relying on the fact that Monty could raise his game, as he had done so many times in the past, to take on the Americans.

If there were remaining doubts about Langer's wisdom when the team reached Oakland Hills, they were dispelled on the first hole of the first match in the first morning's fourballs. Monty and Padraig Harrington were up against the numbers one and three players in the world, Tiger Woods and Phil Mickelson. None of them drove well but Monty was nearest the fairway, in a large bunker to the right. He then struck a superb 7-iron to 15 feet, holed the putt for a winning birdie and walked off the green wearing a facial expression that said: 'You may beat us today, but you'll have to drive over me with a steamroller to do it.' He was more than aided by his team-mate, who couldn't so much talk the hind leg off a donkey as bullshit the balls off a buffalo.

Padraig Harrington is a sunny, loquacious, effervescent Irishman who seems always to appreciate that pushing a small white pill around a manicured field is a pretty bizarre way to make a living. A smile is never more than instant from his lips and if there is a funny side to any

situation, he will be the first to see it. But although he does not take himself or those around him too seriously, he gives every ounce of concentration and effort to the game he plays so well. And despite Monty's superb start, it was Harrington who made the more birdies and played the role of strong man.

Inevitably, though, he was more than happy for Colin to take the lion's share of plaudits and recognition. As a team they dovetailed to excellent effect, raced into an early lead, stood up to an expected comeback and eventually won with more ease than the 2&1 scoreline suggests.

They played twice more together, beating Davis Love and Fred Funk the first afternoon by 4&2, and then losing to Love, this time paired with Stewart Cink, by 3&2 on the second morning in fourballs. It was the cue for Monty to sit out the afternoon matches, the first time he had not played in a session since the second-afternoon fourballs thirteen years earlier at Kiawah Island in 1991. It was a streak of thirty consecutive matches that surpassed the record of even the great Ballesteros.

And then came the draw for the singles, which meant that Montgomerie was to face David Toms, a superb match player who demonstrated his man-on-

man abilities two years before by taking 3½ points from a possible five at the Belfry.

Their match was sixth onto the course but captain Langer had not needed to worry unduly about his order of play for two reasons – all his team members were playing well, and the lead of 11–5 that Europe had amassed was immune to even the most spirited American fight-back. Whether or not the canny German put Monty where he did because he sensed that the contest could be decided there is not certain, but he must have at least been aware of the possibility that this game could wrap up the whole kit and caboodle.

But for a while it didn't look as if the Scotsman would win his point. He took an early lead that was soon cancelled out and should have been ringing up the local lost property office, because somewhere overnight his driving had gone missing. Hitting fairways is the foundation on which Monty's game is based but he only located three of them all day, and in two of those instances he used 3-wood and an iron rather than driver. As his bagman Alastair McLean says in the book *How We Won the Ryder Cup*: 'But he scrambled great. His was real piss-you-off matchplay golf.'

He eventually got to the eighteenth hole with a one-hole advantage and got just through the back of the green in two, while his opponent made a great up-and-down for an excellent par. Colin's ball was in the first cut off the green, and because of the huge amount of borrow he had to allow on a shot that broke massively from right to left, would need to either chip or putt across grass noticeably longer than the green itself, always difficult to judge.

He played a magnificent putt to 5 feet and his caddy reckons that were he given another twenty balls, he could not have replicated the shot. The stage was set for the absolute fitting finale. The man who had never won a Major, who had been abused and vilified by American galleries, who had been through the worst year of his life, who had saved his greatest heroics for the Ryder Cup and who had only been selected because his captain had

faith in him, faced a 5-footer to seal the most decisive European victory ever. He looked it over and stood up to the ball before despatching it with his usual brisk-ness, dead centre. Before the ball dropped, Monty's putter fell from his hands as he turned away in triumph and relief.

Fairy tales do come true, and in the Ryder Cup it happens more often than we have any right to expect.

# An explanation of matchplay

There are two main forms of golf – stroke play and matchplay.

## Stroke play

In this format each competitor competes with all others in the field, and the person who takes the fewest strokes over the course of the event – usually 72 holes, or four rounds  – wins. In the event of a tie there is a play off, during which the tied players compete over one or more additional holes, until one of them completes a hole in a lower score than his fellow competitor(s). So, if three players finish 72 holes on the same low score, and on the first extra, or playoff, hole, one of them takes four strokes while the others take five, he is the winner.

## Matchplay

This format  is used in the Ryder Cup and is man against man or two-man team against two-man team (or pairing). The score is kept by recording the number of holes won or lost, and is usually played over 18 holes. If a competitor takes fewer strokes on a hole than his opponent, he wins the hole and goes one-up. If he wins the next, he goes two-up; if he loses it, he is back to all-square. A match is completed when a player is more holes ahead than there are holes left to play – for example, if he goes four-up with only three holes remaining. In this instance, he has won 4&3. In the event of the opponents being all-square after 18 holes, the match is halved, or shared, with each player collecting half a point.

A player is regarded as 'dormie' when he is ahead by the number of holes remaining to be played. So if he should win the sixteenth to be two-up with two to play, he cannot be beaten. His opponent may, however, win the final two holes to halve the match.

Putts may be conceded, or given, so if a player has putted his ball to within a few inches of the hole, his opponent will probably 'give' him the remaining stroke to save time. Equally, if a player has difficulty on a hole and eventually gets to the green in four strokes and at best can score five, while his opponent is 6 feet away from the flagstick in two, he may well concede the hole, certain that his opponent will do no worse than two-putt. Because of this, scores in matchplay are often estimated.

In the Ryder Cup there are three forms of competition, foursomes, four-balls and singles. The first two days feature foursomes and fourballs, while the third is devoted to singles.

## Foursomes

There are four matches of this type, with each match involving two players from either team, who play in tandem, using one ball. One player from each side tees off and then he and his team-mate play alternate strokes until the hole is completed. Irrespective of who makes the final stroke on that hole, the other player tees off at the next and they again play alternate strokes. For this reason Americans often call foursomes 'alternate shot'.

It is probably the most difficult form of golf for professionals because they only play half the number of shots they usually play, which makes it difficult to get into a rhythm. In addition, it emphasises team work, because each competitor has to play from wherever his partner has left him. Relationships can become strained if the first member of a team hits a shot to within four feet of the hole and his partner then misses the putt or if tactics cannot be agreed.

## Fourballs

This also involves two-man teams, but in this format they each play their own ball, while still working together. An example of this would be a player from Europe getting onto the green in four strokes while his partner and their two opponents are on in two, so he has virtually no chance of winning the hole. He might, however, be facing a similar putt to that of his partner, and play his first, so that his partner can study the speed and line of the putt to help him make his own stroke. Alternatively, on a dangerous driving hole for example, one may play conservatively into the fairway, leaving his partner to take a more aggressive, and dangerous, line from the tee that, if it comes off, offers a better chance of birdie.

## Singles

As it sounds, each member of the twelve-man team is drawn to play a member of the opposing team.

### The current Ryder Cup format
- **Day one**
  Morning foursomes and fourballs; afternoon foursomes and fourballs.
- **Day two**
  Morning foursomes and fourballs; afternoon foursomes and fourballs.
- **Day three**
  Singles.

Before the match begins the team captains have to decide which players to pair and during practice days he will try out different partnerships. In fourballs it is not uncommon to have two aggressive, attacking players in tandem, going on the theory that at any given hole one or other is likely to make a birdie and quite possibly win the hole. However, some prefer to put a straight, dependable golfer in a fourball partnership alongside a more flamboyant stroke-maker, in the belief that the straight hitter will make a string of pars while his partner contributes less often, but with dramatic effect. The cardinal sin in fourball play is to lose a hole to par as at least one player should be able to match regulation figures for the hole.

# Ryder Cup Results

## 1927
**Result:** USA 9½–GB 2½
**Captains:** Walter Hagen (US), Ted Ray (GB)
**Venue:** Worcester CC, Worcester, Massachusetts

### Foursomes
Ted Ray & Fred Robson lost to Walter Hagen & Johnny Golden (2&1)
George Duncan & Archie Compston lost to Johnny Farrell & Joe Turnesa (8&6)
Arthur Havers & Herbert Jolly lost to Gene Sarazen & Al Watrous (3&2)
Aubrey Boomer & Charles Whitcombe (7&5) beat Leo Diegel & Bill Mehlhorn
### Singles
Archie Compston lost to Bill Mehlhorn (1 hole)
Aubrey Boomer lost to Johnny Farrell (5&4)
Herbert Jolly lost to Johnny Golden (8&7)
Ted Ray lost to Leo Diegel (7&5)
Charles Whitcombe halved with Gene Sarazen
Arthur Havers lost to Walter Hagen (2&1)
Fred Robson lost to Al Watrous (3&2)
George Duncan (1 hole) beat Joe Turnesa

## 1929
**Result:** GB 7–USA 5
**Captains:** Walter Hagen (US), George Duncan (GB)
**Venue:** Moortown GC, Leeds

### Foursomes
Charles Whitcombe & Archie Compston halved with Johnny Farrell & Joe Turnesa
Aubrey Boomer & George Duncan lost to Leo Diegel & Al Espinosa (7&5)
Abe Mitchell & Fred Robson (2&1) beat Gene Sarazen & Ed Dudley
Ernest Whitcombe & Henry Cotton lost to Johnny Golden & Walter Hagen (2 holes)
### Singles
Charles Whitcombe (8&6) beat Johnny Farrell
George Duncan (10&8) beat Walter Hagen
Abe Mitchell lost to Leo Diegel (8&6)
Archie Compston (6&4) beat Gene Sarazen
Aubrey Boomer (4&3) beat Joe Turnesa
Fred Robson lost to Horton Smith (4&2)
Henry Cotton (4&3) beat Al Watrous
Ernest Whitcombe halved with Al Espinosa

## 1931
**Result:** USA 9–GB 3
**Captains:** Walter Hagen (US), Charles Whitcombe (GB)
**Venue:** Scioto Country Club, Columbus, Ohio

### Foursomes
Archie Compston & William Davies lost to Gene Sarazen & Johnny Farrell (8&7)
George Duncan & Arthur Havers lost to Walter Hagen & Densmore Shute (10&9)
Abe Mitchell & Fred Robson (3&1) beat Leo Diegel & Al Espinosa
Syd Easterbrook & Ernest Whitcombe lost to Billy Burke & Wilfred Cox (3&2)
### Singles
Archie Compston lost to Billy Burke (7&6)
Fred Robson lost to Gene Sarazen (7&6)
William Davies (4&3) beat Johnny Farrell
Abe Mitchell lost to Wilfred Cox (3&1)
Charles Whitcombe lost to Walter Hagen (4&3)
Bert Hodson lost to Densmore Shute (8&6)
Ernest Whitcombe lost to Al Espinosa (2&1)
Arthur Havers (4&3) beat Craig Wood

## 1933
**Result:** USA 5½–GB 6½
**Captains:** Walter Hagen (US), JH Taylor (GB)

**Venue:** Southport & Ainsdale GC, Southport

## Foursomes

Gene Sarazen & Walter Hagen halved with Percy Alliss & Charles Whitcombe
Olin Dutra & Densmore Shute lost to Abe Mitchell & Arthur Havers (3&2)
Craig Wood & Paul Runyan lost to William Davies & Syd Easterbrook (one-up)
Ed Dudley & Billy Burke (one-up) lost to Alf Padgham & Alf Perry

## Singles

Gene Sarazen (6&4) beat Alf Padgham
Olin Dutra lost to Abe Mitchell (9&8)
Walter Hagen (2&1) beat Arthur Lacey
Craig Wood (4&3) beat William Davies
Paul Runyan lost to Percy Alliss (2&1)
Leo Diegel lost to Arthur Havers (4&3)
Densmore Shute lost to Syd Easterbrook (one-up)
Horton Smith (2&1) beat Charles Whitcombe

### 1935

**Result:** USA 9 –GB 3
**Captains:** Walter Hagen (US), Charles Whitcombe (GB)
**Venue:** Ridgewood Country Club, Ridgewood, New Jersey

## Foursomes

Alf Perry & Jack Busson lost to Gene Sarazen & Walter Hagen (7&6)
Alf Padgham & Percy Alliss lost to Henry Picard & Johnny Revolta (6&5)

Bill Cox & Edward Jarman lost to Paul Runyan & Horton Smith (9&8)
Charles Whitcombe & Ernest Whitcombe (1 hole) beat Olin Dutra & Ky Laffoon

## Singles

Jack Busson lost to Gene Sarazen (3&2)
Richard Burton lost to Paul Runyan (5&3)
Reg Whitcombe lost to Johnny Revolta (2&1)
Alf Padgham lost to Olin Dutra (4&2)
Percy Alliss (1 hole) beat Craig Wood
Bill Cox halved with Horton Smith
Ernest Whitcombe lost to Henry Picard (3&2)
Alf Perry halved with Sam Parks

### 1937

**Result:** USA 8 –GB 4
**Captains:** Ben Hogan (US), Henry Cotton (GB)
**Venue:** Southport & Ainsdale GC, Southport

## Foursomes

Alf Padgham & Henry Cotton (4&2) beat Ed Dudley & Byron Nelson
Arthur Lacey & Bill Cox (2&1) beat Ralph Guldahl & Tony Manero Charles Whitcombe & Dai Rees halved with Gene Sarazen & Densmore Shute Percy Alliss & Richard Burton (2&1) beat Henry Picard & Johnny Revolta

## Singles

Alf Padgham lost to Ralph Guldahl (8&7)
Sam King halved with Densmore Shute
Dai Rees (3&1) beat Byron Nelson

Henry Cotton (5&3) beat Tony Manero
Percy Alliss lost to Gene Sarazen (1 hole)
Richard Burton lost to Sam Snead (5&4)
Alf Perry lost to Ed Dudley (2&1)
Arthur Lacey lost to Henry Picard (2&1)

### 1947

**Result:** USA 11–GB 1
**Captains:** Ben Hogan (US), Henry Cotton (GB)
**Venue:** Portland Golf Club, Portland, Oregon

## Foursomes

Henry Cotton & Arthur Lees lost to Ed Oliver & Lew Worsham (10&8)
Fred Daly & Charles Ward lost to Sam Snead & Lloyd Mangrum (6&5)
Jimmy Adams & Max Faulkner lost to Ben Hogan & Jimmy Demaret (2 holes)
Dai Rees & Sam King lost to Byron Nelson & Herman Barron (2&1)

## Singles

Fred Daly lost to Dutch Harrison (5&4)
Jimmy Adams lost to Lew Worsham (3&2)
Max Faulkner lost to Lloyd Mangrum (6&5)
Charles Ward lost to Ed Oliver (4&3)
Arthur Lees lost to Byron Nelson (2&1)
Henry Cotton lost to Sam Snead (5&4)
Dai Rees lost to Jimmy Demaret (3&2)
Sam King (4&3) beat Herman Keiser

### 1949

**Result:** USA 7–GB 5
**Captains:** Ben Hogan (US), Charles

Whitcombe (GB)
**Venue:** Ganton Golf Club, Scarborough

## Foursomes

Max Faulkner & Jimmy Adams (2&1) beat Dutch Harrison & Johnny Palmer
Fred Daly & Ken Bousfield (4&2) beat Bob Hamilton & Skip Alexander
Charles Ward & Sam King lost to Jimmy Demaret & Clayton Heafner(4&3)
Richard Burton & Arthur Lees (1 hole) beat Sam Snead & Lloyd Mangrum

## Singles

Max Faulkner lost to Dutch Harrison (8&7)
Jimmy Adams (2&1) beat Johnny Palmer
Charles Ward lost to Sam Snead (6&5)
Dai Rees (6&4) beat Bob Hamilton
Richard Burton lost to Clayton Heafner (3&2)
Sam King lost to Chick Harbert (4&3)
Arthur Lees lost to Jimmy Demaret (7&6)
Fred Daly lost to Lloyd Mangrum (4&3)

### 1951

**Result:** USA 9½–GB 2½
**Captains:** Sam Snead (US), Arthur Lacey (GB)
**Venue:** Pinehurst Country Club, Pinehurst, North Carolina

## Foursomes

Max Faulkner & Dai Rees lost to Clayton Heafner & Jackie Burke (5&3)
Charles Ward & Arthur Lees (2&1) beat Ed Oliver & Henry Ransom

Jimmy Adams & John Panton lost to Sam Snead & Lloyd Mangrum (5&4)
Fred Daly & Ken Bousfield lost to Ben Hogan & Jimmy Demaret (5&4)

## Singles

Jimmy Adams lost to Jack Burke (4&3)
Dai Rees lost to Jimmy Demaret (2 holes)
Fred Daly halved with Clayton Heafner
Harry Weetman lost to Lloyd Mangrum (6&5)
Arthur Lees (2&1) beat Ed Oliver
Charles Ward lost to Ben Hogan (3&2)
John Panton lost to Skip Alexander (8&7)
Max Faulkner lost to Sam Snead (4&3)

### 1953

**Result:** USA 6½–GB 5½
**Captains:** Lloyd Mangrum (US), Henry Cotton (GB)
**Venue:** Wentworth Golf Club, Virginia Water

## Foursomes

Harry Weetman & Percy Alliss lost to Dave Douglas & Ed Oliver (2&1)
Eric Brown & John Panton lost to Lloyd Mangrum & Sam Snead (8&7)
Jimmy Adams & Bernard Hunt lost to Ted Kroll & Jack Burke (7&5)
Fred Daly & Harry Bradshaw (1 hole) beat Walter Burkemo & Cary Middlecoff

## Singles

Dai Rees lost to Jack Burke (2&1)
Fred Daly (9&7) beat Ted Kroll
Eric Brown (2 holes) beat Lloyd Mangrum

Harry Weetman lost to Sam Snead (1 hole)
Max Faulkner lost to Cary Middlecoff (3&1)
Peter Alliss lost to Joe Turnesa (1 hole)
Bernard Hunt halved with Dave Douglas
Harry Bradshaw (3&2) beat Fred Haas

### 1955

**Result:** USA 8–GB 4
**Captains:** Chick Harbert (US), Dai Rees (GB)
**Venue:** Thunderbird G&CC, Palm Springs, California

## Foursomes

John Fallon & John Jacobs (1 hole) beat Chandler Harper & Jerry Barber
Eric Brown & Syd Scott lost to Doug Ford & Ted Kroll (5&4)
Arthur Lees & Harry Weetman lost to Jack Burke & Tommy Bolt (1 hole)
Harry Bradshaw & Dai Rees lost to Sam Snead & Cary Middlecoff (3&2)

## Singles

Christy O'Connor lost to Tommy Bolt (4&2)
Syd Scott lost to Chick Harbert (3&2)
John Jacobs (1 hole) beat Cary Middlecoff
Dai Rees lost to Sam Snead (3&1)
Arthur Lees (3&2) beat Marty Furgol
Eric Brown (3&2) beat Jerry Barber
Harry Bradshaw lost to Jack Burke (3&2)
Harry Weetman lost to Doug Ford (3&2)

### 1957

**Result:** GB 7½–USA 4½

**Captains:** Jack Burke (US), Dai Rees (GB)
**Venue:** Lindrick GC, Yorkshire

## Foursomes

Peter Alliss & Bernard Hunt lost to Doug Ford & Dow Finsterwald (2&1)
Ken Bousfield & Dai Rees (3&2) beat Art Wall & Fred Hawkins
Max Faulkner & Harry Weetman lost to Ted Kroll & Jack Burke (4&3)
Christy O'Connor & Eric Brown lost to Dick Mayer & Tommy Bolt (7&5)

## Singles

Eric Brown (4&3) beat Tommy Bolt
Peter Mills (5&3) beat Jack Burke
Peter Alliss lost to Fred Hawkins (2&1)
Ken Bousfield (4&3) beat Lionel Herbert
Dai Rees (7&6) beat Ed Furgol
Bernard Hunt (6&5) beat Doug Ford
Christy O'Connor (7&6) beat Dow Finsterwald
Harry Bradshaw halved with Dick Mayer

## 1959

**Result:** USA 8½–GB 3½
**Captains:** Sam Snead (US), Dai Rees (GB)
**Venue:** Eldorado CC, Palm Desert, California

## Foursomes

Bernard Hunt & Eric Brown lost to Bob Rosburg & Mike Souchak (5&4)
Dai Rees & Ken Bousfield lost to Julius Boros & Dow Finsterwald (2 holes)
Christy O'Connor & Peter Alliss (3&2) beat Art Wall & Doug Ford

Harry Weetman & Dave Thomas halved with Sam Snead & Cary Middlecoff

## Singles

Norman Drew halved with Doug Ford
Ken Bousfield lost to Mike Souchak (3&2)
Harry Weetman lost to Bob Rosburg (6&5)
Dave Thomas lost to Sam Snead (6&5)
Christy O'Connor lost to Art Wall (7&6)
Dai Rees lost to Dow Finsterwald (1 hole)
Peter Alliss halved with Jay Hebert
Eric Brown (4&3) beat Cary Middlecoff

## 1961

**Result:** USA 14½–GB 9½
**Captains:** Jerry Barber (US), Dai Rees (GB)
**Venue:** Royal Lytham & St Annes, St Annes

## Foursomes: Morning

Christy O'Connor & Peter Alliss (4&3) beat Doug Ford & Gene Littler
John Panton & Bernard Hunt lost to Art Wall & Jay Hebert (4&3)
Dai Rees & Ken Bousfield lost to Billy Casper & Arnold Palmer (2&1)
Tom Haliburton & Neil Coles lost to Bill Collins & Mike Souchak (1 hole)

## Foursomes: Afternoon

Christy O'Connor & Peter Alliss lost to Art Wall & Jay Hebert (1 hole)
John Panton & Bernard Hunt lost to Billy Casper & Arnold Palmer (5&4)
Dai Rees & Ken Bousfield (2&1) beat Bill Collins & Mike Souchak
Tom Haliburton & Neil Coles lost to Jerry Barber & Dow Finsterwald (1 hole)

## Singles: Morning

Harry Weetman lost to Doug Ford (1 hole)
Ralph Moffitt lost to Mike Souchak (5&4)
Peter Alliss halved with Arnold Palmer
Ken Bousfield lost to Billy Casper (5&3)
Dai Rees (2&1) beat Jay Hebert
Neil Coles halved with Gene Littler
Bernard Hunt (5&4) beat Jerry Barber
Christy O'Connor lost to Dow Finsterwald (2&1)

## Singles: Afternoon

Harry Weetman lost to Art Wall (1 hole)
Peter Alliss (3&2) beat Bill Collins
Bernard Hunt lost to Mike Souchak (2&1)
Ted Haliburton lost to Arnold Palmer (2&1)
Dai Rees (4&3) beat Doug Ford
Ken Bousfield (1 hole) beat Jerry Barber
Neil Coles (1 hole) beat Dow Finsterwald
Christy O'Connor halved with Gene Littler

## 1963

**Result:** USA 23–GB&I 9
**Captains:** Arnold Palmer (US), John Fallon (GB)
**Venue:** East Lake CC, Atlanta, Georgia

## Foursomes: Morning

Brian Huggett & George Will (3&2) beat Arnold Palmer & Johnny Pott
Peter Alliss & Christy O'Connor lost to Billy Casper & Dave Ragan (1 hole)
Neil Coles & Bernard Hunt halved with Julius Boros & Tony Lema
Dave Thomas & Harry Weetman halved with Gene Littler & Dow Finsterwald

## Foursomes: Afternoon

Dave Thomas & Harry Weetman lost to Billy Maxwell & Bob Goalby (4&3)

Brian Huggett & George Will lost to Arnold Palmer & Billy Casper (5&4)

Neil Coles & Geoffrey Hunt (2&1) beat Gene Littler & Dow Finsterwald

Tom Haliburton & Bernard Hunt lost to Julius Boros & Tony Lema (1 hole)

### Fourballs: Morning

Brian Huggett & Dave Thomas lost to Arnold Palmer & Dow Finsterwald (5&4)

Peter Alliss & Bernard Hunt halved with Gene Littler & Julius Boros

Harry Weetman & George Will lost to Billy Casper & Billy Maxwell (3&2)

Neil Coles & Christy O'Connor lost to Bob Goalby & Dave Ragan (1 hole)

### Fourballs: Afternoon

Neil Coles & Christy O'Connor lost to Arnold Palmer & Dow Finsterwald (3&2)

Peter Alliss & Bernard Hunt lost to Tony Lema & Johnny Pott (1 hole)

Tom Haliburton & Geoffrey Hunt lost to Bill Casper & Billy Maxwell (2&1)

Brian Huggett & Dave Thomas halved with Bob Goalby & Dave Ragan

### Singles: Morning

Geoffrey Hunt lost to Tony Lema (5&3)

Brian Huggett (3&1) beat Johnny Pott

Peter Alliss (1 hole) beat Arnold Palmer

Neil Coles halved with Billy Casper

Dave Thomas lost to Bob Goalby (3&2)

Christy O'Connor lost to Gene Littler (1 hole)

Harry Weetman (1 hole) beat Julius Boros

Bernard Hunt (2 holes) beat Dow Finsterwald

### Singles: Afternoon

George Will lost to Arnold Palmer (3&2)

Neil Coles lost to Dave Ragan (2&1)

Peter Alliss halved with Tony Lema

Tom Haliburton lost to Gene Littler (6&5)

Harry Weetman lost to Julius Boros (2&1)

Christy O'Connor lost to Billy Maxwell (2&1)

Dave Thomas lost to Dow Finsterwald (4&3)

Bernard Hunt lost to Bob Goalby (2&1)

## 1965

**Result:** USA 19½–GB 12½

**Captains:** Byron Nelson (US), Harry Weetman (GB)

**Venue:** Royal Birkdale Golf Club, Southport

### Foursomes: Morning

Lionel Platts & Peter Butler lost to Julius Boros & Tony Lema (1 hole)

Dave Thomas & George Will (6&5) beat Arnold Palmer & Dave Marr

Bernard Hunt & Neil Coles lost to Billy Casper & Gene Littler (2&1)

Peter Alliss & Christy O'Connor (5&4) beat Ken Venturi & Don January

### Foursomes: Afternoon

Dave Thomas & George Will lost to Arnold Palmer & Dave Marr (6&5)

Peter Alliss & Christy O'Connor (2&1) beat Billy Casper & Gene Littler

Jimmy Martin & Jimmy Hitchcock lost to Julius Boros & Tony Lema (5&4)

Bernard Hunt & Neil Coles (3&2) beat Ken Venturi & Don January

### Fourballs: Morning

Dave Thomas & George Will lost to Don January & Tommy Jacobs (1 hole)

Lionel Platts & Peter Butler halved with Billy Casper & Gene Littler

Peter Alliss & Christy O'Connor lost to Arnold Palmer & Dave Marr (6&4)

Bernard Hunt & Neil Coles (1 hole) beat Julius Boros & Tony Lema

### Fourballs: Afternoon

Peter Alliss & Christy O'Connor (2 holes) beat Arnold Palmer & Dave Marr

Dave Thomas & George Will lost to Don January & Tommy Jacobs (1 hole)

Lionel Platts & Peter Butler halved with Billy Casper & Gene Littler

Bernard Hunt & Neil Coles lost to Ken Venturi & Tony Lema (1 hole)

### Singles: Morning

Jimmy Hitchcock lost Arnold Palmer (3&2)

Lionel Platts lost to Julius Boros (4&2)

Peter Butler lost to Tony Lema (1 hole)

Neil Coles lost to Dave Marr (2 holes)

Bernard Hunt (2 holes) beat Gene Littler

Dave Thomas lost to Tommy Jacobs (2&1)

Peter Alliss (1 hole) beat Billy Casper

George Will halved with Don January

### Singles: Afternoon

Christy O'Connor lost to Tony Lema (6&4)

Jimmy Hitchcock lost to Julius Boros (2&1)

Peter Butler lost to Arnold Palmer (2 holes)

Peter Alliss (3&1) beat Ken Venturi

Neil Coles (3&2) beat Billy Casper

George Will lost to Gene Littler (2&1)

Bernard Hunt lost to Dave Marr (1 hole)
Lionel Platts (1 hole) beat Tommy Jacobs

## 1967
**Result:** USA 23½–GB 8½
**Captains:** Ben Hogan (US), Dai Rees (GB)
**Venue:** Champions Golf Club, Houston, Texas

### Foursomes: Morning
Brian Huggett & George Will halved with Billy Casper & Julius Boros
Peter Alliss & Christy O'Connor lost to Arnold Palmer & Gardner Dickinson (2&1)
Tony Jacklin & Dave Thomas (4&3) beat Doug Sanders & Gay Brewer
Bernard Hunt & Neil Coles lost to Bobby Nichols & Johnny Pott (6&5)
### Foursomes: Afternoon
Brian Huggett & George Will lost to Billy Casper & Julius Boros (1 hole)
Malcolm Gregson & Hugh Boyle lost to Gardner Dickinson & Arnold Palmer (5&4)
Tony Jacklin & Dave Thomas (3&2) beat Gene Littler & Al Geiberger
Peter Alliss & Christy O'Connor lost to Bobby Nichols & Johnny Pott (2&1)
### Fourballs: Morning
Peter Alliss & Christy O'Connor lost to Billy Casper & Gay Brewer (3&2)
Bernard Hunt & Neil Coles lost to Bobby Nichols & Johnny Pott (1 hole)
Tony Jacklin & Dave Thomas lost to Gene Littler & Al Geiberger (1 hole)
Brian Huggett & George Will lost to Gardner Dickinson & Doug Sanders (3&2)
### Fourballs: Afternoon
Bernard Hunt & Neil Coles lost to Billy Casper & Gay Brewer (5&3)
Peter Alliss & Malcolm Gregson lost to Gardner Dickinson & Doug Sanders (3&2)
George Will & Hugh Boyle lost to Arnold Palmer & Julius Boros (1 hole)
Tony Jacklin & Dave Thomas halved with Gene Littler & Al Geiberger
### Singles: Morning
Hugh Boyle lost to Gay Brewer (4&3)
Peter Alliss lost to Billy Casper (2&1)
Tony Jacklin lost to Arnold Palmer (3&2)
Brian Huggett (1 hole) beat Julius Boros
Neil Coles lost to Doug Sanders (2&1)
Malcolm Gregson lost to Al Geiberger (4&2)
Dave Thomas halved with Gene Littler
Bernard Hunt halved with Bobby Nichols
### Singles: Afternoon
Brian Huggett lost to Arnold Palmer (5&3)
Peter Alliss (2&1) beat Gay Brewer
Tony Jacklin lost to Gardner Dickinson (3&2)
Christy O'Connor lost to Bobby Nichols (3&2)
George Will lost to Johnny Pott (3&1)
Malcolm Gregson lost to Al Geiberger (2&1)
Bernard Hunt halved with Julius Boros
Neil Coles (2&1) beat Doug Sanders

## 1969
**Result:** USA 16–GB 16
**Captains:** Sam Snead (US), Eric Brown (GB)
**Venue:** Royal Birkdale Golf Club, Southport

### Foursomes: Morning
Neil Coles & Brian Huggett (3&2) beat Miller Barber & Ray Floyd
Bernard Gallacher & Maurice Bembridge (2&1) beat Lee Trevino & Ken Still
Tony Jacklin & Peter Townsend (3&1) beat Dave Hill & Tommy Aaron
Christy O'Connor & Peter Alliss halved with Billy Casper & Frank Beard
### Foursomes: Afternoon
Neil Coles & Brian Huggett lost to Dave Hill & Tommy Aaron (1 hole)
Bernard Gallacher & Maurice Bembridge lost to Lee Trevino & Gene Littler (1 hole)
Tony Jacklin & Peter Townsend (1 hole) beat Billy Casper & Frank Beard
Peter Butler & Bernard Hunt lost to Jack Nicklaus & Dan Sikes (1 hole)
### Fourballs: Morning
Christy O'Connor & Peter Townsend (1 hole) beat Dave Hill & Dale Douglass
Brian Huggett & Alex Caygill halved with Ray Floyd & Miller Barber
Brian Barnes & Peter Alliss lost to Lee Trevino & Gene Littler (1 hole)
Tony Jacklin & Neil Coles (1 hole) beat Jack Nicklaus & Dan Sikes
### Fourballs: Afternoon
Peter Butler & Peter Townsend lost to Billy Casper & Frank Beard (2 holes)
Brian Huggett & Bernard Gallacher lost to Dave Hill & Ken Still (2&1)
Maurice Bembridge & Bernard Hunt

halved with Tommy Aaron & Ray Floyd
Tony Jacklin & Neil Coles halved with Lee Trevino & Miller Barber

### Singles: Morning

Peter Alliss lost to Lee Trevino (2&1)
Peter Townsend lost to Dave Hill (5&4)
Neil Coles (1 hole) beat Tommy Aaron
Brian Barnes lost to Billy Casper (1 hole)
Christy O'Connor (5&4) beat Frank Beard
Maurice Bembridge (1 hole) beat Ken Still
Peter Butler (1 hole) beat Ray Floyd
Tony Jacklin (4&3) beat Jack Nicklaus

### Singles: Afternoon

Brian Barnes lost to Dave Hill (4&2)
Bernard Gallacher (4&3) beat Lee Trevino
Maurice Bembridge lost to Miller Barber (7&6)
Peter Butler (3&2) beat Dale Douglass
Neil Coles lost to Dan Sikes (4&3)
Christy O'Connor lost to Gene Littler (2&1)
Brian Huggett halved with Billy Casper
Tony Jacklin halved with Jack Nicklaus

## 1971

**Result:** USA 9½–GB 2½
**Captains:** Walter Hagen (US), Ted Ray (GB)
**Venue:** Worcester CC, Worcester, Massachusetts

### Foursomes: Morning

Neil Coles & Christy O'Connor (2&1) beat Billy Casper & Miller Barber
Peter Townsend & Peter Oosterhuis lost to Arnold Palmer & Gardner

Dickinson (1 hole)
Brian Huggett & Tony Jacklin (3&2) beat Jack Nicklaus & Dave Stockton
Maurice Bembridge & Peter Butler (1 hole) beat Charles Coody & Frank Beard

### Foursomes: Afternoon

Harry Bannerman & Bernard Gallacher (2&1) beat Billy Casper & Miller Barber
Peter Townsend & Peter Oosterhuis lost to Arnold Palmer & Gardner Dickinson (1 hole)
Brian Huggett & Tony Jacklin halved with Lee Trevino & Mason Rudolph
Maurice Bembridge & Peter Butler lost to Jack Nicklaus & JC Snead (5&3)

### Fourballs: Morning

Christy O'Connor & Brian Barnes lost to Lee Trevino & Mason Rudolph (2&1)
Neil Coles & John Garner lost to Frank Beard & JC Snead (2&1)
Peter Oosterhuis & Bernard Gallacher lost to Arnold Palmer & Gardner Dickinson (5&4)
Peter Townsend & Harry Bannerman lost to Jack Nicklaus & Gene Littler (2&1)

### Fourballs: Afternoon

Bernard Gallacher & Peter Oosterhuis (1 hole) beat Lee Trevino & Billy Casper
Tony Jacklin & Brian Huggett lost to Gene Littler & JC Snead (2&1)
Peter Townsend & Harry Bannerman lost to Arnold Palmer & Jack Nicklaus (1 hole)
Neil Coles & Christy O'Connor halved with Charles Coody & Frank Beard

### Singles: Morning

Tony Jacklin lost to Lee Trevino (1 hole)

Bernard Gallacher halved with Dave Stockton
Brian Barnes (1 hole) beat Mason Rudolph
Peter Oosterhuis (4&3) beat Gene Littler
Peter Townsend lost to Jack Nicklaus (3&2)
Christy O'Connor lost to Gardner Dickinson (5&4)
Harry Bannerman halved with Arnold Palmer
Neil Coles halved with Frank Beard

### Singles: Afternoon

Brian Huggett lost to Lee Trevino (7&6)
Tony Jacklin lost to JC Snead (1 hole)
Brian Barnes (2&1) beat Miller Barber
Peter Townsend lost to Dave Stockton (1 hole)
Bernard Gallacher (2&1) beat Charles Coody
Neil Coles lost to Jack Nicklaus (5&3)
Peter Oosterhuis (3&2) beat Arnold Palmer
Harry Bannerman (2&1) beat Gardner Dickinson

## 1973

**Result:** USA 19–GB&I 13
**Captains:** Jack Burke (US), Bernard Hunt (GB&I)
**Venue:** Muirfield, East Lothian, Scotland

### Foursomes: Morning

Brian Barnes & Bernard Gallacher (1 hole) beat Lee Trevino & Billy Casper
Christy O'Connor & Neil Coles (3&2) beat Tom Weiskopf & JC Snead

Tony Jacklin & Peter Oosterhuis halved with Chi Chi Rodriguez & Lou Graham

Maurice Bembridge & Eddie Polland lost to Jack Nicklaus & Arnold Palmer (6&5)

**Fourballs: Afternoon**

Brian Barnes & Bernard Gallacher (5&4) beat Tommy Aaron & Gay Brewer

Maurice Bembridge & Brian Huggett (3&1) beat Arnold Palmer & Jack Nicklaus

Tony Jacklin & Peter Oosterhuis (3&1) beat Tom Weiskopf & Billy Casper

Christy O'Connor & Neil Coles lost to Lee Trevino & Homero Blancas (2&1)

**Foursomes: Morning**

Brian Barnes & Peter Butler lost to Jack Nicklaus & Tom Weiskopf (1 hole)

Peter Oosterhuis & Tony Jacklin (2 holes) beat Arnold Palmer & Dale Hill

Maurice Bembridge & Brian Huggett (5&4) beat Chi Chi Rodriguez & Lou Graham

Neil Coles & Christy O'Connor lost to Lee Trevino & Billy Casper (2&1)

**Fourballs: Afternoon**

Brian Barnes & Peter Butler lost to JC Snead & Arnold Palmer (2 holes)

Tony Jacklin & Peter Oosterhuis lost to Gay Brewer & Billy Casper (3&2)

Clive Clark & Eddie Polland lost to Jack Nicklaus & Tom Weiskopf (3&2)

Maurice Bembridge & Brian Huggett halved with Lee Trevino & Homero Blancas

**Singles: Morning**

Brian Barnes lost to Billy Casper (2&1)

Bernard Gallacher lost to Tom Weiskopf (3&1)

Peter Butler lost to Homero Blancas (5&4)

Tony Jacklin (3&1) beat Tommy Aaron

Neil Coles halved with Gay Brewer

Christy O'Connor lost to JC Snead (1 hole)

Maurice Bembridge halved with Jack Nicklaus

Peter Oosterhuis halved with Lee Trevino

**Singles: Afternoon**

Brian Huggett (4&2) beat Homero Blancas

Brian Barnes lost to JC Snead (3&1)

Bernard Gallacher lost to Gay Brewer (6&5)

Tony Jacklin lost to Billy Casper (2&1)

Neil Coles lost to Lee Trevino (6&5)

Christy O'Connor halved with Tom Weiskopf

Maurice Bembridge lost to Jack Nicklaus (2 holes)

Peter Oosterhuis (4&2) beat Arnold Palmer

## 1975

**Result:** USA 21–GB&I 11

**Captains:** Arnold Palmer (US), Bernard Hunt (GB&I)

**Venue:** Laurel Valley Golf Club, Ligonier, Pennsylvania

**Foursomes: Morning**

Brian Barnes & Bernard Gallacher lost to Jack Nicklaus & Tom Weiskopf (5&4)

Norman Wood & Maurice Bembridge lost to Gene Littler & Hale Irwin (4&3)

Tony Jacklin & Peter Oosterhuis lost to Al Geiberger & Johnny Miller (3&1)

Tommy Horton & John O'Leary lost to Lee Trevino & JC Snead (2&1)

**Fourballs: Afternoon**

Peter Oosterhuis & Tony Jacklin (2&1) beat Billy Casper & Ray Floyd

Eamonn Darcy & Christy O'Connor Jr lost to Tom Weiskopf & Lou Graham (3&2)

Brian Barnes & Bernard Gallacher halved with Jack Nicklaus & Bob Murphy

Tommy Horton & John O'Leary lost to Lee Trevino & Hale Irwin (2&1)

**Fourballs: Morning**

Peter Oosterhuis & Tony Jacklin halved with Billy Casper & Johnny Miller

Tommy Horton & Norman Wood lost to Jack Nicklaus & JC Snead (4&2)

Brian Barnes & Bernard Gallacher lost to Gene Littler & Lou Graham (5&3)

Eamonn Darcy & Guy Hunt halved with Al Geiberger & Ray Floyd

**Foursomes: Afternoon**

Tony Jacklin & Brian Barnes (3&2) beat Lee Trevino & Bob Murphy

Christy O'Connor Jr & John O'Leary lost to Tom Weiskopf & Johnny Miller (5&3)

Peter Oosterhuis & Maurice Bembridge lost to Hale Irwin & Billy Casper (3&2)

Eamonn Darcy & Guy Hunt lost to Al Geiberger & Lou Graham (3&2)

**Singles: Morning**

Tony Jacklin lost to Bob Murphy (2&1)

Peter Oosterhuis (2 holes) beat Johnny Miller

Bernard Gallacher halved with Lee Trevino

Tommy Horton halved with Hale Irwin

Brian Huggett lost to Gene Littler (4&2)

Eamonn Darcy lost to Billy Casper (3&2)

Guy Hunt lost to Tom Weiskopf (5&3)
Brian Barnes (4&2) beat Jack Nicklaus
**Singles: Afternoon**
Tony Jacklin lost to Ray Floyd (1 hole)
Peter Oosterhuis (3&2) beat JC Snead
Bernard Gallacher halved with Al
Geiberger
Tommy Horton (2&1) beat Lou Graham
John O'Leary lost to Hale Irwin (2&1)
Maurice Bembridge lost to Bob Murphy
(2&1)
Norman Wood (2&1) beat Lee Trevino
Brian Barnes (2&1) beat Jack Nicklaus

## 1977
**Result:** USA 12½–GB&I 7½
**Captains:** Dow Finsterwald (US), Brian
Huggett (GB&I)
**Venue:** Royal Lytham & St Annes, St
Annes

### Foursomes
Bernard Gallacher & Brian Barnes lost to
Lanny Wadkins & Hale Irwin (3&1)
Neil Coles & Peter Dawson lost to Dave
Stockton & Jerry McGee (1 hole)
Nick Faldo & Peter Oosterhuis (2&1) beat
Ray Floyd & Lou Graham
Eamonn Darcy & Tony Jacklin halved
with Ed Sneed & Don January
Tommy Horton & Mark James lost to Jack
Nicklaus & Tom Watson (5&4)
### Fourballs
Brian Barnes & Tommy Horton lost to
Tom Watson & Hubert Green (5&4)
Neil Coles & Peter Dawson lost to Ed

Sneed & Lanny Wadkins (5&3)
Nick Faldo & Peter Oosterhuis (3&1) beat
Jack Nicklaus & Ray Floyd
Tony Jacklin & Eamonn Darcy lost to
Dave Hill & Dave Stockton (5&3)
Mark James & Ken Brown lost to Hale
Irwin & Lou Graham (1 hole)
### Singles
Howard Clark lost to Lanny Wadkins
(4&3)
Neil Coles lost to Lou Graham (5&3)
Peter Dawson (5&4) beat Don January
Brian Barnes (1 hole) beat Hale Irwin
Tommy Horton lost to Dave Hill (5&4)
Bernard Gallacher (1 hole) beat Jack
Nicklaus
Eamonn Darcy lost to Hubert Green (1
hole)
Mark James lost to Ray Floyd (2&1)
Nick Faldo (1 hole) beat Tom Watson
Peter Oosterhuis (2 holes) beat Jerry
McGee

## 1979
**Result:** USA 17–Europe 11
**Captains:** Billy Casper (US), John Jacobs
(Europe)
**Venue:** The Greenbrier, White Sulphur
Springs, West Virginia

### Fourballs: Morning
Antonio Garrido & Seve Ballesteros lost
to Lanny Wadkins & Larry Nelson (2&1)
Ken Brown & Mark James lost to Lee
Trevino & Fuzzy Zoeller (3&2)
Peter Oosterhuis & Nick Faldo lost to

Andy Bean & Lee Elder (2&1)
Bernard Gallacher & Brian Barnes (2&1)
beat Hale Irwin & John Mahaffey
### Foursomes: Afternoon
Ken Brown & Des Smyth lost to Hale
Irwin & Tom Kite (7&6)
Seve Ballesteros & Antonio Garrido (3&2)
beat Fuzzy Zoeller & Hubert Green
Sandy Lyle & Tony Jacklin halved with Lee
Trevino & Gil Morgan
Bernard Gallacher & Brian Barnes lost to
Lanny Wadkins & Larry Nelson (4&3)
### Foursomes: Morning
Tony Jacklin & Sandy Lyle (5&4) beat Lee
Elder & John Mahaffey
Nick Faldo & Peter Oosterhuis (6&5) beat
Andy Bean & Tom Kite
Bernard Gallacher & Brian Barnes (2&1)
beat Fuzzy Zoeller & Mark Hayes
Seve Ballesteros & Antonio Garrido lost
to Lanny Wadkins & Larry Nelson (3&2)
### Fourballs: Afternoon
Seve Ballesteros & Antonio Garrido lost
to Lanny Wadkins & Larry Nelson (5&4)
Tony Jacklin & Sandy Lyle lost to Hale
Irwin & Tom Kite (1 hole)
Bernard Gallacher & Brian Barnes (3&2)
beat Lee Trevino & Fuzzy Zoeller
Nick Faldo & Peter Oosterhuis (1 hole)
beat Lee Elder & Mark Hayes
### Singles: Morning
Bernard Gallacher (3&2) beat Lanny
Wadkins
Seve Ballesteros lost to Larry Nelson
(3&2)
Tony Jacklin lost to Tom Kite (1 hole)

Antonio Garrido lost to Mark Hayes (1 hole)
Michael King lost to Andy Bean (4&3)
Brian Barnes lost to John Mahaffey (1 hole)

### Singles: Afternoon
Nick Faldo (3&2) beat Lee Elder
Des Smyth lost to Hale Irwin (5&3)
Peter Oosterhuis lost to Hubert Green (2 holes)
Ken Brown (1 hole) beat Fuzzy Zoeller
Sandy Lyle lost to Lee Trevino (2&1)
Mark James injured, halved with Gil Morgan (match not played)

### 1981
**Result:** USA 18½ Europe 9 ½
**Captains:** Dave Marr (US), John Jacobs (Europe)
**Venue:** Walton Heath GC, Surrey

### Foursomes: Morning
Bernhard Langer & Manuel Pinero lost to Lee Trevino & Larry Nelson (1 hole)
Sandy Lyle & Mark James (2&1) beat Bill Rogers & Bruce Lietzke
Bernard Gallacher & Des Smyth (3&2) beat Hale Irwin & Ray Floyd
Peter Oosterhuis & Nick Faldo lost to Tom Watson & Jack Nicklaus (4&3)

### Fourballs: Afternoon
Sam Torrance & Howard Clark halved with Tom Kite & Johnny Miller
Sandy Lyle & Mark James (3&2) beat Ben Crenshaw & Jerry Pate
Des Smyth & Jose Maria Canizares (6&5)

beat Bill Rogers & Bruce Lietzke
Bernard Gallacher & Eamonn Darcy lost to Hale Irwin & Ray Floyd (2&1)

### Fourballs: Morning
Nick Faldo & Sam Torrance lost to Lee Trevino & Jerry Pate (7&5)
Sandy Lyle & Mark James lost to Larry Nelson & Tom Kite (1 hole)
Bernhard Langer & Manuel Pinero (2&1) beat Ray Floyd & Hale Irwin
JM Canizares & Des Smyth lost to Jack Nicklaus & Tom Watson (3&2)

### Foursomes: Afternoon
Peter Oosterhuis & Sam Torrance lost to Lee Trevino & Jerry Pate (2&1)
Bernhard Langer & Manuel Pinero lost to Jack Nicklaus & Tom Watson (3&2)
Sandy Lyle & Mark James lost to Bill Rogers & Ray Floyd (3&2)
Des Smyth & Bernard Gallacher lost to Tom Kite & Larry Nelson (3&2)

### Singles
Sam Torrance lost to Lee Trevino (5&3)
Sandy Lyle lost to Tom Kite (3&2)
Bernard Gallacher halved with Bill Rogers
Mark James lost to Larry Nelson (2 holes)
Des Smyth lost to Ben Crenshaw (6&4)
Bernhard Langer halved with Bruce Lietzke
Manuel Pinero (4&2) beat Jerry Pate
JM Canizares lost to Hale Irwin (1 hole)
Nick Faldo (2&1) beat Johnny Miller
Howard Clark (4&3) beat Tom Watson
Peter Oosterhuis lost to Ray Floyd (1 hole)
Eamonn Darcy lost to Jack Nicklaus (5&3)

### 1983
**Result:** USA 14½–Europe 13½
**Captains:** Jack Nicklaus (US), Tony Jacklin (Europe)
**Venue:** PGA National Golf Club, Palm Beach Gardens, Florida

### Foursomes: Morning
Bernard Gallacher & Sandy Lyle lost to Tom Watson & Ben Crenshaw (5&4)
Nick Faldo & Bernhard Langer (4&2) beat Lanny Wadkins & Craig Stadler
JM Canizares & Sam Torrance (4&3) beat Ray Floyd & Bob Gilder
Seve Ballesteros & Paul Way lost to Tom Kite & Calvin Peete (2&1)

### Fourballs: Afternoon
Brian Waites & Ken Brown (2&1) beat Gil Morgan & Fuzzy Zoeller
Nick Faldo & Bernhard Langer lost to Tom Watson & Jay Haas (2&1)
Seve Ballesteros & Paul Way (1 hole) beat Ray Floyd & Curtis Strange
Sam Torrance & Ian Woosnam halved with Ben Crenshaw & Calvin Peete

### Fourballs: Morning
Brian Waites & Ken Brown lost to Lanny Wadkins & Craig Stadler (1 hole)
Nick Faldo & Bernhard Langer (4&2) beat Ben Crenshaw & Calvin Peete
Seve Ballesteros & Paul Way halved with Gil Morgan & Jay Haas
Sam Torrance & Ian Woosnam lost to Tom Watson & Bob Gilder (5&4)

### Foursomes: Afternoon
Nick Faldo & Bernhard Langer (3&2) beat

Tom Kite & Ray Floyd
Sam Torrance & JM Canizares lost to Gil
Morgan & Lanny Wadkins (7&5)
Seve Ballesteros & Paul Way (2&1) beat
Tom Watson & Bob Gilder
Brian Waites & Ken Brown lost to Jay
Haas & Curtis Strange (3&2)
## Singles
Seve Ballesteros halved with Fuzzy Zoeller
Nick Faldo (2&1) beat Jay Haas
Bernhard Langer (2 holes) beat Gil
Morgan
Gordon J Brand lost to Bob Gilder (2
holes)
Sandy Lyle lost to Ben Crenshaw (3&1)
Brian Waites lost to Calvin Peete (1 hole)
Paul Way (2&1) beat Curtis Strange
Sam Torrance halved with Tom Kite
Ian Woosnam lost to Craig Stadler (3&2)
JM Canizares halved with Lanny Wadkins
(Good old Lanny)
Ken Brown (4&3) beat Ray Floyd
Bernard Gallacher lost to Tom Watson
(2&1)

## 1985
**Result:** Europe 16½–USA 11½
**Captains:** Lee Trevino (US), Tony Jacklin
(Europe)
**Venue:** The Belfry G&CC, Sutton
Coldfield

## Foursomes: Morning
Seve Ballesteros & Manuel Pinero (2&1)
beat Curtis Strange & Mark O'Meara
Bernhard Langer & Nick Faldo lost to

Calvin Peete & Tom Kite (3&2)
Sandy Lyle & Ken Brown lost to Lanny
Wadkins & Ray Floyd (4&3)
Howard Clark & Sam Torrance lost to
Craig Stadler & Hal Sutton (3&2)
## Fourballs: Afternoon
Paul Way & Ian Woosnam (1 hole) beat
Fuzzy Zoeller & Hubert Green
Seve Ballesteros & Manuel Pinero (2&1)
beat Andy North & Peter Jacobsen
Bernhard Langer & JM Canizares halved
with Craig Stadler & Hal Sutton
Sam Torrance & Howard Clark lost to Ray
Floyd & Lanny Wadkins (1 hole)
## Fourballs: Morning
Sam Torrance & Howard Clark (2&1)
beat Tom Kite & Andy North
Paul Way & Ian Woosnam (4&3) beat
Hubert Green & Fuzzy Zoeller
Seve Ballesteros & Manuel Pinero lost to
Mark O'Meara & Lanny Wadkins (3&2)
Bernhard Langer & Sandy Lyle halved
with Craig Stadler & Curtis Strange
## Foursomes: Afternoon
JM Canizares & Jose Rivero (4&3) beat
Tom Kite & Calvin Peete
Seve Ballesteros & Manuel Pinero (5&4)
beat Craig Stadler & Hal Sutton
Paul Way & Ian Woosnam lost to Curtis
Strange & Peter Jacobsen (4&2)
Bernhard Langer & Ken Brown (3&2)
beat Ray Floyd & Lanny Wadkins
## Singles
Manuel Pinero (3&1) beat Lanny
Wadkins
Ian Woosnam lost to Craig Stadler (2&1)

Paul Way (2 holes) beat Ray Floyd
Seve Ballesteros halved with Tom Kite
Sandy Lyle (3&2) beat Peter Jacobsen
Bernhard Langer (5&4) beat Hal Sutton
Sam Torrance (1 hole) beat Andy North
Howard Clark (1 hole) beat Mark
O'Meara
Jose Rivero lost to Calvin Peete (1 hole)
Nick Faldo lost to Hubert Green (3&1)
JM Canizares (2 holes) beat Fuzzy Zoeller
Ken Brown beat Curtis Strange (4&2)

## 1987
**Result:** Europe 15–USA 13
**Captains:** Jack Nicklaus (US), Tony
Jacklin (Europe)
**Venue:** Muirfield Village, Columbus,
Ohio

## Foursomes: Morning
Sam Torrance & Howard Clark lost to
Curtis Strange & Tom Kite (4&2)
Ken Brown & Bernhard Langer lost to Hal
Sutton & Dan Pohl (2&1)
Nick Faldo & Ian Woosnam (2 holes) beat
Lanny Wadkins & Larry Mize
Seve Ballesteros & José Maria Olazábal (1
hole) beat Larry Nelson & Payne Stewart
## Fourballs: Afternoon
Gordon Brand Jr & Jose Rivero (3&2)
beat Ben Crenshaw & Scott Simpson
Sandy Lyle & Bernhard Langer (1 hole)
beat Andy Bean & Mark Calcavecchia
Nick Faldo & Ian Woosnam (2&1) beat
Hal Sutton & Dan Pohl
Seve Ballesteros & JM Olazábal (2&1)

beat Curtis Strange & Tom Kite
**Foursomes: Morning**
José Rivero & Gordon Brand Jr lost to
Curtis Strange & Tom Kite (3&1)
Nick Faldo & Ian Woosnam halved with
Hal Sutton & Larry Mize
Sandy Lyle & Bernhard Langer (2&1) beat
Lanny Wadkins & Larry Nelson
Seve Ballesteros & JM Olazábal (1 hole)
beat Ben Crenshaw & Payne Stewart
**Fourballs: Afternoon**
Nick Faldo & Ian Woosnam (5&4) beat
Curtis Strange & Tom Kite
Eamonn Darcy & Gordon Brand Jr lost to
Andy Bean & Payne Stewart (3&2)
Seve Ballesteros & JM Olazábal lost to Hal
Sutton & Larry Mize (2&1)
Sandy Lyle & Bernhard Langer (1 hole)
beat Lanny Wadkins & Larry Nelson
**Singles**
Ian Woosnam lost to Andy Bean (1 hole)
Howard Clark (1 hole) beat Dan Pohl
Sam Torrance halved with Larry Mize
Nick Faldo lost to Mark Calcavecchia (1
hole)
JM Olazabal lost to Payne Stewart (2
holes)
Jose Rivero lost to Scott Simpson (2 & 1)
Sandy Lyle lost to Tom Kite (3&2)
Eamonn Darcy (1 hole) beat Ben
Crenshaw
Bernhard Langer halved with Larry
Nelson
Seve Ballesteros (2&1) beat Curtis Strange
Ken Brown lost to Lanny Wadkins (3&2)
Gordon Brand Jr halved with Hal Sutton

**Result:** Europe 14–USA 14
**Captains:** Ray Floyd (US), Tony Jacklin
(Europe)
**Venue:** The Belfry G&C, Sutton
Coldfield, England

**Foursomes: Morning**
Nick Faldo & Ian Woosnam halved with
Tom Kite & Curtis Strange
Howard Clark & Mark James lost to
Lanny Wadkins & Payne Stewart (1 hole)
Seve Ballesteros & JM Olazabal halved
with Tom Watson & Chip Beck
Bernhard Langer & Ronan Rafferty lost to
Mark Calcavecchia & Ken Green (2&1)
**Fourballs: Afternoon**
Sam Torrance & Gordon Brand Jr (1
hole) beat Curtis Strange & Paul Azinger
Howard Clark & Mark James (3&2) beat
Fred Couples & Lanny Wadkins
Nick Faldo & Ian Woosnam (2 holes) beat
Mark Calcavecchia & Mark McCumber
Seve Ballesteros & JM Olazabal (6&5)
beat Tom Watson & Mark O'Meara
**Foursomes: Morning**
Ian Woosnam & Nick Faldo (3&2) beat
Lanny Wadkins & Payne Stewart
Gordon Brand Jr & Sam Torrance lost to
Chip Beck & Paul Azinger (4&3)
Christy O'Connor Jr & Ronan Rafferty lost
to Mark Calcavecchia & Ken Green (3&2)
Seve Ballesteros & JM Olazabal (1 hole)
beat Tom Kite & Curtis Strange
**Fourballs: Afternoon**
Nick Faldo & Ian Woosnam lost to Chip

Beck & Paul Azinger (2&1)
Bernhard Langer & JM Canizares lost to
Tom Kite & Mark McCumber (2&1)
Howard Clark & Mark James (1 hole)
beat Payne Stewart & Curtis Strange
Seve Ballesteros & JM Olazabal (4&2)
beat Mark Calcavecchia & Ken Green
**Singles**
Seve Ballesteros lost to Paul Azinger (1
hole)
Bernhard Langer lost to Chip Beck (3&2)
JM Olazabal (1 hole) beat Payne Stewart
Ronan Rafferty (1 hole) beat Mark
Calcavecchia
Howard Clark lost to Tom Kite (8&7)
Mark James (3&2) beat Mark O'Meara
Christy O'Connor Jr (1 hole) beat Fred
Couples
JM Canizares (1 hole) beat Ken Green
Gordon Brand Jr lost to Mark McCumber
(1 hole)
Sam Torrance lost to Tom Watson (3&1)
Nick Faldo lost Lanny Wadkins (1 hole)
Ian Woosnam lost to Curtis Strange (2
holes)

**Result:** USA 14½–Europe 13½
**Captains:** Dave Stockton (US), Bernard
Gallacher (Europe)
**Venue:** Ocean Course, Kiawah Island,
South Carolina

**Foursomes: Morning**
Seve Ballesteros & JM Olazabal (2&1)
beat Paul Azinger & Chip Beck

Bernhard Langer & Mark James lost to Ray Floyd & Fred Couples (2&1)
David Gilford & Colin Montgomerie lost to Lanny Wadkins & Hale Irwin (4&2)
Nick Faldo & Ian Woosnam lost to Payne Stewart & Mark Calcavecchia (1 hole)

### Fourballs: Afternoon
Sam Torrance & David Feherty halved with Lanny Wadkins & Mark O'Meara
Seve Ballesteros & JM Olazabal (2&1) beat Paul Azinger & Chip Beck
Steven Richardson & Mark James (5&4) beat Corey Pavin & Mark Calcavecchia
Nick Faldo & Ian Woosnam lost to Ray Floyd & Fred Couples (5&3)

### Foursomes: Morning
David Feherty & Sam Torrance lost to Hale Irwin & Lanny Wadkins (4&2)
Mark James & Steven Richardson lost to Mark Calcavecchia & Payne Stewart (1 hole)
Nick Faldo & David Gilford lost to Paul Azinger & Mark O'Meara (7&6)
Seve Ballesteros & JM Olazabal (3&2) beat Fred Couples & Ray Floyd

### Fourballs: Afternoon
Ian Woosnam & Paul Broadhurst (2&1) beat Paul Azinger & Hale Irwin
Bernhard Langer & Colin Montgomerie (2&1) beat Corey Pavin & Steve Pate
Mark James & Steve Richardson (3&1) beat Lanny Wadkins & Wayne Levi
Seve Ballesteros & JM Olazabal halved with Payne Stewart & Fred Couples

### Singles
Nick Faldo (2 holes) beat Ray Floyd

David Feherty (2&1) beat Payne Stewart
Colin Montgomerie halved with Mark Calcavecchia
JM Olazabal lost to Paul Azinger (2 holes)
Steven Richardson lost to Corey Pavin (2&1)
Seve Ballesteros (3&2) beat Wayne Levi
Ian Woosnam lost to Chip Beck (3&1)
Paul Broadhurst (3&1) beat Mark O'Meara
Sam Torrance lost to Fred Couples (3&2)
Mark James lost to Lanny Wadkins (3&2)
Bernhard Langer halved with Hale Irvin
David Gilford halved with Steve Pate (injured, match not played)

## 1993
**Result:** USA 15–Europe 13
**Captains:** Tom Watson (US), Bernard Gallacher (Europe)
**Venue:** The Belfry G&CC, Sutton Coldfield

### Foursomes: Morning
Sam Torrance & Mark James lost to Lanny Wadkins & Corey Pavin (4&3)
Ian Woosnam & Bernhard Langer (7&5) beat Paul Azinger & Payne Stewart
Seve Ballesteros & JM Olazabal lost to Tom Kite & Davis Love (2&1)
Nick Faldo & Colin Montgomerie (4&3) beat Ray Floyd & Fred Couples

### Fourballs: Afternoon
Ian Woosnam & Peter Baker (1 hole) beat Jim Gallagher Jr & Lee Janzen
Bernhard Langer & Barry Lane lost to

Lanny Wadkins & Corey Pavin (4&2)
Nick Faldo & Colin Montgomerie halved with Paul Azinger & Fred Couples
Seve Ballesteros & JM Olazabal (4&3) beat Davis Love & Tom Kite

### Foursomes: Morning
Nick Faldo & Colin Montgomerie (3&2) beat Lanny Wadkins & Corey Pavin
Bernhard Langer & Ian Woosnam (2&1) beat Fred Couples & Paul Azinger
Peter Baker & Barry Lane lost to Ray Floyd & Payne Stewart (3&2)
Seve Ballesteros & JM Olazabal (2&1) beat Davis Love & Tom Kite

### Fourballs: Afternoon
Nick Faldo & Colin Montgomerie lost to John Cook & Chip Beck (1 hole)
Mark James & Costantino Rocca lost to Corey Pavin & Jim Gallagher Jr (5&4)
Ian Woosnam & Peter Baker (6&5) beat Fred Couples & Paul Azinger
JM Olazabal & Joakim Haeggman lost to Ray Floyd & Payne Stewart (2&1)

### Singles
Ian Woosnam halved with Fred Couples
Barry Lane Lane lost to Chip Beck (1 hole)
Colin Montgomerie (1 hole) beat Lee Janzen
Peter Baker (2 holes) beat Corey Pavin
Joakim Haeggman (1 hole) beat John Cook
Mark James lost to Payne Stewart (3&2)
Costantino Rocca lost to Daris Love (1 hole)
Seve Ballesteros lost to J Gallagher Jr (3&2)

JM Olazabal lost to Ray Floyd (2 holes)
Bernhard Langer lost to Tom Kite (5&3)
Nick Faldo halved with Paul Azinger
Sam Torrance, injured, halved with Lanny
Wadkins (match not played)

### 1995
**Result:** Europe 14½–USA 13½
**Captains:** Bernard Gallacher (Europe),
Lanny Wadkins (US)
**Venue:** Oak Hill Country Club,
Rochester, New York

### Foursomes: Morning
Nick Faldo & Colin Montgomerie lost to
Corey Pavin & Tom Lehman (1 hole)
Sam Torrance & Costantino Rocca (3&2)
beat Jay Haas & Fred Couples
Howard Clark & Mark James lost to Davis
Love & Jeff Maggert (4&3)
Bernhard Langer & Per Ulrik Johansson
(1 hole) beat Ben Crenshaw & Curtis
Strange
### Fourballs: Afternoon
David Gilford & Seve Ballesteros (4&3)
beat Brad Faxon & Peter Jacobsen
Sam Torrance & Costantino Rocca lost to
Jeff Maggert & Loren Roberts (6&5)
Nick Faldo & Colin Montgomerie lost to
Fred Couples & Davis Love (3&2)
Bernhard Langer & Per Ulrik Johansson
lost to Corey Pavin & Phil Mickelson (6&4)
### Foursomes: Morning
Nick Faldo & Colin Montgomerie (4&2)
beat Curtis Strange & Jay Haas
Sam Torrance & Costantino Rocca (6&5)

beat Davis Love & Jeff Maggert
Ian Woosnam & Philip Walton lost to
Loren Roberts & Peter Jacobsen (1 hole)
Bernhard Langer & David Gilford (4&3)
beat Corey Pavin & Tom Lehman
### Fourballs: Afternoon
Sam Torrance & Colin Montgomerie lost
to Brad Faxon & Fred Couples (4&2)
Ian Woosnam & Costantino Rocca (3&2)
beat Davis Love & Ben Crenshaw
Seve Ballesteros & David Gilford lost to
Jay Haas & Phil Mickelson (3&2)
Nick Faldo & Bernhard Langer lost to
Corey Pavin & Loren Roberts (1 hole)
### Singles
Seve Ballesteros lost to Tom Lehman
(4&3)
Howard Clark (1 hole) beat Peter
Jacobsen
Mark James (4&3) beat Jeff Maggert
Ian Woosnam halved with Fred Couples
Costantino Rocca lost to Davis Love (3&2)
David Gilford (1 hole) beat Brad Faxon
Colin Montgomerie (3&1) beat Ben
Crenshaw
Nick Faldo (1 hole) beat Curtis Strange
Sam Torrance (2&1) beat Loren Roberts
Bernhard Langer lost to Corey Pavin
(3&2)
Philip Walton (1 hole) beat Jay Haas
Per Ulrik Johansson lost to Phil
Mickelson (2&1)

### 1997
**Result:** Europe 14½–USA 13½
**Captains:** Seve Ballesteros (Europe), Tom

Kite (US)
**Venue:** Valderrama GC, Sotogrand, Spain

### Foursomes: Morning
JM Olazabal & Costantino Rocca (one-
up) beat Davis Love & Phil Mickelson
Nick Faldo & Lee Westwood lost to Fred
Couples & Brad Faxon (one-up)
Jesper Parnevik & Per Ulrik Johansson
(one-up) beat Tom Lehman & Jim Furyk
Colin Montgomerie & Bernhard Langer
lost to Tiger Woods & Mark O'Meara
(3&2)
### Fourballs: Afternoon
Costantino Rocca & JM Olazabal lost to
Scott Hoch & Lee Janzen (one-up)
Bernhard Langer & Colin Montgomerie
(5&3) beat Mark O'Meara & Tiger Woods
Nick Faldo & Lee Westwood (3&2) beat
Justin Leonard & Jeff Maggert
Jesper Parnevik & Ignacio Garrido halved
with Tom Lehman & Phil Mickelson
### Foursomes: Morning
Colin Montgomerie & Darren Clarke
(one-up) beat Fred Couples & Davis Love
Ian Woosnam & Thomas Bjorn (2&1)
beat Justin Leonard & Brad Faxon
Nick Faldo & Lee Westwood (2&1) beat
Tiger Woods & Mark O'Meara
JM Olazabal & Ignacio Garrido halved
with Phil Mickelson & Tom Lehman
### Fourballs: Afternoon
Colin Montgomerie & Bernhard Langer
(one-up) beat Lee Janzen & Jim Furyk
Nick Faldo & Lee Westwood lost to Scott
Hoch & Jeff Maggert (2&1)

Jesper Parnevik & Ignacio Garrido halved with Justin Leonard & Tiger Woods
JM Olazabal & Costantino Rocca (5&4) beat Davis Love & Fred Couples

**Singles**
Ian Woosnam lost to Fred Couples (8&7)
Per Ulrik Johansson (3&2) beat Davis Love
Jesper Parnevik lost to Mark O'Meara (5&4)
Darren Clarke lost to Phil Mickelson (2&1)
Costantino Rocca (4&2) beat Tiger Woods
Thomas Bjorn halved with Justin Leonard
Ignacio Garrido lost to Tom Lehman (7&6)
Bernhard Langer (2&1) beat Brad Faxon
Lee Westwood lost to Jeff Maggert (3&2)
JM Olazabal lost to Lee Janzen (one-up)
Nick Faldo lost to Jim Furyk (3&2)
Colin Montgomerie halved with Scott Hoch

## 1999
**Result:** USA 14½–Europe 13½
**Captains:** Ben Crenshaw (US), Mark James (Europe)
**Venue:** The Country Club, Brookline, Massachusetts

**Foursomes: Morning**
Paul Lawrie & Colin Montgomerie (3&2) beat David Duval & Phil Mickelson
Sergio Garcia & Jesper Parnevik (2&1) beat Tom Lehman & Tiger Woods

Miguel Angel Jiménez & Padraig Harrington halved with Davis Love & Payne Stewart
Darren Clarke & Lee Westwood lost to Jeff Maggert & Hal Sutton (3&2)

**Fourballs: Afternoon**
Sergio Garcia & Jesper Parnevik (1 hole) beat Jim Furyk & Phil Mickelson
Paul Lawrie & Colin Montgomerie halved with Justin Leonard & Davis Love
MA Jimenez & Jose Maria Olazabal (2&1) beat Jeff Maggert & Hal Sutton
Darren Clarke & Lee Westwood (1 hole) beat David Duval & Tiger Woods

**Foursomes: Morning**
Paul Lawrie & Colin Montgomerie lost to Jeff Maggert & Hal Sutton (1 hole)
Darren Clarke & Lee Westwood (3&2) beat Jim Furyk & Mark O'Meara
MA Jimenez & Padraig Harrington lost to Steve Pate & Tiger Woods (1 hole)
Sergio Garcia & Jesper Parnevik (3&2) beat Justin Leonard & Payne Stewart

**Fourballs: Afternoon**
Darren Clarke & Lee Westwood lost to Phil Mickelson & Tom Lehman (2&1)
Sergio Garcia & Jesper Parnevik halved with Davis Love & David Duval
MA Jimenez & JM Olazabal halved with Justin Leonard & Hal Sutton
Paul Lawrie & Colin Montgomerie (2&1) beat Steve Pate & Tiger Woods

**Singles**
Lee Westwood lost to Tom Lehman (3&2)
Jean Van De Velde lost to Davis Love (6&5)

Jarmo Sandelin lost to Phil Mickelson (4&3)
Darren Clarke lost to Hal Sutton (4&2)
Jesper Parnevik lost to David Duval (5&4)
Andrew Coltart lost to Tiger Woods (3&2)
MA Jimenez lost to Steve Pate (2&1)
Padraig Harrington (1 hole) beat Mark O'Meara (hooray)
Sergio Garcia lost to Jim Furyk (4&3)
Paul Lawrie (4&3) beat Jeff Maggert
Jose Maria Olazabal halved with Justin Leonard
Colin Montgomerie (1 hole) beat Payne Stewart

## 2002
**Result:** Europe 15½–USA 12½
**Captains:** Curtis Strange (US), Sam Torrance (Europe)
**Venue:** The Belfry, Sutton Coldfield

**Fourballs: Morning**
Darren Clarke & Thomas Bjorn (1 hole) beat Tiger Woods & Paul Azinger
Sergio Garcia & Lee Westwood (4&3) beat David Duval & Davis Love
Colin Montgomerie & Bernhard Langer (4&3) beat Scott Hoch & Jim Furyk
Padraig Harrington & Niclas Fasth lost to Phil Mickelson & David Toms (1 hole)

**Foursomes: Afternoon**
Darren Clarke & Thomas Bjorn lost to Hal Sutton & Scott Verplank (2&1)
Sergio Garcia & Lee Westwood (2&1) beat Tiger Woods & Mark Calcavecchia

Colin Montgomerie & Bernhard Langer halved with Phil Mickelson & David Toms
Padraig Harrington & Paul McGinley lost to Stewart Cink & Jim Furyk (3&2)

### Foursomes: Morning

Pierre Fulke & Phillip Price lost to Phil Mickelson & David Toms (2&1)
Lee Westwood & Sergio Garcia (2&1) beat Jim Furyk & Stewart Cink
Colin Montgomerie & Bernhard Langer (1 hole) beat Scott Verplank & Scott Hoch
Darren Clarke & Thomas Bjorn lost to Tiger Woods & Davis Love (4&3)

### Fourballs: Afternoon

Niclas Fasth & Jesper Parnevik lost to Mark Calcavecchia & David Duval (1 hole)
Colin Montgomerie & Padraig Harrington (2&1) beat Phil Mickelson & David Toms
Sergio Garcia & Lee Westwood lost to Tiger Woods & Davis Love (1 hole)
Darren Clarke & Paul McGinley halved with Scott Hoch & Jim Furyk

### Singles

Colin Montgomerie (5&4) beat Scott Hoch
Sergio Garcia lost to David Toms (1 hole)
Darren Clarke halved with David Duval
Bernhard Langer (4&3) beat Hal Sutton
Padraig Harrington (5&4) beat Mark Calcavecchia
Thomas Bjorn (2&1) beat Stewart Cink
Lee Westwood lost to Scott Verplank (2&1)
Niclas Fasth halved with Paul Azinger

Paul McGinley halved with Jim Furyk
Pierre Fulke halved with Davis Love
Phillip Price (3&2) beat Phil Mickelson (you beauty)
Jesper Parnevik halved with Tiger Woods

## 2004

**Result:** Europe 18½–USA 9½
**Captains:** Hal Sutton (US), Bernhard Langer (Europe)
**Venue:** Oakland Hills CC, Bloomfield, Michigan

### Fourballs: Morning

Colin Montgomerie & Padraig Harrington (2&1) beat Tiger Woods & Phil Mickelson
Darren Clarke & Miguel Angel Jimenez (5&4) beat Davis Love & Chad Campbell
Paul McGinley & Luke Donald halved with Chris Riley & Stewart Cink
Sergio Garcia & Lee Westwood (5&3) beat David Toms & Jim Furyk

### Foursomes: Afternoon

MA Jimenez & Thomas Levet lost to Chris DiMarco & Jay Haas (3&2)
Colin Montgomerie & Padraig Harrington (4&2) beat Davis Love & Fred Funk
Darren Clarke & Lee Westwood (1 hole) beat Tiger Woods & Phil Mickelson
Sergio Garcia & Luke Donald (2&1) beat Kenny Perry & Stewart Cink

### Fourballs: Morning

Sergio Garcia & Lee Westwood halved with Jay Haas & Chris DiMarco

Darren Clarke & Ian Poulter lost to Tiger Woods & Chris Riley (4&3)
Paul Casey & David Howell (1 hole) beat Jim Furyk & Chad Campbell
Colin Montgomerie & Padraig Harrington lost to Stewart Cink & Davis Love (3&2)

### Foursomes: Afternoon

Darren Clarke & Lee Westwood (5&4) beat Jay Haas & Chris DiMarco
MA Jimenez & Thomas Levet lost to Phil Mickelson &David Toms (5&4)
Sergio Garcia & Luke Donald (1 hole) beat Jim Furyk & Fred Funk
Padraig Harrington & Paul McGinley (4&3) beat Davis Love & Tiger Woods

### Singles

Paul Casey lost to Tiger Woods (3&2)
Sergio Garcia (3&2) beat Phil Mickelson
Darren Clarke halved with Davis Love
David Howell lost to Jim Furyk (6&4)
Lee Westwood (1 hole) beat Kenny Perry
Colin Montgomerie (1 hole) beat David Toms
Luke Donald lost to Chad Campbell (5&3)
Miguel Angel Jimenez lost to Chris DiMarco (1 hole)
Thomas Levet (1 hole) beat Fred Funk
Ian Poulter (3&2) beat Chris Riley
Padraig Harrington (1 hole) beat Jay Haas
Paul McGinley (3&2) beat Stewart Cink

# Ryder Cup Records

**Biggest margin of victory**
**USA:** 1967: Champions GC, Texas, 23½–8½
**Europe:** 2004: Oakland Hills, Michigan, 18½–9½

**Most Ryder Cup appearances**
**Europe:** Nick Faldo 11 (1977, '79, '81, '83, '85, '87, '89, '91, '93, '95, '97)
**USA:** Lanny Wadkins 8 (1977, '79, '83, '85, '87, '89, '91, '93)
Ray Floyd 8 (1969, '75, '77, '81, '83, '85, '91, '93)
Billy Casper 8 (1961, '63, '65, '67, '69, '71, '73, '75)

**Youngest player**
**Europe:** Sergio Garcia in 1999 – 19 years, 8 months, 15 days
**USA:** Horton Smith in 1929 – 21 years, 4 days

**Oldest player**
**USA:** Raymond Floyd in 1993 – 51 years, 20 days
**Europe:** Ted Ray in 1927 – 50 years, 2 months, 5 days

**Most matches played**
**Europe:** Nick Faldo 46
**USA:** Billy Casper 37

**Most points won**
**Europe:** Nick Faldo 25
**USA:** Billy Casper 23.5

**Most matches won**
**Europe:** Nick Faldo 23
**USA:** Arnold Palmer 22

**Most singles won**
**USA:** Arnold Palmer, Billy Casper, Lee Trevino, Sam Snead 6
**Europe:** Peter Oosterhuis, Nick Faldo 6

**Most foursomes won**
**Europe:** Bernhard Langer 12
**USA:** Arnold Palmer, Lanny Wadkins 9

**Most Fourballs won**
**Europe:** Ian Woosnam 10
**USA:** Lanny Wadkins 7

**Most matches lost**
**GB&I:** Christy O'Connor Sr 21
**USA:** Ray Floyd 16

**Most singles lost**
**GB&I:** Christy O'Connor Sr 10
**USA:** Ray Floyd, Jack Nicklaus 4

**Most foursomes lost**
**Europe:** Bernard Hunt 9
**USA:** Ray Floyd 8

**Most Fourballs lost**
**Europe:** Nick Faldo 9
**USA:** Curtis Strange 5

**Most halves**
**USA:** Gene Littler 8
**GB&I:** Tony Jacklin 8

**Pairings with most wins**
**Europe:** Seve Ballesteros/Jose Maria Olazabal
11 wins, 2 losses, 2 halves
**USA:** Larry Nelson/Lanny Wadkins
4 wins, 2 losses, 0 halves

# Bibliography

Barkow, Al, *Gettin' to the Dance Floor: The Early days of American Pro Golf*, Heinemann Kingswood, 1986

Bubka, Bob; Clavin, Tom, *The Ryder Cup*, Crown Publishers, 1999

Callahan, Tom, *In Search of Tiger*, Mainstream, 2003

Campbell, Malcolm, *The New Encyclopedia of Golf*, Dorling Kindersley, 2001

Chieger, Bob, and Sullivan, Pat, *The Book of Golf Quotations,* Stanley Paul, 1987

Dabell, Norman, *How We Won the Ryder Cup: The Caddies' Stories*, Mainstream, 2005

Dusinberre Durham, Shirley, *Mr Ryder's Trophy*, Sleeping Bear Press, 2002

Evans, Alun, *The Golf Majors: Records and Yearbook 2002*, A&C Black, 2002

Faldo, Nick, *Life Swings*, Headline, 2004

Feherty, David; Frank, James A, *David Feherty's Totally Subjective History of the Ryder Cup*, Rugged Land, 2004

Feinstein, John, *A Good Walk Spoiled*, Little, Brown, 1995

Frost, Mark, *The Greatest Game Ever Played*, Time Warner, 2002

James, Mark, *Into the Bear Pit*, Virgin, 2001

James, Mark, *After the Bear Pit*, Virgin, 2002

Laidlaw, Renton (Ed), *Royal & Ancient Golfer's Handbook 2005*, Macmillan, 2004

Langer, Bernhard, *My Autobiography*, Hodder and Stoughton, 2002

Lawrenson, Derek, *The Complete Encyclopedia of Golf*, Carlton, 1999

Macwilliam, Rab, *Who's Who in Golf*, Hamlyn, 2001

McDonnell, Michael, *Classic Golf Quotes*, Robson Books, 2004

McMillan, Robin, *Us Against Them: An Oral History of the Ryder Cup*, Harper Collins, 2004

Montgomerie, Colin, *The Real Monty*, Orion, 2003

Musgrove, David, and Hopkins, John, *Life with Lyle*, Heinemann, 1989

Rosaforte, Tim, *Heartbreak Hill: Anatomy of a Ryder Cup*, St Martin's Press, 1996

St John, Lauren, *Seve: The Biography*, Partridge Press, 1993

Tait, Alastair, *Seve: A Biography of Severiano Ballesteros*, Virgin, 2005

Torrance, Sam, *Sam: The Autobiography of Sam Torrance*, BBC Books, 2003

Wodehouse, PG, *The Golf Omnibus*, Hutchinson, 1973